Driven to Innovate

A Century of Jewish Mathematicians and Physicists

Ioan James

Peter Lang Oxford

First published in 2009 by

Peter Lang Ltd
International Academic Publishers
Evenlode Court, Main Road, Long Hanborough, Witney
Oxfordshire OX29 8SZ
England

www.peterlang.com

Ioan James has asserted his moral right under the Copyright, Designs
and Patents Act of 1988 to be identified as the Author of this Work.

© Peter Lang Ltd 2009

A catalogue record for this book is available from the British Library

ISBN 978-1-906165-22-2

DESIGN Kara Trapani, Peter Lang Ltd
COVER ILLUSTRATIONS (clockwise from top left):
Albert Michelson; Emmy Noether; Alfred Tarski; Paul Ehrenfest;
Tullio Levi-Civita; J. J. Sylvester; Albert Einstein; Lise Meitner.

Every effort has been made to trace copyright holders and to obtain their permission
for the use of copyright material. The publisher apologizes for any errors or omissions
and would be grateful for notification of any corrections that should be incorporated
in future reprints or editions of this book.

Printed in the United Kingdom
by the MPG Books Group

Contents

Preface

There is extraordinary overrepresentation of Jews, relative to their numbers, in the top ranks of the arts and sciences, in the professions of law and medicine, and in many other activities. It is far greater than would be expected from the proportion of Jews in the general population, which is estimated to be about two-tenths of 1 per cent. Take physics, for example. Everyone knows about Albert Einstein, but there were so many others. Nobel Prizes, a convenient measure of excellence, have been awarded annually since 1901. In the first half of the twentieth century 14 per cent of the prize-winners in physics were Jewish, in the second half it was 32 per cent, and since then it has continued to rise. The first American Nobel laureate, in any field, was the Jewish physicist Albert Michelson. There have never been Nobel Prizes for mathematics, but the list of outstanding Jewish mathematicians is equally impressive.

Most of these Jewish mathematicians and physicists were victims of anti-Semitism in some form. They were confronted with prejudice, against which they had to struggle, especially when they were trying to get started. Some left their country of origin to start again in another country. A few left voluntarily, in search of better prospects, but many had to flee from pogroms in the territories controlled by the tsars or from persecution in countries where the Nazis enforced their racial policies. Most of those who stayed behind were murdered in the Holocaust.

Jews are reluctant to talk about Jewish accomplishment. This book was written by one who has neither the advantages nor the disadvantages of being Jewish, as a non-technical tribute to the contribution to mathematics and physics made by Jewish men and women. I have profiled a constellation of twenty Jewish mathematicians and fifteen Jewish physicists, from a wide range of countries, who were born in the century beginning in 1801. I write about them as human beings, trying to understand the difficulties they encountered and how they surmounted them. Although they were chosen because of the variety of their life-stories, they were all in the forefront of research in their respective fields.

There may be no simple answer to the old question of why Jewish people have been so successful, particularly in the closely related fields of mathematics and physics, but various theories have been advanced in the literature. The individual profiles throw some light on the matter. Of course there were also outstanding Jewish scientists in other disciplines, such as astronomy, biology, and chemistry; some of the newer sciences, such as psychology, were pioneered by Jews. Of the people profiled here I have had the privilege of knowing, or at least meeting, ten of them, as well as many of the outstanding Jewish mathematicians and physicists of today. Among the many people, Jewish and otherwise, who have helped me in various ways I would particularly like to thank Simon Altmann, Judith Goodstein, David Hollinger, John Tyrer, and Beruriah Wiegand.

Introduction

The Subjects of the Profiles

Although so much has been published about Jewish culture, not much of it refers to scientific Jews. *The Jews in Science* by Louis Gershenfeld (1934) and *Judaism and Science* by Noah Efron (2006) make useful background reading. The books of David Nachmansohn (1978) and R. Siegmund-Schultze (1998, 2002) are also relevant, as are those of Laura Fermi (1961) and Jean Medawar and David Pyke (2000). Ulrich Charpa and Ute Deichmann have edited a volume of articles entitled *Jews and Science in German Contexts* (2007) including a comprehensive list compiled by Simone Wenkel of German-speaking Jewish scientists in academia. Max Pinl and Lux Furtmüller (1973), D. E. Rowe (1986, 2007), and Sanford Segal (2003) have written about the mathematicians.

Full-scale biographies have been published for about twenty of the Jewish mathematicians and physicists to be profiled here. The case of Albert Einstein is exceptional: there is a wide choice of biographies. There are also works entitled *Einstein on Religion, Einstein on Politics, Einstein and Judaism, Einstein in Love,* and so on. His collected works have been published, also his correspondence. The Einstein Project regularly publishes articles about aspects of his life and work. The Einstein literature would fill a small library.

In selecting the thirty-five Jewish mathematicians and physicists for profiling here I have been guided by a number of considerations. It is tempting to begin in the eighteenth century, when the two great processes of Jewish Emancipation and Jewish Enlightenment originated, but the beginning of the nineteenth makes a more natural starting-point, because of the paucity of suitable subjects before that. It is more difficult to draw the line at the beginning of the twentieth century, particularly in physical science, which was developing rapidly. Given a few more years I might have added another chapter including profiles of two more physicists, the Hungarian Eugene Wigner and the American J. Robert Oppenheimer, also two more mathematicians, the Hungarian John von Neumann and the Frenchman André Weil. Even within the constraints I have imposed upon myself there are many distinguished Jewish physicists, even Nobel laureates, for whom I have not been able to find room, and the same is true of mathematicians. The political geography of Europe changed so much in the nineteenth century that an arrangement by countries of origin would be too difficult, especially as the subjects moved around so much, and so the profiles are arranged chronologically by birth-date of the subjects instead. This produces some interesting contrasts, for example between the enlightened Jewish society of western Europe and the traditional Jewish society of the east. The five chapters of profiles each contain the life-stories of seven Jewish mathematicians and physicists born in the periods 1804–1854, 1857–1877, 1878–1882, 1882–1893, and 1894–1901. Many of their careers extend into the twentieth century.

Of course they only form a minority of the most remarkable mathematicians and physicists born in the nineteenth century, but an important minority, by any standards. Some were relatively unaffected by anti-Semitism. Others were forced to make changes of career which often turned out well—but not always. Decisions made under pressure sometimes turned out badly. There are undoubtedly many whose careers were so blighted that they never had a chance to show what they could achieve. I greatly regret that, out of thirty-five profiles, there is only one female mathematician, Emmy Noether, and only two female physicists, Hertha Ayrton and Lise Meitner; their life-stories illustrate some of the difficulties that women used to face in making a career in science, especially Jewish women.

The thirty-five I have chosen for profiles, and a few others mentioned in passing, give a strong impression of the enormous contribution that Jewish people have made to mathematics and physics. They come from a wide range of countries of origin: Germany fifteen; Russia (including Ukraine, White Russia, and the Baltic States) four; Austria three; Denmark,

England, Hungary, Italy, Poland, and the United States two each; France one. Towards the end of their careers eleven of my subjects were living in the United States, eight in Germany, seven in Britain, two each in Italy, Russia, and Switzerland, one each in Denmark, France, and the Netherlands. Country of residence is easier to determine than nationality: when someone is described as German, say, it does not necessarily mean to imply they were necessarily of German nationality.

The question of whether or not a particular person should be classified as Jewish is not one in which I would wish to become too involved. Converts to Judaism become Jews, as do their descendants. Strictly speaking what matters is having a Jewish mother; the father is disregarded for this purpose, although not for membership of the priestly castes. Someone whose father was Jewish but whose mother was not I would describe as partly Jewish; sometimes it is difficult to be sure. Most of those profiled here are undoubtedly of Jewish descent, and it seems reasonable to suppose that there may be genetic factors involved which arise from this. There may also be cultural factors at work, certain traditions and values which are distinctively Jewish.

Secrets of Success

As the social theorist Thorstein Veblen wrote in 1919, 'it is a fact that must strike any dispassionate observer that the Jewish people have contributed much more than an even share to the intellectual life of modern Europe. Particularly is this true of the modern sciences, and it applies perhaps especially in the field of scientific theory.' 'Men of Jewish extraction', he went on to say, 'continue to supply more than a proportionate quota to the rank and file engaged in scientific and scholarly work ... and, more importantly, a proportionate number of the men to whom modern science and scholarship look for guidance and leadership are of the same derivation.' What Veblen wrote almost a century ago is even more true today.

Explanations of Jewish success in the arts and sciences, in law, medicine, finance, entrepreneurship, and the media, range from the racial,

through combinations of environmental and genetic, to the purely psychological. Elevated intelligence provides one explanation. It has often
been found (see, for example, Murray (2003) and Storfer (1990)) that, on
average, Ashkenazim perform better in intelligence tests than Sephardim
or gentiles. Moreover, they display high verbal and mathematical ability
but relatively low visuospatial skills. In a recent article Cochran, Hardy,
and Harpending (2006) maintain that 'the unique demography and socio-
logy of Ashkenazim in medieval Europe selected for intelligence; the
high IQ test scores of Ashkenazim, along with their unusual pattern
of abilities, are a product of natural selection, stemming from their
occupation of an unusual social niche.' Between the ninth century and
the sixteenth, as Botticini and Eckstein (2005) have shown, these Jews
generally selected occupations involving sales, finance, and trade, where
intelligence is important for success, while the chief occupation of non-
Jews was agriculture. However, it was the Sephardim, not the Ashkenazim,
who contributed so much to scholarship in this period, so that intelligence
cannot be the only factor at work.

In *The Jewish Mind* (1997) Raphael Patai reviews some of the theories
for the disproportionate success of the Jews which have been advanced in
the literature. He identifies a number of factors as being mainly responsible
for Jewish excellence and genius (the term 'genius' has a long history but
nowadays is usually taken to mean exceptional creativity) and selects
the following:

> First of all, two probably selective factors—the pressure of the Gentile
> persecution, or at least discrimination, which made for the survival of the
> most intelligent; and the advantages enjoyed by the best scholars in mating
> and procreation. The latter was the direct outcome of factor three; the religio-
> cultural tradition of considering learning the highest value. Factor four,
> derived from or correlated with the third, was the extremely stimulating
> character of the home environment. The fifth was the age-old preference
> for urban living and the actual concentration in towns and cities. The sixth
> consisted of being forced by the Gentiles to eke out a livelihood in commercial
> occupations in which intelligence is a sine qua non. And the seventh was
> the challenge of the Gentile cultural atmosphere. Exposure to these factors

for many generations tended to raise the level of general Jewish intelligence, by increasing the percentage of the gifted among the Jews, and produce among them a remarkable number of men of genius whose works and words changed the world.

Patai thus emphasizes a more Darwinian approach. The selective factors are applicable not necessarily to the individuals in question but to their ancestors, otherwise 'the advantages of discrimination' could hardly be a factor in the more recent successes of American or Israeli Jews. Whenever we can trace a Jewish family history back a few generations we may expect to find people who must have suffered from serious persecution, even if their descendants have not. For example, the parents of Hertha Ayrton fled the pogroms of the Pale of Settlement, while the Nazis drove others from their homeland.

Darwin himself, we recall, never claimed that natural selection was the sole cause of evolution of a species, i.e. what came to be called survival of the fittest. Sexual selection, he argued, was also important, and explained things that natural selection alone could not. There is a long tradition of cultured Jewish families with highly talented and scholarly sons trying to find equally gifted marriage partners. The advantages enjoyed by the best scholars in mating and procreation are obviously an important factor but here again the effect will not be evident until later generations. We must look back to the parents and grandparents for examples where this factor may operate. Jewish families tend to progress through the various social strata in a predictable way. Many start out in trade, moving in later generations into the professions—medicine and law—and eventually the world of scholarship. The goal of achieving an academic appointment is consistent with the long-held respect for learning in Jewish culture.

In most of our profiles the father of the subject is a successful professional man, who married a social and intellectual equal or superior. Thus the fathers of Emmy Noether, Max Born, Niels Bohr, Norbert Wiener, and Wolfgang Pauli were academics; the fathers of Heinrich Hertz, Tullio Levi-Civita, James Franck, and George Pólya were lawyers; the fathers of Edmund Landau and Max Dehn were in medicine; Jacques Hadamard's father was a schoolteacher; most of the rest were in business of one kind or another ranging from peddling to running large industrial enterprises. Traditionally, raising and educating children is one of the most important components of Jewish family life. Jewish parents give their children everything, writes Patai. Population geneticists, from Galton onwards, have contrasted the Jewish tradition with the Catholic one, whereby the Church recruits talented boys to be trained as priests and then the rule of celibacy prevents them from marrying and having legitimate children.

As Patai points out, sexual selection is closely connected with the third factor, the old Jewish religio-cultural tradition of considering learning the highest value. The talented child may receive any necessary financial support from members of the extended family. We see this in the cases of Vito Volterra, who was supported in various ways by his relative Edouardo Almagià; of Albert Einstein, who was seen through school and university by his aunt; and of Oscar Zariski, who was similarly supported by a rich uncle.

In the first and second centuries Judaism transformed itself from a religion based on rites and sacrifices to a religion centred on prayer and study of the Torah, including an exhaustive analysis of the Talmud and its commentators. This involved comparison of different interpretations, discussing all aspects of a given problem, and arriving at a conclusion through mental activity involving penetration, scholarship, memory, logic, wit, and subtlety. This religious and educational reform gave Jews a comparative advantage in occupations where the return from this investment in education was greater than that from agriculture. At times when literacy was uncommon among the gentile poor, Jewish men were usually literate if not numerate. Jewish women were not encouraged to have anything but the most basic formal education, but were not necessarily uneducated. The ability to communicate in Hebrew with other Jews, whatever the vernacular of the country they were in, was an important commercial and cultural advantage. The life of a peasant farmer may have had its compensations, but commerce and entrepreneurship provide better training for the mind.

The fourth factor is the provision of a stimulating home environment. The importance of this to the intellectual development of children is well established by modern psychologists who write about the education of children, particularly gifted children. The parents' intellectual aspirations for the child, their reinforcements of different types of intellectual performance, the opportunities for learning provided both inside and outside the home, the value placed by parents on the child's intellectual performance, and work habits emphasized in the home are all important. We cannot hope to discover such details in each of the cases we discuss, but something is known. For example, both parents of Abram Ioffe, we read, were much interested in intellectual pursuits and undoubtedly greatly encouraged and influenced their son, who showed early signs of exceptional intelligence. Emmy Noether grew up in a home constantly visited by members of a stimulating circle of scholars. The Bohr brothers benefited from being brought up in a patrician home of culture where they were exposed to a world of ideas in animated debates in which conflicting views were examined rationally and in good humour. The family home of Max Born, with its atmosphere of scientific and general culture, provided him with a stimulating environment during his formative years. His mother was an excellent pianist; one of his most treasured possessions was an album of hers containing autographs of the many celebrated musicians with whom his parents were acquainted. The Gabor brothers also grew up in a home of culture. The family took lunch and dinner together and, especially in later years, mealtimes were like the meetings of a discussion group.

Studies comparing the quality of the home environment maintained by a Jewish family as compared with a gentile family in the same socio-economic stratum show that learning is more highly valued in the Jewish home. In practice this translates into the higher intellectual aspirations which Jewish parents have for their children. Even the poorest Jewish home was a place permeated by the age-old Jewish emphasis on learning, where parents did everything they could to enable their children to study, to stimulate them to study, and, if necessary, to bully them into studying. Further up the socio-economic ladder the physical environment they can create for their children may be better, and the means the parents employ to motivate them may be different, but their intention remains the same. The Jewish child can read long before he enters the school system; the home will provide magazines and books, probably an illustrated encyclopedia as well. Sometimes parents go too far, as in the case of Leo Wiener, the father of Norbert, who exercised an excessively strong influence over the education of his son. Psychologists warn that while there is much to be said for early intellectual stimulation, there are also likely to be costs that may keep the child from making the best of his or her abilities later in life. Children whose early years are filled with learning sessions may have insufficient time to play with other children and learn to make friends. A child whose activities are largely determined by a parent's bidding may be over-conscious of the necessity to please other people and may fail to develop personal enthusiasms and interests.

The fifth factor is the age-old Jewish preference for urban living. It is remarkable that when Jews were allowed to move into the towns and cities a surge of talent followed within one or two generations. This happened in the Habsburg Empire in 1848, for example. It is well established (see Klineberg 1971) that children brought up in a stimulating urban environment tend to be more intelligent than those raised in rural areas, quite apart from the opportunity the former may have of attending better schools and having a richer social life.

The sixth factor, competing with the gentiles, needs less explanation. Jews have often been forced into occupations where intelligence is needed for success. For academics, this competitive spirit came out through performance in examinations. Although J. J. Sylvester came only second in the highly competitive Cambridge mathematical Tripos, some years later Numa Hartog became the first Jewish Senior Wrangler. Jacques Hadamard came out first in the national French examinations, and later won every prize offered by the Paris Academy. Jews have carried off many Nobel Prizes in science (none is awarded in mathematics), and here too the competitive spirit is strong.

The last factor in the list is the challenge of the gentile cultural atmosphere. As I understand it, Patai means that success is relative: the outstanding man or woman needs to surpass the achievement of others, the revolutionary has to have something to revolutionize. Einstein, for example, revolutionized classical physics.

There have been other theories as to why the Jews have been so successful. For example, in the much-quoted article cited above Veblen argues that

> It was a dynamic, changing society that let the Jews out of the ghettos, but it was only those Jews eager for change who came forth. Not being conservatives in the Jewish tradition, they had even less cause to be conservative in non-Jewish terms and so became pioneers of change. … Scientific progress presupposes a degree of exemption from hard and fast preconceptions, a sceptical animus, *unbefangenheit*, release from the dead hand of finality, and the reason the intellectually gifted Jew is everywhere on top is that he is the most unattached, the most marginal, and therefore the most sceptical and unconventional of all scientists. It is by loss of allegiance, or at the best by force of the divided allegiance to the people of his origin, that he finds himself in the vanguard of modern enquiry. He becomes a disturber of the intellectual peace, but only at the cost of becoming an intellectual wayfaring man, a wanderer in the intellectual no man's land, seeking another place to rest, farther along the road, somewhere over the horizon.

David Hollinger, in his interesting critique (2002) of Veblen's thesis, points out that it actually explains very little and begs a host of questions. He argues that Veblen's extravagant admiration for a sensibility of alienation and his almost fanatical antipathy for commercial pursuits blinded him to a number of facets of Jewish history that could help solve the puzzle. He further argues that we need a demystified approach to the study of Jewish overrepresentation, according to which we would analyse Jewish intellectual pre-eminence alongside, rather than in isolation from, Jewish pre-eminence in many other callings, including the arts, the service professions, and finance.

According to Sigmund Freud, the anti-Semitic sentiments which were almost universal at German universities tended to encourage 'a certain independence of judgment' in many Jewish intellectuals, and the status of outsider, no matter how it is attained, often makes for creativity. Shulamit Volkov, in her original discussion (2001) of the social causes for the large number of Jews successfully active in German science during the nineteenth and early twentieth centuries, also reached this conclusion. 'Since the early nineteenth century,' she argued,

> Jews were allowed to study even at the best universities in the country and they seem to have made ample use of this opportunity. After graduation, however, their careers were obstructed by discrimination in various guises. As a result they found themselves as mature scientists either in marginal fields of research, or in comparatively marginal, less central and less prestigious institutions of higher learning, or both. They were thus often placed in apparently unfavourable academic positions; in the prevailing circumstances, however, these might unexpectedly turn out to be particularly creative niches where their talents found ample room for development. Conditions in these niches placed a higher premium on inventiveness than elsewhere, and were particularly conducive to professional breakthroughs of all kinds. Jews accordingly enjoyed, so to speak, the advantages of discrimination, and these may have been the ultimate source of their unusual accomplishments.

In her second paper Volkov withdrew this statement, which in any case was chiefly applicable to Wilhelmine Germany.

Jewish Mobility

Mobility is often mentioned as a Jewish characteristic, a willingness to start again in another country, but it is difficult to generalize. Some of the subjects of my profiles showed no inclination to leave the land of their birth. Hertha Ayrton remained in England, Jacques Hadamard in France, Carl Jacobi, Gotthold Eisenstein, Leopold Kronecker, Heinrich Hertz, Felix Hausdorff, and Edmund Landau in Germany, Tullio Levi-Civita in Italy, Abram Ioffe and Igor Tamm in Russia, Niels Bohr in Denmark, Norbert Wiener in America. Sylvester spent a substantial period in America, but regarded England as his homeland.

It could be argued that only the most enterprising take the major step that emigration entails and experience the stimulus that settling in a new country provides. 'Emigration', explained Nina Courant, 'was something we could never have brought ourselves to do on our own, but when it was forced upon us and there was nothing else we could do, it was wonderful—like being young all over again.' Many of the émigré scientists, even those who were middle-aged or elderly, spoke of this feeling of rejuvenation on reaching Britain or the United States. It stimulated them both personally and intellectually. However there were those who did not find it easy to settle in countries so different from the one they had always regarded as their homeland. For example they missed the formality and deference to which they had been accustomed.

Wherever they went, Jews could expect to find a ready-made social and professional network among their co-religionists, what Heine described as a portable homeland. The question arises: was there ever anything in the nature of an 'invisible college' of Jewish mathematicians and physicists? Perhaps one can see signs of this amongst the Hungarians, but it seems it was more their Hungarian background, and their similar scientific interests, that brought them together. Nevertheless, there was certainly some interaction, for instance a Jewish mentor who may have acted as a role model. Ehrenfest, for example, was strongly influenced by Einstein, Born by Minkowski, Zariski by Lefschetz, Pauli by Born. But how important the common Jewish heritage was in these relationships seems unclear.

Just over half of my subjects changed countries, willingly or not, at some stage in their lives. When Hermann Minkowski, Heinz Hopf, or Wolfgang Pauli moved from Germany to Switzerland, there was not much cultural shock. Obviously there was no language problem for them, nor was there for others who moved around in *Mitteleuropa* where a knowledge of German was taken for granted among educated people. Movement to other parts of Europe was another matter, as when Moritz Jacobi moved from Germany to Russia, or when Lise Meitner moved from Germany to Sweden, or Paul Ehrenfest from Austria to the Netherlands, or Max Born from Germany to Scotland, or Abram Besicovitch from Russia to England, or Franz Simon from Germany to England, or Dennis Gabor from Hungary to England.

However, the majority emigrated from Europe to America, the 'land of opportunity'. Albert Michelson did so at such an early age that he might almost count as American-born. Solomon Lefschetz grew up in Paris and was unusual in that he went to America at the start of his professional career. Most of the others did so at a later stage when they had already established a reputation. Albert Einstein would have been welcome anywhere apart from Germany; he chose the United States, as did Emmy Noether, James Franck, George Pólya, Richard Courant, Oscar Zariski, and Max Dehn. Alfred Tarski happened to be in America when Poland was invaded and never went back.

For many years the American government had been encouraging immigration, and large numbers of Europeans had taken advantage of this, but in 1925 a quota system was introduced. Academics appointed to American universities were exempt from the quota, as were their dependants, but obtaining such an appointment was difficult, even for highly qualified people in the prime of their professional lives, especially if they were Jewish. In 1927 one of the former students of Oswald Veblen (nephew of Thorstein) wrote to him from Ohio State University about 'the alarming degree of animosity towards Jews displayed by almost everyone in the university'. In 1931 a mathematician at the University of Chicago writing about a Jewish colleague said 'he is one of the few men of Jewish descent who does not get on your nerves and really behaves like a gentile to a satisfactory degree'. In physics, by the end of the decade, Jews already occupied a disproportionately large place in the intellectual leadership of the profession, making it all the more difficult to find positions for further Jewish émigrés. When seeking to fill vacancies some administrators flatly excluded Jews. Elsewhere, if a department already had one Jewish member a problem arose when there was a suggestion of hiring another. One wrote 'there is a question of two Jewish men in the same department, and a somewhat small one,' another that 'you know you have to be careful about getting too many Jews together.' 'Other things being equal,' said a third, 'we would rather not take a man of the Jewish faith, but we can see that some Jews might be more acceptable than some Protestants.' Of course similar attitudes existed in other countries.

The Jewish Mind

The idea that Jews tend to have a different cognitive style from non-Jews has a long history. Are Jews more likely to be visual thinkers than non-Jews? The German physicist Arnold Sommerfeld (1868–1951), for example, suspected that Einstein's work 'expressed the abstract conceptual thinking of the Semite'. The German mathematician Carl Weierstrass (1815–1897), on the other hand, maintained that Jewish mathematicians were less imaginative than non-Jewish mathematicians. The Austrian philosopher Ludwig Wittgenstein (1889–1951) claimed that it was typical of the Jewish mind (perhaps he was thinking of the Jewish elements in his own nature) to understand the work of another better than the other understood it himself. In an influential lecture he gave in America Felix Klein (1849–1925) maintained that 'the degree of exactness of the intuition of space may be different in different individuals, perhaps even in different races. It would seem as if a strong naive space intuition were an attribute pre-eminently of the Teutonic race, while the critical, purely logical sense is more fully developed in the Latin and Hebrew races.' Klein's remarks on the subject were seized upon by supporters of the Nazis like Ludwig Bieberbach (1886–1982), who fulminated against what he called Jewish mathematics, and the situation was similar in physics. Do Jews have a preference for pure mathematics rather than applied, for theoretical physics rather than experimental physics?

In the early twentieth century the unscientific theory that different 'races' had different psychological types, developed by E. R. Jaensch, was popular in America as well as Germany. More recently research has been carried out to see whether any particular medical conditions, such as diabetes or myopia, are unusually prevalent among Jewish people. For example, a few of the people profiled in this book, namely Sylvester, Cantor, Ehrenfest, and Wiener, suffered from bipolar disorder: is this significant? Goodman (1979), Goodman and Motulsky (1979), Patai and Wing (1989), Bonne-Tamir and Adam (1994), and Jones (1997) have written about the prevalence of genetic disorders, such as Tay-Sachs disease, among the Jewish people. Recently there have been several articles about the Ashkenazim in the *American Journal of Human Genetics;* the latest research seems to confirm that there are few special genetic characteristics of Jewish people but that, through intermarriage, they take on any special characteristics of the non-Jewish people around them.

In fields like mathematics and physics exceptional creativity is often associated with mild disorders on the autistic spectrum, which can provide the single-mindedness that gets things done. Those with Asperger's syndrome who are not retarded or afflicted with extreme rigidity of thinking can excel. Emotional detachment and social isolation are one characteristic of the syndrome. Einstein, for example, was little attached to the people around him and said that he had no desire to be emotionally involved in the society in which he lived. Other people profiled in this book who show distinct signs of autistic behaviour include Wolfgang Pauli, Norbert Wiener, and Alfred Tarski. This seems like a remarkably high proportion, when the highest estimate for the general population is no more than 1 per cent.

Jews may forsake Judaism yet still take pride in the achievements of Jewish people. Judaism meant more to some of the people profiled here than to others. Most, if not all, of them would be described as assimilated. A number were converted to Christianity, at least nominally; others like Paul Ehrenfest declared themselves officially without religion. Those who professed Judaism, in some degree, included Carl and Moritz Jacobi, J. J. Sylvester, Leopold Kronecker, Hertha Ayrton, and Felix Hausdorff, but only Edmund Landau could be described as observant. Some were brought up in one of the Christian faiths, or were converted, usually as a matter of expediency. Thus Gotthold Eisenstein, Georg Pólya, Wolfgang Pauli, and Alfred Tarski were officially Catholics, while Georg Cantor, Heinrich Hertz, Max Dehn, Harald and Niels Bohr, and Heinz Hopf were officially Protestants. Leopold Kronecker is said to have converted at the end of his life. Albert Einstein's Jewish identity emerged more and more strongly as the years went by, but it was only as a boy that he felt drawn towards Judaism. Some, including Norbert Wiener and Wolfgang Pauli, did not realize that they were Jewish until after childhood. In tsarist Russia converted Jews officially ceased to be regarded as Jews, but elsewhere it was a racial matter. Abram Besicovitch converted to the Russian Orthodox Church in order to marry.

'The aggressive clannishness of Jews', writes Bell (1937) in early editions of his popular *Men of Mathematics*, 'has often been remarked, sometimes as an argument against employing them in academic work.' The popular stereotype of Jewish people as 'pushy, belligerent and quarrelsome' is not entirely unearned but of the people profiled in this book it is only Carl Jacobi and Solomon Lefschetz who seem to come at all close. Certainly J. J. Sylvester, Leopold Kronecker, Edmund Landau, Richard Courant, Norbert Wiener, and Wolfgang Pauli had their faults, but they hardly seem to conform to the stereotype. Others, notably Jacques Hadamard and Emmy Noether, seem remarkable for their attractive human qualities. Patai (1997) emphasizes that after a time the personality and character of Jews reflect those common in the gentile environment in which they lived. Thus German Jews have German characteristics, Russian Jews have Russian characteristics, French Jews have French characteristics, Italian Jews have Italian characteristics, Polish Jews have Polish characteristics, and so on. He concludes that in America and other English-speaking countries the Jewish personality is characterized by greater intensity, greater sensitivity, and greater impatience. In those areas where originality is valued, the greater intensity of the Jewish mind is reflected in an incessant striving for greater originality. In the words of Sigmund Freud, they are full of the urge to innovate.

1

Historical Background

Jewish Communities

This is not an account of the endless troubles of the Jewish people through the ages; there are plenty of books on Jewish history, some of which are mentioned in the Bibliography. However the reader may find it useful to have an outline of the historical background to the main events in the lives of the people to be profiled later.

The two major Jewish communities, the Sephardim and the Ashkenazim, are distinguished from one another by certain differences of background, liturgy, and Hebrew pronunciation. There are also some smaller communities such as the oriental Jews, who until recently had always lived in the Middle East. Nowadays they are mainly to be found in Israel; they have never been very numerous and are irrelevant to the purpose of this book. In classical times some of the original Jewish population began to migrate in a westerly direction into Egypt and beyond. Although many remained in North Africa, others followed the westward thrust of Islam into Iberia, where they settled. Strictly speaking the Sephardic (or Spanish) Jews are those that settled in Moorish Spain but the term is now applied more broadly to those of a Levantine or North African origin.

The Ashkenazim (strictly speaking, German Jews, but extended to all parts of northern Europe where their descendants settled) established themselves in central Europe after the collapse of the Byzantine Empire. They spoke Yiddish, a blend of Hebrew, medieval German, and Slavonic elements, whereas the Sephardim spoke Ladino, a blend of Hebrew and Spanish. The most important Ashkenazi settlements were in France and the Rhineland, especially the borderlands of Alsace and Lorraine;

it has been suggested that they originally came from southern Europe, especially Italy. Most of the individuals to be profiled here are of Ashkenazi descent, but a few are definitely or probably Sephardic. The Karaites are also represented. They are a breakaway sect of Judaism which originated in Persia and later spread among Jews all over the world. Although they accept the written tradition of Judaism they reject rabbinical learning, and orthodox Jews therefore consider them heretics.

Throughout the Middle Ages western Jews were too severely persecuted to be able to make much contribution to civilization. As well as normal taxes they suffered from various imposts. They were denied full civic rights, such as the right to own property. There were restrictions on where they could live. They were only allowed to engage in certain occupations. In 1215 the pope promulgated an edict requiring all Jews to wear the yellow badge, and in 1239 another pope ordered all copies of the Talmud to be seized and burnt. In 1290 the king of England expelled the Jews from his domains and about twenty years later the king of France did the same. Christians persecuted Jews, especially at times of religious excitement; the Crusades were associated with appalling pogroms, a later Russian term for a violent attack by one section of the population on another, usually but not always on the Jews.

In most towns with a substantial Jewish population a Jewish quarter arose, since the Jews, like other minorities, preferred it so. These typically contained no more than a few hundred families, who needed to live near to their synagogues. However, in 1555 the virulently anti-Semitic pope directed that they must be confined to closed ghettos, surrounded by walls and entered through gates which were locked at night. Within such ghettos, isolated from the gentile community, Jewish traditions were preserved but without room to expand they soon became overcrowded and rather squalid. Their inhabitants were subject to hostility from the surrounding population, ranging from sporadic acts of violence to organized pogroms. Gradually these lawless outbreaks, which were a frequent occurrence, were replaced by legalized oppression as laws passed in the Middle Ages which had fallen into abeyance were enforced rigorously, causing much suffering.

Let us now turn our attention to central and eastern Europe, coming back to western Europe later. In the latter part of the fourteenth century the Grand Duchy of Lithuania, then a vast territory, was united with the kingdom of Poland by the Treaty of Lublin. By this time the quality of Jewish life in the west had deteriorated to such an extent that many Jews migrated east to Poland-Lithuania, where they were welcomed by the Polish kings, who granted the immigrants privileges and liberties, religious freedom, and cultural autonomy. Polish noblemen, as feudal lords, valued Jewish expertise in commerce and industry and employed Jewish agents to develop their backward provinces economically. The majority engaged in service occupations, acting as middlemen between the peasantry and various urban markets. They also set up small businesses such as innkeeping, dealing in furs and lumber, and the production of vodka. Jewish artisans practised their traditional arts and crafts, such as shoemaking. Eastern Jews tended towards ultra-orthodox hasidic Judaism, a ritual-bound way of life that is celebrated with much romantic nostalgia in Jewish literature and folklore.

Thus the nucleus of the Jewish population of eastern Europe was formed as the result of migration from west to east through Germany, but there were migrants from other regions, some of whom were Jewish. There has been a historic tendency for there to be a flow of migrants into Europe from Asia, particularly the Russian steppes. As explained by Dunlop (1954) and Koestler (1976), the once pagan kingdom of the Khazars which stretched between the Dnieper and the Volga rivers and was torn between the Christianity of Byzantium and the Islam of the Baghdad Caliphate, formally converted to Judaism around 740 AD. After the collapse of the Khazar empire in the thirteenth century its inhabitants began to migrate westwards into Hungary, Lithuania, Poland, and the Balkans. Inevitably the Jewish migrants from western Europe would have mingled with Khazar Jews. Several Jewish Khazar tribes joined forces with their pagan Magyar neighbours and migrated as far as Hungary. In imperial Russia, Khazar Jews were exempt from some of the disabilities to which other Jews were subject, because they had not been in Palestine at the time of Christ's crucifixion.

As a result of persecution there had also been a major Jewish migration from central Europe back into the lands of what had become the Ottoman Empire. By the end of the sixteenth century, Polish-Lithuanian Jewry and Ottoman Jewry had become the most important Jewish communities both numerically and intellectually. Fifty years later the former community suffered heavy losses through an invasion by Swedes from the north and by the Cossack rebellion in 1648, essentially a clash between the Polish monarch and his eastern subjects, which involved a brutal massacre of thousands of Jews, the most traumatic event until the Nazi Holocaust. Almost a century later there was another disaster when the Russian empress Elizabeth ordered the expulsion of all Jews from Russian territory in 1742. Most of them went to eastern Poland.

Thirty years later the first partitioning of Poland—agreed upon by Austria, Prussia, and Russia—resulted in all of eastern Poland, Lithuania, White Russia, Podolia, and Ukraine being incorporated into Russia, which became much larger as a result. Prussia (and other German states) already had a substantial Jewish population but this was greatly increased by the inclusion of Jews living in Posen (now Poznan), the part of Poland assigned to Prussia. That left Galicia, a backward area, which was annexed to Austria. Another partition took place at the Congress of Vienna (1814–1815), the same as the earlier one except that the region around Warsaw, called Congress Poland, was nominally independent but in practice a Russian dependency.

In eastern Europe, and especially in Russia, there were many instances of discriminatory legislation particularly affecting the Jews. The type of proscription under which they lived varied in different countries and at different times—for example they were subject to more official prohibitions in Russia, and more informal interference in Poland. Where they might live, where they might go, what they might do for a living were strictly defined, with major consequences for their habits, behaviour, and attitudes. They experienced not only the sudden institution of new regulations but also the varying enforcement of old ones. The constant need to adjust to these resulted in a high degree of adaptibility and a corresponding adjustment to instability and insecurity. Although other minorities were also subject to oppression no other group in the region was the target of so much discriminatory legislation.

In 1804, to exclude the Polish Jews from Great Russia, where they might upset the old manorial system which prevailed in the countryside, Tsar Alexander instituted what became known as the Pale of Settlement. Extending from the Baltic in the north to the Black Sea in the south, the Pale covered a million square kilometres of land. Legally, Jews were not allowed to reside outside the Pale, although it was possible for individuals to purchase exemption. The Pale was mainly rural but it contained many towns and important cities like Odessa, the port on the Black Sea founded by Catherine the Great. Within its confines the Ashkenazi population grew rapidly for several generations, as it did in Congress Poland. Jews dominated commercial life within the Pale throughout the nineteenth century. Jewish businesses were usually family concerns, relying on a network of contacts within the Jewish community. Finance, always a Jewish speciality, caused Jewish entrepreneurs to lead the industrialization of Russia in the late nineteenth century, and some of them became very wealthy as a result.

Western and Central Europe

The seventeenth century marked the start of the reintegration of Jews into western European society and the positive transformation of their social and economic status, after a long period of cultural isolation. A new era dawned around 1800, when the reforms associated with the Age of Enlightenment were welcomed by leading members of the Jewish community. The process of emancipation started in the late eighteenth century, when the political upheavals in France led to profound social and economic changes, sometimes reversed by later events. It would take up too much space to deal with developments in each European country in detail; instead the relevant material will be added in the individual profiles as necessary.

In 1787 the Austrian emperor issued a proclamation requiring the Austrian Jews to adopt German surnames and Germanized first names, to simplify administration. Prussia and other German states followed suit, and later other countries made similar regulations. In revolutionary France, one of the first acts of the Constituent Assembly was to secularize education, a prerequisite for emancipation, and soon afterwards to annul all anti-Jewish regulation. Educational reforms opened up opportunities of which the French Jews were quick to take advantage, and educated Jews began to use French as their main language. After his crucial victory over the Prussians at Jena in 1806, Bonaparte introduced reforms in the status of Jews throughout the German and Austrian lands. In France itself the Napoleonic decree of March 1808, usually called the decree of Bayonne, reimposed various restrictions on the Jews of France, but the secularization of education remained. Further reversals followed the restoration of the monarchy in 1816, but much survived of what had been achieved.

What happened in France was gradually propagated throughout western Europe, at a pace which varied from country to country. Take Italy, for example. Jews had been driven out of the Papal States in 1555, apart from Rome and Ancona. Under pressure from the Vatican some northern cities followed suit, but the free city of Livorno was a great exception. Legalized oppression was endemic. Venice, for example, as late as 1777, was suddenly brought into line with Rome so that Jews were forbidden to employ Christians, to own property, or to engage in manufacturing, thus ruining a useful and prosperous community. Bonaparte brought reforms to the parts of Italy which he conquered, but there was a reaction when the French left and the Austrians moved in. It was not until 1847 that in Rome, home of the largest of the Italian Jewish communities, the walls of the ghetto were torn down.

The settlement at the Congress of Vienna had left the Holy Roman Empire with thirty-nine German states, comprising thirty-five states and four free cities. Catholic Austria and Protestant Prussia were the largest and most powerful of these states; the rest varied greatly in size and importance. The two areas of densest Jewish population were the former Polish territories of Posen and West Prussia in the east and the area of the middle and upper Rhine and Main river valleys to the southwest. In between there were a few areas of moderate Jewish population in Silesia, Southern Hanover, Ostfriesland, and the cities of Berlin and Hamburg.

In Prussia, at the time of the Napoleonic wars, political and military leaders realized that their feudal society needed reform if it was to be able to overcome French hegemony. One reform, granted in 1812, was that Jews were declared to be of Prussian nationality rather than foreigners. They were granted freedom of movement and free choice of occupation, but they continued to have no access to public office or to a military career. Moreover this law did not hold in the whole of Prussia, in particular not in the former Polish territories. Also, only a few years later, certain parts of the law were rescinded. In 1847 another law was passed giving equal rights and duties to all citizens, but with numerous exceptions for Jews. For example, they were still barred from certain professions and access to public office was still difficult. As a result their abilities and energies could find expression only in commerce and industry. Around the middle of the nineteenth century a new upper-middle class in comfortable economic positions began to emerge, whereas the previously dominant nobility, the Junkers, as well as the artisans, the peasants, and the landowners, lost many of their privileges. Those who had suffered because of these developments became bitter opponents of the Jews and a potent source of anti-Semitism.

Through leaders such as Moses Mendelssohn, the eighteenth-century Jewish philosopher, Jewish emancipation began to spread in Germany and the German-speaking countries, as it had in France. Yiddish-speaking Jews began to learn to speak German. Jews had been encouraged to settle in Berlin since the late seventeenth century; they were therefore well established. Towards the end of the eighteenth, a small group of highly intelligent Jewish families who had made fortunes in trade and industry showed an active interest in literature, the arts, and the sciences and would discuss them in the salons which were presided over by rich, well-educated, and spirited Jewish women. Balanced precariously between the nobility and the bourgeoisie, they succeeded in transforming Berlin into a major cultural centre. Salons of this type arose elsewhere in Europe.

Lower down the social scale the coffee houses which were such a feature
of old Europe also provided a forum where members of the intelligentsia
could meet and discuss the issues of the day.

In 1848, the year of revolution, the Habsburg Empire followed the
German example by greatly relaxing the laws controlling and restricting
Jewish life. Jews were permitted to reside in the major cities of the empire,
and many took advantage of this. Budapest, Cracow, and Prague soon
acquired large Jewish populations. By 1867 Jews could live anywhere in the
land; they were eligible for all occupations and eventually were admitted
even into the hereditary nobility. In Vienna, the seat of government,
Jews began first to enter and then to dominate intellectual and cultural
life. By the end of the century, most of the lawyers and half the doctors
and dentists of *Mitteleuropa* were Jewish. Although anti-Semitism was
rife in Vienna, especially after the Jews were blamed for the financial
crash of 1873, there was less resistance to the appointment of Jews to
the professoriate than there was in Germany; one quarter of the total
university faculty was Jewish.

In the last third of the nineteenth century the political geography of
what had been the Holy Roman Empire changed radically. After a series
of wars most of the independent north German states were incorporated
in a new north German confederation under Prussian leadership. The
process of German unification was completed after the Franco-Prussian
war: the outcome was a German Reich consisting of the many formerly
independent German states; four kingdoms, five grand duchies, thirteen
duchies and principalities, three free cities, and Alsace-Lorraine, the last
ceded by France and treated as conquered territory.

In imperial Germany Jews finally acquired the same rights and
duties as other citizens. Once they were able to move into the cities,
talented, intelligent Jews, with their will-power and drive for better
living conditions, rapidly began to exercise influence on the burgeoning
economy. When German industry started its rapid rise and Germany
overtook France and England to become the leading industrial power
in Europe, Jews played an important role in this success. Especially in
Berlin, the headquarters of German Jewry, but also in other important
commercial centres, such as Breslau and Hamburg, Jewish businessmen

prospered and some not only became very wealthy but moved upwards socially. The mathematicians Leo Kronecker, Felix Hausdorff, Emmy Noether, Edmund Landau, and Max Dehn and the physicists James Franck, Max Born, and Franz Simon grew up in this milieu. They had no financial problems, so far as we know, unlike Albert Einstein whose father was a rather unsuccessful businessman. In Wilhelmine Germany, Jews were also strongly represented in the various professions, especially those which it was possible to practise independently. By 1907, 6 per cent of physicians and dentists, and 14 per cent of lawyers were Jews, although Jews only made up around 1 per cent of the total population. The number of Jewish students at most universities also rose rapidly. Berlin and Breslau proved to be the most popular. Among the scientists to be profiled here Eisenstein, Kronecker, Cantor, and Landau studied in Berlin, where nearly 20 per cent of the students were Jewish, while Hausdorff, Born, Courant, Simon, and Hopf chose Breslau, the capital of lower Silesia, which also had a large Jewish population, being the hub of the textile industry, a Jewish speciality.

Prior to emancipation there had been a small number of 'court' Jews in comfortable and privileged positions, who acted as agents for the rulers of the states in which they lived. The Habsburg rulers particularly valued their intelligence, skill, and knowledge, and permitted them to trade without restriction. Among other privileges their sons were permitted to study in universities, and gradually the doors were opened to other Jews. In most of Europe, well before the end of the century, Jews at least had access to secular education and to professions from which they had previously been excluded. Educated Jews rapidly adopted the culture of the countries in which they lived, including a fierce patriotism. French Jews became enthusiastic about French culture, German Jews about German culture, Russian Jews about Russian culture, and so on. Generally speaking, western Jews regarded themselves as superior to eastern Jews. There was, moreover, a certain pecking order. Frankfurt Jews looked down on Berlin Jews, Berlin Jews looked down on Viennese Jews, and Viennese Jews looked down on Warsaw Jews.

Individual Jews had to decide whether to remain in the closed world of traditional Judaism or to become assimilated into the surrounding gentile community. Many became non-observant, and some converted to Christianity, usually for pragmatic reasons: as Christians they were spared some of the more overt forms of anti-Semitism, and career possibilities opened up which had not previously been available. From the 1880s on it was common in Germany for the sons of Jewish parents to be baptized or at least officially registered as without religion, but even these were only admitted to public office and the civil service in very limited and insignificant numbers.

Eastern Europe and Russia

In eastern Europe hopes of reform, which had fuelled widespread unrest against absolute rule, ended in reaction and, for the Jews, a wave of pogroms. The situation for the Jews of the Pale took a sharp turn for the worse when the bigoted Tsar Alexander III ascended the throne in 1881 determined to avenge the assassination by nihilists of his relatively liberal father. He encouraged a new series of pogroms on a scale and of a character not seen since the Middle Ages. Under the reactionary advisers of his successor, the weak-willed and superstitious Tsar Nicholas II, the persecution intensified still further. The territory allotted to the Pale of Settlement was reduced in size. The pogroms were accompanied by the May Laws, economic and social restrictions unprecedented in scope. Western European countries protested but to no avail. By the end of the century Jewish economic and social life became completely demoralized. For example, the Black Sea port of Odessa, which had attracted many Jewish merchants from elsewhere in the Pale, experienced a series of pogroms, culminating in a particularly dreadful one in 1905. This led to a major exodus of Jews from what had become one of the major commercial and cultural centres of eastern Europe.

Waves of immigration to other parts of the world followed on a huge scale, and within a few decades the composition of European Jewry changed entirely. Earlier pogroms had driven many Polish Jews into Germany, but now a huge number fled in terror into any country which would receive them. Altogether 3.5 million Jews left central and eastern Europe between 1880 and 1925, with 100,000 settling in France, 112,000 in Canada, 150,000 in Argentina, 210,000 in England, and 2.65 million in the United States. Among them were the parents of the physicist Albert Michelson and those of the mathematician Norbert Wiener, who emigrated to the United States in the nineteenth century, while entry was still unrestricted. The Jewish communities of western Europe—particularly that of England—were greatly reinforced, but far more significant was the mass migration of European Jews to the United States, which was ready to accept large numbers of emigrants at this period (it is estimated that almost twenty-three million Europeans, many of them Jews, emigrated to America between 1881 and 1914).

By 1925 no fewer than 1.75 million Jews were living in New York, which overtook Warsaw as the city with the largest Jewish population; Chicago also had a large Jewish community, and there were substantial communities elsewhere. Before the middle of the nineteenth century the Jewish population of the United States had been quite small. The first major wave of Jews to arrive from central Europe were mainly middle-class. They adapted to American ways fairly easily but were looked down upon by the Protestant elite, typically alumni of the Ivy League colleges. When the lower-class eastern European Jews arrived later they found the earlier Jewish immigrants kept themselves well apart. The sons and daughters of these later immigrants naturally took full advantage of the educational opportunities available to them. By the end of the nineteenth century Jews already comprised half the student body of City College and Hunter College in New York, and there was also a high proportion at New York University. At the end of the First World War the proportion of Jewish students at Columbia University approached two out of five, at Harvard one in five, at Yale more than one in ten. When Jewish admission quotas were introduced after the war the limits were 21 per cent at Columbia, 12 per cent at Harvard, and 7 per cent at Yale. The restriction was applied quite mechanically: after Columbia had all but accepted Richard Feynman's application he was told the Jewish quota for the year was already full, so as a result the most brilliant physicist of his generation went to MIT instead. Similar policies operated in many law and medical schools, and spread to state universities.

In imperial Russia between 1853 and 1886 the total number of gymnasium students increased six-fold, while the number of Jewish gymnasium students soared by a factor of almost fifty. Over the same period the number of university students also increased six-fold while the number of Jews among them increased over a hundred times. Law and medicine were the preferred subjects. In Odessa it was recorded that 'all the schools are filled with Jewish students from end to end and ... the Jews are always at the head of the class,' while at the university every third student was Jewish. This led to the introduction of a *numerus clausus*, which restricted access of Jews to high schools and universities. The quota was 3 per cent in St Petersburg and Moscow, 5 per cent elsewhere, except in the Pale where it was set at 10 per cent. There were no restrictions on the proportion of Jewish students at German universities until the Nazi period, when it was limited to 1.5 per cent in 1933; later, Jewish students were barred altogether.

When the First World War broke out, although so many had left the Russian Empire, most of Europe's Jews (5.2 out of about 8.7 million) still lived in territories subject to the tsar, where they formed about 4 per cent of the total population. In 1915 the Pale was dissolved and although Jews were still not allowed to live in Moscow or Petrograd (St Petersburg) they could settle (but not acquire property) in other towns. The peace treaty after the end of the war assigned more than half of these Russian Jews to the new Republic of Poland, but 2.5 million remained in what became the Soviet Republic. During the war a large number had been accused of spying for the Germans and deported in cattle trucks from the border areas to the interior of the country where they had nowhere to live and no means of livelihood.

The October Revolution of 1917 was followed by civil war between the Bolsheviks (the Reds) and the Mensheviks (the Whites), ending in defeat for the Whites. Leading Jewish Bolsheviks included Trotsky but the Mensheviks were also led by Jews. By the eve of the Second World War well over a million Jews were living in areas that had been closed to them a quarter of a century earlier. They mainly settled in the cities of Moscow, Leningrad (St Petersburg), Kiev, and Kharkov.

The Nazi Period

But this is taking us too far into the twentieth century, and it is time we went back to record historical developments further west, particularly in Germany. During the First World War around 100,000 Jews served in the German army. About 3000 served as officers, since the army had relaxed its previous policy of excluding Jews from the officer corps. However, in some circles the defeat of Germany, which was followed by hyper-inflation and mass unemployment, was blamed on a sinister alliance between socialists and Jews. Eventually, political unrest undermined the fragile Weimar Republic and led to the rise of the Nazi (National Socialist) party. There was a crisis in 1932 when the veteran Hindenburg barely succeeded in winning an election for the German presidency ahead of the upstart Adolf Hitler, leader of the Nazis. Hindenburg appointed him as chancellor, an action which he was soon to regret. Within a few months Hitler had secured absolute dictatorial power and every attempt at opposition to the Nazis was ruthlessly crushed. Many highly educated Germans did not think Nazism could possibly last, that it was far too extreme an ideology to have any chance of real acceptance by Germans. By the time they began to realize its disastrous impact it was too late for any serious opposition. Few people outside Germany were aware of the brutality of the terror, organized with great efficiency and applied against the slightest signs of opposition, using assassinations, executions, and forced labour camps.

Almost at once the Nazi propaganda machine started attacking the Jews and others classed as non-Aryans. A nationwide boycott of Jewish businesses was announced, and a general campaign began to remove Jews from professions of all kinds, in government, medicine, law, education, and the arts. Jews and other non-Aryans in the civil service were forced to retire or dismissed. Communists, gypsies, Jehovah's Witnesses, and homosexuals were also rounded up and sent to concentration camps, but in this book we are mainly concerned with the fate of the Jews. The Nazis considered anyone Jewish if they had one Jewish parent or grandparent. Another wave of legislation in 1935 attacked 'racial defilement'. Sexual relations between Aryans and non-Aryans were forbidden, in or out of marriage; the penalties for the non-Aryan were severe and there were grounds for dismissal if the Aryan was a civil servant. Existing marriages were not affected until later, but the mathematicians Emil Artin and Hermann Weyl, whose wives were Jewish, thought it wise to emigrate, as did the physicist Enrico Fermi when similar laws was introduced in Italy.

At this stage it was still relatively easy to emigrate and many left as soon as they could. Often they were from families that had lived in Germany for generations and regarded it as their homeland. The influx of immigrants greatly enriched the cultural life of the countries to which they emigrated. Although the United States was often the final destination, the emigrants usually began by taking refuge in countries neighbouring Germany in the hope that the situation might improve and they might be able to resume their former lives. France and Italy, especially, became places of asylum for German, and later Austrian, Jews fleeing from the Nazis. Jewish asylum-seekers later feared that Europe would be completely overrun by the Nazis and that while Britain and other unoccupied countries might serve as useful stepping-stones they needed to go on to places more remote from the Nazi menace, preferably the United States.

The Nazis went on, in stages, to make life as difficult as possible for the remaining Jews. Ghettos were reintroduced. All Polish Jews living in Germany were required to leave the country without delay. At the end of 1938 the situation took a sharp turn for the worse, starting with the large-scale burning of synagogues, destruction of Jewish homes and other property, beatings and arrests, known as the *Kristallnacht* pogrom. Up to this point many of the more important Jewish firms had been allowed to stay in business, perhaps because the German economy was still so precarious, although some of the less important firms had already been 'Aryanized'. Now Jews were required to cease all business activity and sell to the state any investments or property they might own; in addition, heavy fines were imposed on the Jewish community. Before long, the concentration camps, which until then had mainly been used to detain political opponents of the regime, were filled to overflowing with Jews who had been dragged from their homes. Previously it had been possible for emigrants to arrange to transfer their assets to their country of adoption, albeit after paying heavy taxes, but now they had to give up almost everything they possessed.

Next, measures were taken to obtain a complete list of all Jews living in Germany. They were issued with new identity documents, stamped with the letter J. Men had to add 'Israel' to their names, women had to add 'Sara'. They were persecuted and humiliated, denied all civic rights, but still worse was to come: at the height of the war in Europe (when Germany was obviously losing), the Nazis adopted the Final Solution, which was to exterminate the Jews completely. This operation was carried out with great efficiency, even to the detriment of the German war effort. It was not confined to Germany but extended to other parts of Europe which came under Nazi control, including France, Belgium, Luxemburg, the Netherlands, Italy, Norway, Denmark, Finland, Austria, Czechoslovakia, Hungary, Romania, Bulgaria, Yugoslavia, Greece, Poland, Estonia, Latvia, Lithuania and parts of the Soviet Union. (Detailed accounts of what happened in Europe during this terrible period can be found in the literature, for example Dawidowicz (1975).)

2

Jews in Academia

The German System

Although a few were independently wealthy, most of the mathematicians and physicists we are concerned with needed to earn a living, and that usually meant obtaining employment in a university. Again we focus on the situation in the German-speaking countries of central Europe, since it is most germane to what follows. German universities, like their counterparts elsewhere, had been centres of training for the professions of law, medicine, and the ministry since the Middle Ages. In the seventeenth and eighteenth centuries they also assumed responsibility for the education of the professional civil service. A university existed in every German state that could afford to support one; the larger states maintained more than one, while Prussia had six. Later, three new urban universities were founded in Cologne, Frankfurt, and Hamburg, making nineteen German universities altogether, each constituted in much the same way with professional schools, called faculties, for medicine, law, and theology and a fourth faculty, philosophy, which represented the humanities, mathematics, and some of the natural sciences, and which provided general education as a service for the other three.

After Prussia lost substantial amounts of territory in the Napoleonic wars the king urged his state to replace intellectually what it had lost physically. During the intense reform movement which followed, the University of Berlin played a leading role after it opened its doors in 1810. Wilhelm, the elder of the von Humboldt brothers, was the driving force behind this development. As minister of education in the Prussian government he promoted the model of the modern university, combining teaching with original scholarship and first-class research. He introduced the radical ideas that professors should lecture on whatever they wished and that students could take whatever courses they preferred. Moreover the faculty of philosophy, to which the scientists belonged, replaced medicine, law, and theology as the heart of the university. These reforms then spread to other universities, old and new, throughout Germany. At the same time the over-emphasis on classical studies at school was ended and at the new secondary schools mathematics, seen as an essential preparation for science, became an important part of the curriculum.

To graduate from a gymnasium (elite secondary school, similar to a French lycée) and be qualified to enter a university or equivalent institution of higher education it was necessary for a student to pass an examination called the *Abitur*. This also allowed the student to volunteer to serve just one year in the army, rather than be conscripted for three years. It was possible to obtain the *Abitur* at other types of school, but the great majority of university students had received their secondary education at a gymnasium. At university, attendance at lectures was optional, and there was no set syllabus. There were no tutorials, and no organized contact between teachers and students. Professors gave their lectures and then disappeared. A student was not obliged to limit himself to a single institution but could attend the lectures of particular professors wherever they might be found. After at least three years of study he took an examination, either for the certificate required for entry into one of the professions or for a doctorate, comparable to a master's degree elsewhere.

To become a *Privatdozent*, the first step in an academic career, the aspirant next needed to obtain the *venia legendi* or *venia docendi* (licence to teach independently) by presenting a *Habilitationsschrift,* essentially a thesis, and delivering a *Habilitationsvortrag,* a trial lecture before the faculty on a subject chosen from a short list provided by the candidate. Once habilitated, the aspirant was eligible to become a *Privatdozent*. (Felix Hausdorff complained that at Leipzig *Privatdozenten* were hardly treated as human beings.) *Privatdozenten* were expected to survive on the fees they collected from the students who attended their lectures. A *Privatdozent* might remain in this lowly status indefinitely but the next stage to aspire to was that of *ausserordentliche Professor* (in Latin *professor extra-ordinarius).* The final step was up to the rank of *ordentliche Professor* (in Latin *professor ordinarius)* with a substantial advance in salary and status. The *Ordinarius* would often delegate various chores to an unpaid assistant, usually a promising graduate student who had not yet habilitated. The duties might include researching the literature for the professor's lectures and writing them up afterwards. Professors, but not *Privatdozenten,* ranked as state officials, their appointment subject to ministerial approval. Although the terms *Ordinarius, Extra-Ordinarius,* and *Privatdozent,* and their equivalents in other languages, are often translated in American literature as full professor, associate professor, and instructor, this is misleading.

At German universities, there was unlikely to be an *Ordinarius* in mathematics or physics before the nineteenth century. When it became normal to appoint one for mathematics, some theoretical physics might be included in this, but not experimental physics. Once physics began to emerge as a separate discipline, with its own *Ordinarien,* laboratories were needed, since for a degree in the subject practical classes were a requirement. By 1870 most German universities also had at least one *Extra-Ordinarius* in physics, as well as an *Ordinarius.*

After unification German universities continued much as before under the control of the separate states. Physics continued to be taught to an assortment of professionals in training, who were required in increasing numbers and variety by modern Germany. It continued to be taught to the small number of intending physicists as well, but with an important difference, since the training led not only to school-teaching but also to careers in industry. Because the traditional universities were unable or unwilling to meet the demands of commerce and industry for well-trained and competent people the polytechnics or *technische Hochschulen* (technical universities) had been established, somewhat on the model of the French *école polytechnique.* By the end of the nineteenth century there were nine of these in Germany; two more were established early in the twentieth. The teaching was of a high standard, the professors in several cases being Nobel laureates. In another important development, the Kaiser Wilhelm Gesellschaft, founded in 1911, established a network of well-equipped research institutes, sponsored partly by industry, in

Berlin, Munich, Göttingen, and other major centres. Thus although anti-Semitism was strongly entrenched in the universities, there were alternative opportunities for Jews in these and other new instutions.

Notoriously, at Prussian universities Jewish *Privatdozenten* were not easily promoted (neither, for that matter, were Roman Catholics). The much-honoured experimental physicist Eugen Goldstein (1850–1930), for example, declined offers of senior university posts because he was not prepared to relinquish Judaism; instead he spent most of his long professional career as a physicist at the Potsdam astronomical observatory and other bodies which did not require this. The theoretical physicist Felix Auerbach remained a *Privatdozent* in Breslau for ten years, during which the faculty twice proposed him for *Extra-Ordinarius* but the Prussian minister of culture declined, although Helmholtz and other senior physicists supported the proposal. When Kiel proposed him for a similar position the minister of culture explained to the finance minister that he did not want to increase the Jewish element in Kiel but would not object if he went to Jena instead. However at Jena the faculty opposed the appointment of Auerbach because he was a Jew and because he had been a *Privatdozent* for so long. Nevertheless he was duly appointed *Extra-Ordinarius* over their objections but ran into further opposition later when it was proposed to promote him to *Ordinarius*.

Some of the career difficulties experienced by Jewish academics may be attributed to anti-Semitism when there may in fact be other explanations. For example, a belief in socialism certainly posed an obstacle to career advancement, as we will see in the cases of George Pólya and Emmy Noether. There were, of course, personality problems in particular cases. No doubt a combination of various factors might be responsible for unusual delay in career advancement. Nevertheless there was undoubtedly strong resistance to the appointment of Jews to regular positions in universities, especially at the top rank of *Ordinarius*. During the period 1882–1909 the number of Jewish *Ordinarien* at German universities was never more than twenty-five, but by 1917 had fallen to only thirteen, out of over a thousand such posts. However these figures do not include converted Jews who were more numerous at the top level. Eleven universities, including Berlin, had no Jewish *Ordinarien* at all. Resistance came primarily from the faculties themselves: anti-Semitism was strongest in some fields of humanities and in law, less strong in medicine, and least strong in mathematics and science.

The Third Reich

There was no security of tenure for university professors in the Third Reich. Anyone could lose their position if he or she incurred the displeasure of the Nazis. The racial laws which the Nazi government introduced in 1933 effectively terminated the employment of almost all Jewish university teachers, from *Privatdozenten* to professors. From 1938 those dismissed were not only forbidden to teach, they were no longer allowed to enter university buildings, including libraries. There had been certain exceptions in the original legislation, namely those who had been state officials before the First World War or else had fought or had lost a father or son in the fighting, but later these exceptions were partially abolished. Young people who were hoping to begin an academic career were also affected, as were many others who for reasons of circumstance, conviction, or character were considered undesirables by the Nazi regime. By April 1936 more than 1600 scholars, about a third of them scientists, had been dismissed from German universities and scientific institutions, among them 313 *Ordinarien*. An estimated 80 per cent of them were dismissed on 'racial' grounds, i.e. because they were classed as Jewish. Some were suspected of left-wing political sympathies. A few of their fellow academics, such as James Franck, openly protested at the dismissals, but the majority felt this would be unwise. They reasoned, 'if I protest I shall be removed from my post, where I have influence; then I'll have none. So I had better keep quiet and see what happens.' Some may have hoped to fill the vacancies thus created themselves, but found that ill-qualified Nazi supporters were appointed instead.

As a result of the racial laws, about 1150 Jewish scientists, many of them of great distinction, left Germany between 1933 and 1935. Max Pinl and Lux Furtmüller (1973) have collected information about over a hundred mathematicians of Jewish descent who were victimized in that period. Eight Jewish mathematicians were deported to the death camps, two of them with their wives. Only two survived. Three Jewish mathematicians committed suicide to escape deportation, one of them with his wife. Altogether ninety-six Jewish men and five women, all mathematicians, were directly affected. Four-fifths of them, eighty-two out of 101, emigrated to sixteen different countries, often in stages. Among the receiving countries, the United States accepted three-fifths of the total, forty-nine emigrants, of whom two returned, one each to Austria and Germany. Great Britain led the others with seven, followed by Israel with five. Canada, the Netherlands, and the Soviet Republic accepted three each, Switzerland and Australia two; Denmark, Norway, Sweden, Ireland, Brazil, Chile, Turkey, and India one each. Similar details have not been collected for Jewish physicists but we know that by 1935 one in four of them had lost their positions, including some of the most distinguished. By 1941 over a hundred had emigrated from Germany to the United States.

The impact of the racial laws varied considerably from place to place. Where the senior faculty members worked together as a team and staff–student relations were close the effects of the Nazi purge were reduced. In Berlin, regarded by many as Germany's flagship for research in physics, there was a mathematical-physical working group of faculty and students which helped to preserve good relations. In Frankfurt the atmosphere in the Mathematical Institute was particularly harmonious, and the constitution of the university forbade discrimination of any kind. In Munich fewer academics were affected by the racial laws because not many Jews had been appointed to academic positions in the first place. The opposite was true at Göttingen, where the Jewish exodus essentially ruined Germany's flagship for research in mathematics. At a banquet there in 1934 the Nazi minister of culture asked David Hilbert whether it was true, as rumoured, that the Mathematical Institute had suffered after the removal of the Jews and their friends. Hilbert's famous reply was 'Suffered? It hasn't suffered, Herr Minister. It just doesn't exist any more.' But, as David Rowe (1986) has remarked, it had rather gone underground, like so many other remnants of Weimar culture, and reappeared in the United States.

Displaced Scholars

In these pages we trace the fortunes of many of the Jewish mathematicians and physicists who left their central European homelands in the 1930s and early 1940s, at least partly to escape the threat of Nazi oppression. In countries where they sought asylum, committees were set up to render assistance; in Britain, for example, there was the Academic Assistance Council (AAC), a voluntary organization funded by donations from British academics, later known as the Society for the Protection of Science and Learning (SPSL), and there was also the Professional Committee for German Jewish Refugees. The AAC was set up 'to help scholars displaced from university or research positions for reasons of racial origin, political or religious opinion'; it provided maintenance for displaced scholars, from whatever country, and acted as a centre for information, to put them in touch with institutions that could best help. The government was sympathetic, regarding it as in the public interest to try and secure for the United Kingdom prominent Jews who were expelled from Germany and who had achieved distinction whether in pure science, applied science, music or art. Of the 2600 Jews assisted by the AAC/ SPSL, twenty became Nobel laureates, fifty-four were elected Fellows of the Royal Society, thirty-four became Fellows of the British Academy, and ten received knighthoods.

Often emigration was a two-stage process. The first priority was to escape the Nazis. Many obtained temporary refuge in England, France, or other countries, where the authorities usually required some guarantee that the immigrant would not become a liability to the state. Owing to the international character of science, mathematicians and physicists usually had professional contacts who were able to help provide this. The displaced scholar would then have time to arrange a more permanent means of livelihood, perhaps in a different country. Often that would be the United States but American immigration laws were strictly enforced and officialdom moved slowly. There was no American committee dealing with individuals, like the British AAC, but the Emergency Committee in Aid of Displaced German Scholars managed to persuade a large number of universities and colleges, including many which were not of the first rank, to provide positions for Jewish émigrés.

Much was also achieved by the efforts of individuals. For example, the Oxford physicist Frederick Lindemann quickly realized that Hitler's folly and brutality could be turned to the advantage of British universities, especially his own university of Oxford. Lindemann was a passionate, combative champion of scientific and technological education, who combined private wealth, a cosmopolitan background, and considerable personal eccentricity (see Fort (2003) for details of his life-story). He already knew personally many of the German scientists, having taken his PhD in Berlin under Nernst. Lindemann had no love for Jews but deplored the way they were treated by the Nazis. A strong believer in private initiative, he wasted no time, going at once to visit those under threat and arranging for some of them to continue their work in Britain.

Another possible place of asylum for the Jews was British-administered Palestine, where the Hebrew University had opened its doors in 1925. The Göttingen number-theorist Edmund Landau was one of the first invited to lecture; he quickly learnt enough Hebrew to give his talk in that language instead of German. Two years later when he returned for a year as visiting professor, he was invited to become head of the department of mathematics but declined. The mathematical logician Abraham Fraenkel, from Kiel, was appointed to a post in the department in 1929. Two years later he returned to Kiel, where his post as *Ordinarius* had been held open, but in 1933 he changed his mind again and returned to Jerusalem where he played a major role in developing the university's reputation for mathematics. When Albert Einstein was asked by Weizmann if he would like to move to the Hebrew University he refused outright because he was highly critical of the university's administration. Later, Einstein, liaising with Fraenkel, was always on the lookout for physicists who might be persuaded to go there and lead a department in the subject, but Max Born and Franz Simon, among others, found reasons for refusal. Among the last of the handful of Jewish mathematicians to emigrate to Palestine was the elderly Issai Schur, who was already in poor health when he arrived from Berlin in 1938; he died soon afterwards. Once the Second World War had broken out the necessary transport was no longer available, but Otto

Toeplitz left Bonn just in time and took up an administrative post at the Hebrew University. After the independent state of Israel was established in 1948 other universities were founded to meet the demand for higher education from the growing population.

The mathematicians and scientists who left Nazi Germany early, in particular those in the prime of life, were mostly successful in obtaining suitable positions, especially since there was widespread sympathy with their plight, but later this became extremely difficult or impossible, due to the widespread unemployment during the Great Depression. When positions became available there was a reluctance to appoint foreigners. Both India and Turkey were trying to recruit physicists, especially, and there were opportunities in the Soviet Republic, which often ended in disaster, as we shall see in the case of the unfortunate Fritz Noether.

In the 1920s the Rockefeller Foundation had established a programme of international fellowships, administered by an office called the International Education Board. The fellowships were tenable by young European scientists who wished to visit centres of excellence other than their own, either in America or in other European countries. Initially the programme focused on physics and chemistry, but then mathematics was included and later biology. The fellowships were awarded for one year at a time, but could be renewed. Up to 1930, 135 were awarded to physicists, including thirty-one from Germany, twenty-two from Russia, and eighteen from England, mostly for study in the United States. Many Jews benefited from the fellowship programme but even the officers of the International Education Board were not immune from prejudice. After interviewing an applied mathematician one of them noted 'while he is a Jew, he has developed a typical British appearance that impresses me rather favourably. He is tall, stocky and well-built, with a ruddy complexion. Nothing of the obnoxious Jewish traits were in evidence.'

When the Nazis rose to power and the exodus from Germany got under way the Rockefeller fellowship programme could not be adapted to help the displaced scholars because of a regulation that fellowships could only be awarded to those who had a position to go to afterwards. Consequently an emergency programme was set up in 1933, supplemented by two others in 1940; altogether about 300 displaced scholars were assisted, either in the United States or in Europe, in addition to the regular fellowship programme. About forty mathematicians and physicists, mostly Jewish, received Rockefeller assistance to restart their careers in the United States.

When G. H. Hardy, as Secretary of the London Mathematical Society, wrote to the International Education Board about the difficulty of finding suitable positions for displaced mathematicians in England one of the officers replied, 'I feel that some of the considerations you bring forth about the situation in England are about equally applicable to the United States, where foreigners are very hard to place, since generally along with any position … there goes the necessity of contact with undergraduates, and these youngsters are inexperienced enough to regard a foreign accent as indicative of individual and intellectual incapacity.' Jews had the additional problem that the prevalence of anti-Semitism in the American academic world seriously impeded efforts to place Jewish émigrés. Although the United States eventually admitted more émigrés from the Reich than any other single country, its record in relation to capacity was less than generous. One reason was the strongly negative attitude of the existing Jewish community to the prospect of any further large influx of Jewish immigrants, and the resultant refusal of the community's leaders to urge more than token changes in immigration law or procedures. A proposal in 1939 to admit up to 20,000 Jewish children failed to reach the floor of Congress after a bitter debate; at the same time hospitality was being mobilized on a large scale to bring 10,000 child refugees into Britain. Most of them never saw their parents again.

There can be no doubt of the importance of émigré mathematicians, as a group, during the 1930s, for the development of the subject in the United States. The president of the Rockefeller Foundation summed up the situation when he wrote, '[If] Hitler had set out, with benevolent intent, to build up America as one of the world's great mathematical centers, he could hardly have achieved more successfully the result, which his ruthlessness has accomplished.' As Medawar and Pyke explain in *Hitler's Gift* (2000), the same was true in the case of science, and the story has often been told of how Jewish physicists, driven from Germany by Nazi policies, were able to contribute to the Allied war effort and help to make victory possible.

The Scientific Academies

As we shall see, the Prussian Academy of Sciences did not elect a professed Jew until 1848. This delay seems exceptional; otherwise there seems to have been little, if any, discrimination in the scientific academies. The Royal Society of London, for example, elected its first Jewish fellow as early as 1723. In the United Kingdom, during the first half of the twentieth century, the proportion of Jews in the general population was less than 1 per cent, but the proportion in the Royal Society rose steadily from 1 per cent to 5 per cent. No fewer than eighteen of the Jewish émigré mathematicians were elected to the highest learned societies of their adoptive countries, three of them successively in two countries. They include four Fellows of the Royal Society and nine members of the United States National Academy of Sciences. Today over 40 per cent of the members of the physics divisions of the latter are Jewish.

Shortly before deciding he had to leave Germany, Albert Einstein resigned from the Bavarian Academy, writing, 'To the best of my knowledge the learned societies of Germany have stood by passively and silently while substantial numbers of scholars, students and academically-trained professionals have been deprived of employment and livelihood. I do not want to belong to a society which behaves in such a manner, even if it does so under compulsion.' He also resigned from the Berlin Academy, where a personal chair had been created for him. Max Planck wrote to thank him for doing so and hoped that they would remain friends. Abram Ioffe also resigned from his corresponding membership of the Berlin Academy in protest against the actions of the Nazi regime. In Italy Mussolini suppressed the Accademia Nazionale dei Lincei and replaced it by the Accademia d'Italia, excluding members of the Lincei, such as Vito Volterra, who publicly opposed his fascist regime.

3

Some Forerunners

Sephardic Scholars

During the Middle Ages, Jewish scholars shared with their Arabian contemporaries the task of preserving the achievements of Greek mathematics and astronomy, and partly those of Indian mathematics, and transmitting them to the Occident. Both the main branches of Judaism had important contacts with the world of Islam and came under the influence of the Arab scientific renaissance. Muslim scholars studied the heritage of the classical world and, in science, developed what they learnt. Their knowledge was passed on to both Christian and Jewish scholars, the latter mainly in Iberia, where Jews were able to pursue philosophy and enlightened speculation (Langerman 1999). Jewish scholars translated into Hebrew not only from Arabic but also from Greek and Latin. Translations of Arabic scientific works into Latin (or Spanish) were also produced mainly by Jews. Astronomy was considered by Arab scientists one of the seven disciplines which were comprised in mathematics, the other six being arithmetic, algebra, geometry, astrology, optics, and music.

The expulsion of the Moors from Spain in 1492 was a calamity for the Jews as well. It is estimated that 150,000 Jews were expelled from Spain and Sicily, then under Spanish rule. Some settled along the North African coast and in Italy, Egypt, Palestine, and Syria, but the majority went to the Balkans and the central provinces of the Ottoman Empire. The conversos, those Jews who chose to convert, were not allowed to leave the country. Among them there were some who still observed Jewish rites in secret. These marranos (swine), as they were insultingly called, often occupied high position in the state. The Holy Office of Inquisition, although established to root out heresy in the Catholic Church, was increasingly used to persecute the Jews. In Spain one of its duties was to discover and punish marranos, usually by death, after dramatic autos da fé (acts of faith). Whereas Spanish Jews had the option of leaving, Portuguese Jews had no choice but to convert, although many became marranos. When eventually the marranos succeeded in leaving Iberia they settled in certain areas of Flanders, Provence, and southwest France. Important Sephardic communities arose in Amsterdam, Bordeaux, and Bayonne, also in London and Hamburg. They brought with them a distinctive Jewish culture, regarded themselves as superior, and did not mingle with their Ashkenazi brethren.

No less an authority than George Sarton found that 15 per cent of the known scientists working in the Western world between 1150 and 1300 were Jewish. Historians of science such as Moritz Steinschneider have found much of interest in the earlier period, but until the eighteenth century the advancement of mathematics owed little to Jewish scholars, and the same is true of secular science. In the words of Thorstein Veblen (1919) 'the intellectual pre-eminence of Jews in modern Europe was due to a break with the past, not its resurrection. The cultural heritage of the Jewish people may be very ancient and very distinguished but these achievements of the Jewish ancients neither touch the frontiers of modern science nor do they follow in the lines of modern scholarship.' This may have been due to rabbinical objections to the pursuit of secular science, the rabbis regarding this as a pagan invention, outside the Jewish tradition. However, the study of law and medicine was permissible, as were logic, astronomy, and even mathematics. The vast majority of observant Jews held rabbinical authority superior to scientific authority; this was an obvious barrier to their acceptance in the scientific community.

The Early Modern Period

In his account of the work of the astronomer and cosmographer David Gans (1541–1613), André Neher (1986) has given a description of how Jewish scholars struggled to accommodate the new astronomical theories which emerged in his lifetime. Gans, a free-thinking rabbi who spent most of his career in Prague, provided the first references to Nicholas Copernicus, Tycho Brahe, and Johannes Kepler to be found in a Hebrew text; the latter two astronomers he knew personally. In many ways heliocentric cosmology posed less of a problem to Jews than to Christians. Ruderman (1995) has written more generally about the impact of scientific discoveries on Jewish thought in the early modern period.

There is a notable absence of Jewish physicists before the first half of the nineteenth century, although Jewish mathematicians emerged considerably earlier. In *The Jew in Science* Gershenfeld (1934) lists the names of some shadowy figures who appear to have been commentators on or translators of textbooks rather than researchers. These include the Germans Meier Hirsch (1765–1851) and Michael Creizenach (1789–1842), the Russian Jakob Eichenbaum (1796–1861), the Lorrainer Moses Ensheim (1750–1839), the Czech Simon Gunz (1743–1824), the Dutchman Rehuel Lobatto (1797–1866), and the Silesian Elkan Markus (1781–1861). To these should be added the cosmopolitan Mordechai Schnaber Levison (1741–1797), who moved between England, Germany, and Sweden. A prolific writer, he produced the first book in Hebrew giving an account of Newton's scientific theories.

Another, who is also not listed by Gershenfeld, is the mathematical rabbi Abraham Jakub Stern (1768–1842), an account of whose life has been given by Jacob Schatzky (1954). Stern was born in an obscure shtetl of Lublin province; his parents were desperately poor. At first he made a living as a watchmaker, while teaching himself astronomy and mathematics, and also learnt to speak French, German, and Polish. He invented a 'complicated' calculating machine which in 1813 he demonstrated to the 'German sages' of Halle and Furth. Two years later he was introduced to Tsar Alexander I as 'the Jewish mechanical engineer', and granted an annual pension from the Russian state. He designed a new calculating machine, still more complex than the first, and a rapid automated plough. In Warsaw, where he was respected for his great erudition, he was the first Jew to be elected a member of the Royal Society of Friends of the Sciences. Short in stature, with beautiful, good-natured eyes and a long beard, he was the subject of pictures showing him lecturing to the society which were was used to create a false impression of how liberal and tolerant the government of Congress Poland was towards Jews. Although consulted by the government on Jewish affairs, politically he was a naive reactionary, trying to preserve the traditional Jewish way of life against the forces of Enlightenment.

Stern had a protégé named Chaim Selig Slonimski (1810–1904), who became his son-in-law. Born in Bialystock, Slonimski received a traditional Jewish education until the age of eighteen. Afterwards he studied foreign languages and acquired mathematical and astronomical knowledge, mostly from medieval Hebrew works. In addition to several treatises on algebra and astronomy he wrote important books on the Jewish calendar, and one on astronomy entitled *The History of the Heavens*, with help from Stern. These works are not as well known as they might be because they have not been translated from Hebrew. He also wrote an interesting memoir of Alexander von Humboldt, which has been translated into German by Kurt-Jurgen Maass (Slonimski 1997). After Slonimski settled in Warsaw, he was a frequent guest at the home of Stern, who saw him as a potential husband for his youngest daughter, Sarah; the marriage took place in 1842, just before Stern died. Until then Stern had kept secret from Slonimski the details of his calculating machine, fearing that the latter would claim it as his own. This just what happened, after Stern's death; Slonimski took out patents on the machine and exhibited it in Berlin where it impressed the mathematicians and was praised by the younger Humboldt, but like other designs of this period it was unsuitable for commercial exploitation.

English Forerunners

As explained by Roth (1941) and Endelman (2000), in England, after the Commonwealth, Jews could settle wherever they pleased, and enjoyed social tolerance but not full civic rights. Initially the numbers involved were quite small but in the Hanoverian period the prosperity of the Netherlands declined and many Jews transferred their activities from Amsterdam to London. By 1734 there were estimated to be 6000 Jews in England. A further influx from Bohemia and Poland brought the Jewish population in London alone to 20,000 by the end of the eighteenth century. Biblical Hebrew was taught at universities, and even in some humanist schools, and Hebrew literature was studied by scholars, but professed Jews could not matriculate at Oxford, or proceed to a degree at Cambridge. Such disabilities, which they shared with non-Anglicans, such as Catholics, dissenters, and atheists, were not completely removed until 1871.

Although no Jews played a prominent role in the scientific revolution which began in the seventeenth century and continued into the eighteenth, in England there were several who might be described as disciples of Isaac Newton. One was Israel Lyons, whose remarkable career as mathematician, botanist, and astronomer has been described by Glyn (2002). His father, an Ashkenazi Jew of Polish origin who was known as the 'ingenious silversmith', taught Hebrew in Cambridge and published an excellent grammar of the language. Israel, born in 1739, was something of an infant prodigy. He could well have entered the university if he was prepared to convert, but loyalty to his father prevented this. Largely self-taught, he wrote a successful *Treatise of Fluxions* at the age of nineteen, but after this he turned to natural history and astronomy. He wrote a handbook of the flora to be found in the neighbourhood of Cambridge and in 1764 gave a summer course on botany in Oxford 'to great applause'. These lectures were arranged by Joseph Banks, who was an undergraduate at the time. Many years later Banks was able to help him find employment, but meanwhile Lyons earned his living as a coach for the Cambridge Tripos. He also used his knowledge of astronomy to work on the Nautical Almanac at the request of the Board of Longitude. Towards the end of the 1760s, however, he took to drink and by 1770 was described as a pathetic figure.

In 1773 Lyons had recovered enough to sail on a scientific expedition into the Arctic, making astronomical observations. The next year he married 'a most agreeable young lady with a considerable fortune', which freed him from financial constraints. They moved to London, where he started to write a biography of the late Astronomer Royal Sir Edmond Halley, but after barely a year of married life he died at the early age of thirty-six, apparently from measles. Lyons' publications include a paper on 'some calculations in spherical trigonometry' in the *Philosophical Transactions* of the Royal Society and an article on astronomy, published posthumously. He was clearly a remarkable man, although not a mathematician of any great distinction.

Lyons was apparently known to the father of the novelist Maria Edgeworth who found him a sufficiently interesting character to depict him, as himself, in her novel *Harrington* of 1819. During the hero's sojourn in Cambridge, he encounters Lyons: 'He had little of the Jew in his appearance. … a gay looking man … with quick sparkling black eyes, and altogether a person of modern appearance both in dress and address … though he was a Hebrew teacher … I found him by his conversation … a man of remarkably fertile genius. He was proud of shewing himself to be a man-of-the-world. I found him in the midst of his Hebrew scholars, and moreover with some of the best mathematicians, and some of the first literary men in Cambridge.'

Another Jewish scientist who worked in London at a slightly later period was considered one of the outstanding amateur scholars of his day. This was the mathematician, actuary, and astronomer Benjamin Gompertz. His brother Ephraim was also known as a mathematician and political economist, and another brother Lewis, known for his kindness to animals, was a prolific inventor of ingenious but rather impractical devices. They were members of a distinguished mercantile family in the diamond trade that had branched out from the Netherlands in the eighteenth century.

Born in London on 5 March 1779 and largely self-educated, Benjamin Gompertz has been described as the last of the learned Newtonians;

out of respect for the memory of Sir Isaac he continued to use the old language of fluxions, when it had been obsolete for nearly half a century. His speciality was actuarial science, particularly life contingencies, where his 'law' on mortality marked the beginning of a new era. In 1824 he was appointed actuary and head officer of the newly formed Alliance British and Foreign Life and Fire Assurance Company, and chief manager of the Alliance Marine Assurance Society founded by his brother-in-law Moses Montefiore and Nathan Rothschild. According to Hooker (1965) he held these offices with great distinction until he retired in 1847, owing to failing health. As we shall see, the French mathematician Olinde Rodrigues was also engaged in the business of life insurance, shortly before Gompertz published his major papers on life contingencies, as was the British mathematician Sylvester somewhat later. Perhaps this type of business should be added to the list of occupations to which Jews were particularly attracted.

Gompertz was active in various scientific societies. Elected to the Royal Society in 1819, he became a member of the Council in 1832. He was also active in the newly formed Astronomical Society, today the Royal Astronomical Society. Although not an observational astronomer himself, the computations he made were of great value to those who were. He was president of the Spitalfields Mathematical Society at the time it was absorbed into the Astronomical Society, and he helped to promote the formation of the Royal Statistical Society. The London Mathematical Society, of which he became one of the original members, was founded not long before his death in 1865.

French Forerunners

In pre-revolutionary France, education was in the hands of the Catholic Church, and there was not much sign of Jewish interest in science. However, Lorraine, where fewer restrictions were imposed on Jews than in the rest of France, was an exception. There was a major Jewish settlement of long standing in Metz, the principal city of the duchy, where the many-sided

Jewish scholar Olry Terquem was born in 1782. In 1801 he became only the second Jew to be admitted to the École Polytechnique in Paris. He began his teaching career as professor of higher mathematics at the Lycée Imperial in Mainz, then under French control. He was also professor at a succession of royal artillery schools, first in Mainz, then in Grenoble, and finally in Paris, where he organized a school library. In 1842 he founded, and for many years edited, a mathematical journal, the *Nouvelles annals de mathematiques*. He produced textbooks of algebra, geometry, and mechanics, especially the military applications of mathematics. When he died, at the age of eighty, he left the manuscript of a history of the artillery. For his 'services of erudition' he was made an officer of the Legion of Honour by Napoleon III. As Landau (2001) makes clear, Terquem's reputation rests much more on his contributions to Jewish scholarship than his mathematical work. He was one of the leaders of the movement to take full advantage of the elimination of anti-Jewish legislation by the French National Assembly.

The last of these mathematical precursors to be mentioned here was also French. He has some claim to be regarded as the first modern Jewish mathematician, but although he had the ability he lacked the opportunity to contribute much to the development of the subject, and so must yield the place to Carl Jacobi, whose profile is the first of the series.

The parents of Olinde Rodrigues belonged to prominent Sephardic families which were long settled in the city of Bordeaux. His father Isaac, who married Sara-Sophie Lopes-Fonseca in 1794, was in business as an accountant at the time. Olinde, the first of seven children, was originally given the first name of Benjamin but changed it later. He was born in Bordeaux on 6 October 1795. Later the family moved to Paris where Isaac worked first as an exchange dealer and then as a stockbroker. He was one of those selected for the assembly of Jewish notables convened by Bonaparte in 1806. He took advantage of the secularization of public education to send both his sons to the Lycée Imperial (later Louis-le-Grand) in Paris where Michel Chasles, who later became famous as a geometer, was one of Olinde's contemporaries. Although Rodrigues beat Chasles for first place in the final examination, which would have ensured his admission to one of the Grandes Écoles, the Polytechnique or the Normale, he did not enter either of these elite establishments although they admitted Jews at the time. Presumably he went to the Sorbonne instead, since he obtained a university degree in 1815; his thesis contained the famous formula for Legendre polynomials which nowadays bears his name.

When the Catholic Church regained control of education it was determined not to allow Jews into teaching positions. This prevented Rodrigues from embarking on an academic career, although he was able to accept private pupils. During the next few years he worked for a recently founded insurance company, helping to create actuarial tables of life expectancy. In 1817 he married a Catholic who adopted the name Euphrasie; she was an accomplished pianist and shared with her husband a love of music and an interest in social reform. She bore him two sons and two daughters.

Although the main interests of Rodrigues lay elsewhere he did not give up mathematical research altogether. He lived during an exciting period for the development of modern mathematics, in which the mathematicians of Paris played a leading role. The results he published appeared in three clusters, with substantial gaps in between; there were several papers on differential geometry, others on the principle of least action, and one on the motion of a rigid body.

To earn a living Rodrigues followed in his father's footsteps by becoming a stockbroker at the Paris Bourse before taking up banking as director of a Caisse Hypothecaire, a type of housing-loan association. Towards the end of his life he wrote a book on the practice of such associations; there is also an earlier work on accountancy. However, Rodrigues is better known for his involvement in Saint-Simonism, and we need to recall what this was about.

Charles Henri de Rouvnoy, comte de Saint-Simon, was born in 1760, fought alongside George Washington in the American War of Independence, and on his return to France not only survived the Terror but became wealthy through land speculation. At thirty-eight he studied mathematical physics at the École Polytechnique; Gaspard Monge, Joseph Lagrange, and Jean-le-Rond d'Alembert became his friends as well as his teachers. He had a vision of a secular religion and proposed the public worship of Isaac Newton. More sensibly, he devoted himself to drawing up plans for the reorganization of society on socialist lines. A charismatic leader, he inspired his followers with a quasi-religious fervour, but his personal life left much to be desired and he quickly ran through his fortune and fell into debt. After the Restoration he became more and more isolated, felt betrayed by his friends, and in March 1823 injured himself in a suicide attempt which left him an invalid.

It was at this point that Rodrigues met Saint-Simon and was strongly impressed by his ideas for social reform. During the next two years he was the count's constant companion. Not only did he support Saint-Simon financially, he also helped the master complete his last work, *Nouveau Christianisme*, and financed its publication. In May 1825 Saint-Simon died in the arms of his disciple, placing on him the mantle of leadership of the movement he founded, in which Jews were prominent.

As well as five sisters, Olinde had a gifted brother, Eugène, to whom he was devoted. By this time a student at the Sorbonne, Eugène began to assist Olinde and with infectious enthusiasm play a major role in the movement. Eugene reorganized it on the lines of a religious community, while Olinde provided help, advice, and above all finance. Unfortunately Eugène was already near the end of his short life; he suffered from asthma and declined in health until his death at the age of twenty-three, leaving Olinde desolate. He was replaced as leader of the movement by Prosper Enfantin, a former pupil of Olinde's, while Olinde kept control of the finances. Enfantin reconstituted the Saint-Simonians in a way that is reminiscent of some of the strange cults which have arisen in modern times. He required his followers to make public confessions, no personal trait, however intimate, being beyond discussion. Such confessions could last ten hours at a stretch. Enfantin also believed he was entitled to have sex with his female followers. Before long the authorities clamped down on the movement; Enfantin was imprisoned and Rodrigues fined.

Still very much a divided country, France was subject to recurrent political unrest throughout most of the nineteenth century. During the 'three glorious days' of 1830, when there was a rebellion against the reactionary government of Charles X, Rodrigues helped to man the barricades. Later he played an active part in the campaign for the abolition of slavery. Another uprising in 1848 gave him the opportunity to propose a new constitution for what became the Second Republic on

Saint-Simonian principles. The same year he went to London, where the Chartists, in sympathy with what was happening in France, organized a large demonstration, in which he took part. Rodrigues died on 17 December 1851, apparently as the result of a minor accident. We do not know much about the closing years of'his life. Rodrigues is described as small and bony, without being thin, his features regular, with hair and sideboards curly. His walk was described as quick but uneven, his talk brief and brusque, with 'prophetic accents', whatever that may mean.

Fortunately, a brief but well-researched biography by Altmann and Ortiz (2005) is contained in the recent volume on various aspects of the career of this remarkable man. As well as Rodrigues, there were other notable Sephardic mathematicians and physicists, such as the Italian mathematician Federigo Enriques (1871–1946) and the Austrian physicist Wolfgang Pauli (1900–1958). Another was the British physicist E. N. da C. Andrade (1887–1935), whose ancestors were Portuguese; one of them was the marques do Pombal, statesman and leading figure of the Enlightenment in Portugal.

In politics, emancipated Jews tended to be radicals, yearning for a world of equality and brotherhood, as we have just seen in the case of Rodrigues, and there will be others later in this book. For example, Carl Jacobi was also involved in the unrest of 1848, the year of revolution, when he petitioned the king of Prussia to transfer power to parliament. Gotthold Eisenstein shared his republican leanings. Hertha Ayrton was an early supporter of the Labour Party in Britain. Jacques Hadamard and Emmy Noether could be described as communists, while Tullio Levi-Civita, George Pólya, and Oscar Zariski also had left-wing sympathies. Abram Ioffe and Igor Tamm were radicals in their youth. Discrimination on political grounds was not uncommon, often linked with anti-Semitism. As Hitler told Max Planck, he was not against Jews, only communists, 'but all Jews are communists'.

German Forerunners

In the early years of the nineteenth century there were several German Jews who were active in experimental physics, of which the first is Moritz Jacobi (1801–1874), elder brother of the more famous mathematician Carl, whose profile comes later. The Jacobis, who lived in Potsdam, were a cultured household. Simon, the head of the family, was a banker, who ran into financial difficulties towards the end of his life. Little is known about his wife except that her maiden name was Lehmann. They had four children: three sons, Moritz, Carl, and Eduard, and a daughter Therese. The first two, at least, converted to Christianity.

Encouraged by his parents Moritz had originally tried to make a career in architecture. He studied this at the University of Göttingen, known as the Georgia Augusta because it was founded in 1727 by King George II of Great Britain, who was also Elector of Hanover. Although modelled on Oxford and Cambridge in some respects it was still in many ways a typical German university of the period, but with more generous endowments and greater autonomy. The Georgia Augusta attracted students from all over Germany and from elsewhere in Europe as well.

After leaving the university Moritz spent some years gaining professional experience until at the age of thirty-two he set up in architectural practice at Königsberg, where his younger brother Carl had just become *Ordinarius* in mathematics. In 1835 he moved for two years to the University of Dorpat as professor of civil engineering. While there he married Anna Grigorjowna (née Kochanowskaya), known in the family as Annette. They had several children but lost their eldest son in 1838 and their two youngest sons within one week in 1849.

Moritz Jacobi's next and last career move was to St Petersburg where he worked for the Imperial Academy of Sciences from 1837 under the name of Boris Semionowitsch Jacobi. He was appointed adjunct member in 1839, promoted to *Extra-Ordinarius* three years later and *Ordinarius* in 1847. In 1840 he attended the Glasgow meeting of the British Association for the Advancement of Science, the 'Parliament of Science' where professionals and amateurs gathered periodically to hear about the latest discoveries.

Moritz Jacobi devoted his energies to pioneering research into the practical applications of the theory of electricity, based on principles laid down by Ampère, Coulomb, Oersted, and Ohm. Scientific discoveries are often made by several people working independently at about the same time. Handicapped by his isolation from the main centres of research, Moritz Jacobi found that his discoveries in Russia were often anticipated by his near-contemporaries Michael Faraday in England and Joseph Henry in the United States.

Historians of science and technology tend to be rather dismissive of the work of Moritz Jacobi if they mention it at all, but he was famous in his lifetime. Most of the practical applications he developed during his thirty-seven years in St Petersburg turned out to be premature, in that the appropriate technology had not been developed sufficiently to make them viable. Nevertheless his research was of value in the design of electric motors and generators. He is best known for realizing that the dynamo is essentially an electric motor in reverse. Moritz Jacobi also developed a version of electric telegraph similar to the first design of Samuel Morse and he discovered the process of reproduction by electrodeposition which he called galvanoplasty but which is nowadays known as electrotyping. He also studied the practical use of electromagnetism for driving machinery and experimented with the electric arc.

Throughout the latter part of his life Moritz was in regular correspondence with his younger brother Carl; their lively letters tell us something about his life in the period 1822 to 1851. This correspondence was published in a volume, admirably edited by Ahrens (1907), which includes photographic portraits of the two brothers. After Carl died in 1851 we know little about the later life of Moritz except that in 1859 he was elected a corresponding member of the Prussian Academy of Sciences. In 1867 he went to Paris for the Universal Exhibition and addressed the international commission to standardize the system of weights and measures; two years later he attended another meeting of the British Association, this time in Exeter. In 1870 he experienced the first episode of an illness which was to prove fatal four years later.

It is unfortunate that we know so little about the life of the man who appears to have been the first Jewish physicist of the modern school. The second, perhaps, was the experimental physicist Peter Theophil Riess (1804–1883), an old friend of Carl Jacobi. His research interests were similar to those of Moritz Jacobi, but he was much more in touch with other scientists; for example he was in correspondence with Michael Faraday and collaborated with Alexander von Humboldt on surveys of the earth's magnetic field. Both the Humboldt brothers had been introduced into Jewish society by one of their tutors, and became greatly influenced by the ideas discussed at the salons which were such a feature of social and cultural life in that period. The elder brother, Wilhelm, believed that professed Jews should be excluded from official positions, but the more philo-Semitic Alexander did not agree and used his influence with the king to secure royal approval for the election of Riess to the Prussian Academy of Sciences in 1848 (for further details, see Honigmann (1997)). The first professed Jew to be so honoured, Riess came of a wealthy and cultured family, settled in Berlin for generations; Honigmann (1985) has collected the little that is on record about him.

The first professed Jew to be appointed *Ordinarius* at any German university was the mathematician Moritz Stern. Born in Frankfurt in 1807, only three years after Carl Jacobi, Stern was educated at home by his father and grandfather who hoped he would enter the rabbinate. Instead he turned to mathematics, after a year at Heidelberg, and completed his education at Göttingen under Gauss. He was awarded the doctoral degree with distinction and in 1830 became a *Privatdozent*. After some years the faculty of the Georgia Augusta proposed to promote him but the Hanoverian ministry was adamant, insisting that a Jew could never become a professor. So Stern continued to survive on a meagre income from the fees of students who attended his lectures, and from writing popular works and making translations, supplemented by occasional small grants from the university. Eventually there was a change of policy at the ministry and the Georgia Augusta was able to appoint Stern as *Extra-Ordinarius* in 1848. When the diarist Thomas Archer Hirst interviewed Stern in 1852 he was a widower; his wife had committed suicide after becoming insane. Hirst described his manner as gentle and quiet; he was much impressed by Stern's 'beautifully clear' lectures on integral calculus and mechanics. Dedekind attended Stern's course on number theory which he described as 'very interesting'. As well as numerous mathematical publications Stern also wrote an early work of Jewish interest and a centenary address on the life and work of Gauss. Stern was not appointed *Ordinarius* until 1859, some thirty years after he received the *venia legendi*. In 1885 he moved to the Federal Polytechnic in Zurich, where he died on 30 January 1894. Further information about his most interesting life can be found in Küssner (1982) and in the memoir by his son, the historian Alfred Stern, extracts from which can be found in Richarz (1974).

Another early Jewish physicist was Benjamin Goldschmidt, whose career is also described by Küssner (1982). Born on 4 August 1807 in Brunswick, the son of a money-changer, he became the first Jew to be admitted to the Carolinum Collegium, at which the great Carl Friedrich Gauss (1777–1855) was an alumnus. At the age of twenty Goldschmidt matriculated at Göttingen University to study mathematics and science. Four years later he graduated with high honours, and after habilitation he was appointed *Privatdozent*. At the time Gauss, in collaboration with the physicist William Weber, was engaged in electrical research, especially geomagnetism, in which Alexander von Humboldt was also involved. Gauss chose Goldschmidt to act as his assistant, and became very fond of him. He assisted Gauss not only in his scientific research but also in the trigonometric survey of the Duchy of Brunswick, which was one of Gauss's official responsibilities. Goldschmidt took the first name of Benedikt after he converted to Christianity in 1832. Twelve years later he was awarded the title of *Extra-Ordinarius*. His 'very sudden' death at the age of forty-four on 15 February 1851 caused Gauss great distress.

4

Years of Opportunity

In this chapter the birth-dates of the subjects span, more or less, the eventful first half of the nineteenth century. For Jews in central and western Europe, this was the century of emancipation and enlightenment. By 1880 the legal process of emancipation was complete; once they had the opportunity, Jews were not slow to show how they could contribute to the arts and sciences. In science, particularly in mathematics and physics, they soon became known internationally for their research. Emancipation was slow to reach eastern Europe, the stronghold of traditional Judaism. In 1804 the Pale of Settlement had been created, as we have seen; and Jews who were confined to this region were isolated from developments further west.

Forceful Personality, Sweeping Enthusiasm
Carl Jacobi (1804–1851)

In the first part of the nineteenth century Berlin, the Prussian capital, was not a large city, but it was already important. It was the seat of government, in which the elder von Humboldt, Wilhelm, was minister of education. It housed the university, which he had reformed, and the academy of sciences. It was also remarkable for its flourishing Jewish society, founded by Moses Mendelssohn and known as the Berlin

Enlightenment. A small group of highly intelligent Jewish families who had made fortunes in trade and industry showed an active interest in literature, the arts, and the sciences and would discuss them in their salons, which were attended by non-Jewish members of the intelligentsia as well. The scientist Alexander von Humboldt, the younger of the two brothers, was at home in this society. He included mathematicians and physicists among his friends and was helpful to them in various ways. For example, we have already seen how he used his influence to persuade the king of Prussia that the physicist Peter Theophil Riess should be appointed to the academy. The younger Humboldt will figure several times in this chapter.

Of the German-Jewish mathematicians who were born in the first decade of the nineteenth century, by far the most successful was Carl Jacobi, the younger brother of Moritz, who was born in Potsdam on 10 December 1804 and quickly recognized as a prodigy. Historians of mathematics regard him as the first Jewish modern mathematician. He was taught classics and mathematics by an uncle on his mother's side up to the age of twelve. When he entered the Potsdam gymnasium in 1816 he rose to the highest class almost at once, and four years later, in 1821, he graduated with top marks in classics, history, and mathematics. He then enrolled at the University of Berlin, where for the first two years he divided his time between classics, philosophy, and mathematics. Since the teaching of mathematics in German universities of this period never rose above the elementary level, he continued studying the mathematical classics in the works of Euler, Lagrange, and others on his own, as he had at school.

After qualifying as an *Oberlehrer* at the age of nineteen, Carl Jacobi was offered a teaching post at the prestigious Joachimsthal Gymnasium in Berlin. Instead of taking this up he set out to qualify as a university teacher. In 1823 he wrote a doctoral thesis on partial fractions, and completed the process of habilitation the following year, when he also converted to Protestantism—although he continued his subscription to the synagogue. Already a *Privatdozent* at the age of twenty, Jacobi gave his first lecture course at the university; apparently the audiences were much impressed by the clarity and liveliness of his delivery. Since there did not seem much hope of obtaining a senior post in Berlin, in 1826 he moved to Königsberg, where the prospects at the ancient university known as the Albertina seemed brighter. Within a year he had been appointed *Extra-Ordinarius*, and five years later *Ordinarius*. Jacobi remained there for eighteen years, the best part of his career.

During his student years Jacobi had developed the practice of frequently exchanging letters with other mathematicians, such as Adrien-Marie Legendre in Paris. In the summer of 1829 Jacobi, by then twenty-five, made a visit to Paris, paying his respects to Gauss en route. The purpose of the visit was partly to call on Legendre but also to make contact with Joseph Fourier, Siméon-Denis Poisson, and other leading French mathematicians of the period. There is no evidence that he contacted Rodrigues or Terquem. In his inaugural address as *Ordinarius* at the Albertina Jacobi criticized the French for being too interested in the application of mathematics to physical problems.

Stubhaug (2000) describes in detail Jacobi's rivalry with the Norwegian mathematician Niels Abel, who had developed a general theory of the doubly periodic elliptic functions. Jacobi published a more limited theory and has been criticized for using Abel's ideas without acknowledgement. Abel, on his deathbed, repeatedly said that Jacobi was the man who best understood what his own work was all about. Moreover, in 1829, shortly after his rival's tragically early death, Jacobi failed to give the young Norwegian proper credit in his successful textbook *Fundamenta nova theoriae functionum ellipticarum*, although he acknowledged Abel's influence in his correspondence with Legendre.

In spite of a reputation for bluntness and sarcasm, Jacobi proved himself to be an exceptional teacher. He presented himself to his students as one who knew a little and wished to know more. He introduced new mathematical ideas into his classwork, so that the students could follow the course of his investigations. So great was his enthusiasm that he often told them of results which he never found time to publish. There already existed research seminars in the humanities, in which students played an active role, but Jacobi organized the first in mathematics and physics, in collaboration with the theoretical physicist Franz Neumann. This was so successful that it was soon copied elsewhere.

In 1833 Carl Jacobi was elected to the Royal Society of London. In 1842 the king of Prussia sent him, with his colleague the astronomer Wilhelm Bessel, to attend the Manchester meeting of the British Association for the Advancement of Science, where he gave a lecture on analytical dynamics and reported to his brother Moritz afterwards, 'there I had the courage to make the valid point that it is the glory of science to be no use. This caused a vehement shaking of heads.' When asked who he thought was the leading British mathematician at that time he replied, 'there is none.' However he was ready to praise the Anglo-Irish prodigy William Rowan Hamilton, who had already published the first part of his planned treatise on geometrical optics and whose masterpiece, *The General Method of Dynamics*, was almost complete. Jacobi referred to Hamilton as 'the illustrious Astronomer Royal of Dublin' and, later, as 'the Lagrange of your country'.

One of Carl Jacobi's close friends was Lejeune Dirichlet, under whose enlightened leadership the University of Berlin began to establish a strong reputation in mathematics. In personality the pugnacious Jacobi was a direct contrast to the good-natured Dirichlet, and it may seem surprising that they became such close friends. Dirichlet's wife Rebecca recalled how 'his relation with Dirichlet was wonderful: they would sit together for hours— I called it "silent mathematical conversation"—and as they would not hold back and Dirichlet would often tell him the most bitter truths, and Jacobi understood this so well and knew how to bow his great spirit before Dirichlet's great character.' In 1831 Jacobi married Marie Schwink, the daughter of a formerly wealthy *Kommerzierat* who had lost his fortune through speculative investments. His own father Simon had also once been wealthy but when he died serious financial problems in his bank emerged. Carl's younger brother Eduard took over the firm but Carl, who was already overworked, collapsed under the stress of assisting him in dealing with these problems.

No one found Jacobi an easy person to be with. According to Felix Klein he encountered difficulty in gaining acceptance as a member of the Albertina faculty, because he had something unpleasant to say to every one of his colleagues. As Rebecca Dirichlet wrote to her sister Fanny, 'Jacobi has called several times during the last few weeks. How rude he can be! But really these rude people have rather the best of it, that is if, like Jacobi, they have redeeming qualities, for if they do but take the trouble to be ordinarily polite, people are amazed, charmed and grateful into the bargain.'

Carl Jacobi suffered from diabetes and in 1839 he took the cure at the spa of Marienbad. However by 1842 the condition had become much worse. Through Alexander von Humboldt Dirichlet arranged for the Prussian government to grant Jacobi a pension which would enable him to spend some time convalescing in Italy, as prescribed by his doctors. The Jacobis spent the next year in Rome and Dirichlet was given leave of absence so that he and his family could join them there. Rebecca Dirichlet gave her sister Fanny some glimpses on their life in the Eternal City. On one occasion they met Mary Somerville, the Scottish 'queen of science', who annoyed Jacobi by talking all the time about his brother Moritz. They also had an audience with the pope who talked with them for more than half an hour, all about mathematics and mathematicians, and showed much more knowledge of the subject than Mary Somerville. 'It must have been a sight', Fanny wrote, 'to see Dirichlet on his knees kissing the pope's toe, and Jacobi kissing his hand.'

After a pleasant extended convalescence in Rome, where some other leading mathematicians were living at the time, including Schäfli and Steiner, Jacobi returned to Germany in 1844 and, fearing that the more severe climate of Königsberg would be bad for his health, he decided to move to Berlin. He had been a corresponding member of the Prussian Academy of Sciences for some years but now he became a full member; as such he was entitled to give lectures at the university. The Dirichlets remained in Rome but they too experienced ill-health; the doctors advised a change of air, and so they moved to Florence. Although not in the best of health himself, Jacobi volunteered to deputize for his friend in Berlin, so that Dirichlet was able to be absent for a further year.

The year 1848 saw a tide of revolutions against established authority sweep across Europe. In Prussia, although the bureaucratic monarchy succeeded in retaining control, there was a great deal of unrest. Jacobi was active in politics and at a political meeting he made some incautious remarks which led to his being treated as an object of suspicion by the

government. He signed a petition to the king, asking him to divest himself
of authority and pass it on to the parliament. As a result his efforts to
become more closely associated with the university were blocked at
ministerial level, and a salary bonus he had been granted to meet the
additional cost of living in the capital was temporarily suspended. This
meant that the family had to give up the home they had established in
Berlin. He moved his wife and children to the small town of Gotha near
Leipzig, where the cost of living was less, while he took rooms in an inn
in the city. Towards the end of 1849 he accepted the offer of a chair at
the University of Vienna. When it was realized that Prussia was about
to lose one of its foremost scientists, he was persuaded not to take this
up. However, on a visit to his family early in 1851, he caught influenza,
followed by smallpox, and this led to his death in Berlin on 18 February
at the age of forty-six, leaving a wife, five sons, and three daughters.

Dirichlet, in a memorial lecture at the Berlin Academy, described
Jacobi as its greatest member since Lagrange, while Klein recorded that:

> Jacobi possessed not only the impulse to acquire pure scientific knowledge,
> but also the desire to impart it. This drive to activate others manifested
> itself, on the one hand, in a brilliant pedagogical talent, and on the other,
> in a strong determination to assert his personality, even to the point of
> inconsiderateness. The keenness and versatility of his brilliant mind, together
> with an infamous and often feared sarcastic wit, supplied him with most
> effective weapons for his incessant battles, although he was often seduced
> into using them imprudently.

Always Fighting the World
J. J. Sylvester (1814–1897)

The life of the British mathematician James
Joseph Sylvester has been closely studied,
by Karen Parshall (1998 and 2006), among
others, who sees him as the founder of the mathematical research
community in the United States. He had his faults, as a man and as a
mathematician, but his life displays vividly some of the difficulties faced by
a Jew in the Anglo-Saxon world in the middle of the nineteenth century.
He was born on 3 September 1814, the youngest child in the family of
five sons and five daughters of Abraham Joseph, merchant in the City of
London, and his wife Miriam. The family were Ashkenazim who settled
in England in 1754, making Liverpool their main base, but the branch we
are concerned with here had moved to London not later than 1810. All
the children, but not their parents, adopted the surname of Sylvester. The
two oldest sons, Nathaniel and Sylvester Joseph, emigrated to the United
States, where they set up in New York as contractors of state lotteries,
which were used to raise capital for major projects.

James Joseph attended Jewish schools in north London, where his
mathematical ability was quickly recognized. At the age of fourteen he
transferred to the new secular University College London, where he was
taught by Augustus De Morgan, among others. Sylvester was only there
briefly before his father withdrew him after an incident in the refectory
where he allegedly attacked a fellow student with a knife. The next year
he made a fresh start at the Royal Institution School in Liverpool, where
another branch of the Joseph family provided him with somewhere to
live. One of his schoolmates recalled, 'I have more than once seen him
hunted by his schoolfellows, in the open street, for no worse reason than

that he was a Jew, and very much cleverer, especially in mathematics, than they were.' Another recalled that one classmate fought a long battle with Sylvester, and punished him a good deal, but did not succeed in making him give in. He defended his race, it was said, with more courage than skill. James Joseph became so unhappy with this that he ran away to Dublin where he was found by chance by another member of the Joseph clan who sent him back to face further bullying at school.

His life as a teenager was not all misery, however. His brothers told him of a large prize being offered for the solution of a combinatorial problem which had arisen in the lottery business; he won the prize for his solution. We next hear of Sylvester at Cambridge, where he was matriculated in 1831 as a member of St John's, one of the largest and wealthiest colleges. His residence was interrupted by episodes of serious illness, possibly the depression from which he suffered later in life. It was not until 1837 that he took the highly competitive Mathematical Tripos and came second.

As a non-Anglican, Sylvester could not supplicate for a Cambridge degree. Later he obtained a BSc from Trinity College, Dublin, on the strength of his Cambridge record, but because of the religious test he remained ineligible for a college fellowship at Cambridge. Many years later, after the test had been abolished, the perceived injustice still rankled:

> If I speak with some warmth on this subject, it is because it is one that comes home to me—because I feel what irreparable loss of facilities for domestic and foreign study, for full mental development, and the growth of productive power, I have suffered, what opportunities for usefulness I have been cut off from, under the effect of this oppressive monopoly, this baneful system of protection of such long standing and inveterate tenacity of existence.

At University College London there were no such disabilities. In 1838 Sylvester was appointed professor of natural philosophy, thus becoming a colleague of his former teacher De Morgan. His duties included the teaching of science in general and physics in particular. He was not a success as a lecturer. 'When he was with us', said De Morgan later, 'he was an entire failure; whether in lecture room or in private exposition he could not keep his team of ideas in hand.'

Sylvester resigned after three years and crossed the Atlantic to become professor of mathematics at the University of Virginia, founded at Charlottesville by Thomas Jefferson in 1819 to offer Southerners an alternative to the New England colleges. Before leaving London he had been elected to the Royal Society on the strength of his early papers on mathematical physics. When the assistant secretary called on Sylvester for his subscription 'he took offence at what he called "my peremptory prescribing of a time in which he should pay" … he insisted also that I should address him as "sir" with every sentence, query or rejoinder.'

Sylvester, the first Jewish professor to teach a non-Semitic subject in America, received a warm welcome when he arrived at Charlottesville but he left in a hurry after only a few months. There was, at this time, a good deal of student unrest in the university, partly due to resentment at the importation of too many foreign professors. Sylvester, as an Englishman and a Jew, was a natural target. When one of the students assaulted him Sylvester defended himself with his metal-pointed cane, and, believing quite wrongly that he had killed his assailant, fled to join his brothers in New York. He tried to obtain another academic post in America, but without success. At Columbia College, in the city of New York, he thought he stood a good chance, since its charter expressly forbade religious discrimination, but a spokesman for the selection board told him point blank that the election of a Jew would be repugnant to the feelings of every member of the board. 'The opposition', it was said, 'was not at all on the ground of him being a foreigner; it would have been the same had he been born of Jewish parentage in the United States.'

Sylvester returned to England thoroughly disheartened and extremely depressed. A year later he was appointed to the responsible post of secretary and actuary of a life assurance company, the Equity and Law, possibly introduced by his co-religionist Benjamin Gompertz. He made a success of this work, where his mathematical skills came in useful, and since a legal qualification was an advantage in the actuarial profession he began to study law. He entered the Inner Temple in 1846 and was called to the bar four years later. During this period he met another Cambridge mathematician, Arthur Cayley, who was starting his pupillage as a barrister. Although very different in personality—Sylvester proud, turbulent, and argumentative, Cayley calm, patient, and methodical—they developed a lifelong friendship based on shared mathematical interests. It was due to Cayley that Sylvester regained his lost confidence and began to flourish once more as a creative mathematician. In 1863 Cayley married and returned to Cambridge for a productive and uneventful career as first Sadleirian professor of pure mathematics. From then on he only met Sylvester occasionally but they continued to exchange letters.

At this time continental mathematicians regarded England as something of a mathematical backwater, but there was interest in the theory of invariants which Cayley and Sylvester had been developing. Sylvester set out to reinforce this through personal contacts. He was fluent in French and able to converse easily in German and Italian. Travel had become much easier thanks to the construction of the railway network. In Paris he made the acquaintance of several of the French mathematicians, particularly Charles Hermite, one of the rising stars. At least as early as 1851 he had established contact with his co-religionist Olry Terquem, to whose journal he contributed several articles. In 1857 he made an Italian tour, in the course of which he met Enrico Betti and other Italian mathematicians, and two years later he was back for another working holiday. In 1863 he was elected corresponding member of the Paris Academy of Sciences; soon afterwards several other foreign academies followed suit.

Meanwhile Sylvester carried on with his actuarial work. He made regular valuations for the Equity and Law and acted as check officer and scientific adviser to the directors of other insurance companies. He was also instrumental in founding the Institute of Actuaries, serving as vice-president for the first five years of its existence, and later being elected an honorary member. However what he needed was an academic post where he could concentrate on mathematical research. When a professorship of mathematics at the Royal Military Academy in Woolwich fell vacant he applied for the post, but an internal candidate was promoted instead. However this man died soon afterwards, and Sylvester was appointed to succeed him, thus becoming the opposite number of his co-religionist Rodrigues.

Sylvester moved into the official residence at Woolwich, where he spent a fruitful and rewarding fifteen years, especially the first ten. He frequently entertained his London friends and distinguished foreign mathematicians in the commodious house provided for him. He served on the council of the Royal Society. To provide himself with a base in central London he joined the Athenacum, the club founded in 1824 for 'gentlemen distinguished in science, literature or the arts, or in public services'.

Sylvester's research achievements during this fruitful period were recognized by the award of a Royal Medal by the Royal Society. After the London Mathematical Society was formed in 1865 Sylvester played an active part and succeeded De Morgan as president. He also presided over the mathematics and physics section of the British Association for the Advancement of Science, the meetings of which he freqently attended. In his presidential address he took issue with T. H. Huxley's views on science education.

Sylvester's appointment at Woolwich was not an unqualified success. In the classroom, the cadets infuriated him with their practical jokes. He antagonized the authorities with arguments about his rights and responsibilities. His post was combined with the professorship of natural philosophy but his lectures in that capacity were described as 'ill-prepared and inefficient'. Unfortunately for Sylvester, an administrative reform in military establishments such as the Royal Military Academy forced him to retire at the age of fifty-five, and that led to another lull in his mathematical productivity. He stood, unsuccessfully, for election to the London School Board; apparently his unmistakable Jewishness counted against him. At London's Royal Institution he gave one of the series of Friday evening discourses, made famous by Michael Faraday. He made another continental tour, this time to Poland, Russia, and Sweden. Being fond of singing, he took some lessons from the composer Charles Gounod, who was living in London at the time. But his main interest, apart from mathematics, was in versification. 'He led himself to believe he could rival the majestic cadences of Milton,' according to one of his friends 'and would be remembered quite as much for his verse as for his mathematics.' He wrote a monograph on the subject, entitled *The Laws of Verse*. One critic dismissed it with the comment 'chiefly valuable for the light it throws on his personality'.

As it turned out, Sylvester's academic career was not at an end; the best was still to come. In 1875 he put his name forward for the chair of mathematics at the newly established Johns Hopkins University in Baltimore, Maryland. The Hopkins was to be the first research-level university in the United States to emphasize both undergraduate and graduate teaching, while stressing original research and the training of future researchers, and it was to be non-sectarian. On the recommendation of Joseph Henry, Sylvester was appointed and, after some argument about the salary, took up the post as soon as the school opened in 1876.

The seven years Sylvester spent at Johns Hopkins were a great success. The opportunity to build a mathematics programme, to teach able and motivated students, and to pursue his own research interests in a supportive intellectual environment was just what he wanted. While not overburdened with routine administration, he was surrounded by able assistants and talented pupils. The Mathematical Seminary which he founded amounted to a research school in mathematics, the first in America, and those who attended it went out to promote mathematical research elsewhere. He published much of his new work in the pages of the *American Journal of Mathematics*, which he founded in 1878 and edited until 1884. These years also brought him further recognitions of distinction: for example, the Royal Society awarded him the prestigious Copley Medal and Oxford an honorary doctorate; later Cambridge was to follow suit. Some of his students later recalled the impression he made in his lectures:

> The one thing which constantly marked [them] was the enthusiastic love of the thing he was doing …we were set aglow by the delight and admiration which, with perfect naiveté and with that luxuriance of language peculiar to him, Sylvester lavished upon his own results. That in this enthusiastic admiration he sometimes lacked a sense of proportion cannot be denied. A result announced at one lecture and hailed with loud acclaim as a marvel of beauty was by no means sure of not being found before the next lecture to be quite erroneous … He was a very interesting man but it was practically impossible to take any notes on what he said as he spoke very rapidly and always on the subject which interested him at the monment. He could never

stop to pick up an eraser, but when he wanted to erase anything he rubbed it out with his hand and then wiped his hand on his forehead …

I can see him now, with his white beard and few locks of grey hair, his forehead wrinkled o'er with thought, writing rapidly his figures and formulae on the board. But stop, something is not quite right; he pauses, his hand goes to his forehead to help his thought, he goes over the work again, emphasizing the leading points and finally discovers his difficulty. Perhaps it is some error in his figures, perhaps an oversight in the reasoning, sometimes, however, the difficulty is not elucidated and there is not much to the rest of the lecture. But at the next lecture we would hear of some new discovery which was the outcome of that difficulty, and of some article for the Journal which he had just begun. If a textbook had been taken up at the beginning with the intention of following it that textbook was most likely doomed to oblivion for the rest of term, or until the class had been made listeners to every new thought and principle that had sprung from the laboratory of his mind, in consequence of that first difficulty. Other difficulties would soon appear so that no textbook could last more than half the term.

He always spent his summers in England. I remember one summer he found, when he was crossing the Atlantic, that he had left behind his papers on the subject he was then interested in. When he had got to Liverpool he crossed over to a boat that was sailing to New York and returned to Baltimore to get his papers. He was very likely to forget that he had to give a lecture. He always came into the library in the middle of the forenoon and I made a point of being in the library at the same time. He lectured at one o'clock and as one o'clock approached he became uneasy, knowing that he had something to do. He would get up and leave the room and I would follow him across the street. He would start for his club downtown. I walked faster than him and got ahead of him and crossed over to intercept him. Then I would say 'Professor, no lecture today?' His reply invariably was 'Bless my soul, I had forgotten. Let's go back.'

At seventy Sylvester wished to return home to England. The prestigious Savilian professorship of geometry had fallen vacant with the sudden death of the incumbent Henry Smith and now Sylvester applied for the chair. After some hesitation, perhaps because of his age, he was appointed and in 1884 became the first professed Jew to hold an Oxford chair. He was elected to a fellowship at New College, where he resided. He was not the first Jew to be elected a fellow of an Oxford or Cambridge college; that distinction belongs to the philosopher Samuel Alexander who was elected a Fellow of Lincoln College, Oxford in 1882. He entertained a succession of mathematical visitors in New College, including Cayley, of course, and his old friend Henri Poincaré, also Leopold Kronecker with his wife and daughter. His inaugural lecture, on the analytic geometry of Descartes, was a success, but he soon became disillusioned with Oxford, where the students were not as tolerant of his eccentricities as they had been at Johns Hopkins.

Sylvester's circle included the diarist Hirst, professor at University College London, whose profiles of some of the leading mathematicians of the period make such interesting reading. In his diary, quoted by Gardner and Wilson (1993), there are several entries which throw some light on Sylvester's personality. At first Hirst found Sylvester 'excessively friendly, wished we lived together, asked me to go live with him at Woolwich and so forth. In short he was eccentrically affectionate.' However this did not last, for some years later Hirst records 'Sylvester's animus against me was disagreeably manifest. It has lasted now for years and the cause of it is just as unknown to me now as it was on its first appearance.' Not long afterwards we find Sylvester describing Hirst as thoroughly insincere, an inveterate plotter. Parshall (1998) suggests a plausible explanation. Hirst and Sylvester were both members of a dining club called the Royal Society Club, but Hirst belonged to another, more exclusive, dining club, also associated with the Royal Society, called the X-club. Its nine members formed the most powerful and influential scientific coterie in England. Sylvester was offended not to be invited to join. Further on in Hirst's diary we are told that '(Sylvester) voluntarily shook hands with me, and thus at last there is a kind of reconciliation between us. I am very glad of it for I have learned to my sorrow that our former intimacy can never be renewed. What the exact cause of our original estrangement was I never knew, but I know that he suspected me most unjustly of incessantly plotting to undermine his influence in the scientific and mathematical circles. He misconstrued every act and word of mine to such an extent that intercourse was impossible.'

Sylvester was described as being of less than average height, with a large and massive head, regular features, and fine grey eyes. He was often photographed, and had his portrait painted twice, first as a young man seated, by George Patten, and the second time, in old age, by Alfred Emslie. The resulting full-length portrait, for his alma mater, was all too true to life; Sylvester seemed old and tired, and cataracts were affecting his eyesight. When he was approaching the age of eighty, declining health caused him to hand over to a deputy.

Sylvester spent his last years in and around London, with the Athenaeum as his base. Cambridge University Press was in process of publishing his collected works, as well as those of Cayley, but he dreaded the amount of effort that would entail. Cayley's death in 1895 left him deeply saddened; he felt too ill to go to Cambridge for the funeral. Sylvester died at his lodgings in Mayfair on 15 March 1897, following a paralytic stroke, and was buried in the Jewish cemetery. His many friends, especially in the Jewish community, subscribed for a medal, to be awarded triennially by the Royal Society, in his honour. The first recipient of the Sylvester Medal was Poincaré.

As a schoolboy Sylvester had been described as kindly and brave, but unduly sensitive. 'Sensitive to a painful degree', wrote the *Oxford Magazine* after his death, 'the good opinion of others and appreciation from them were at all times necessary for his happiness.' 'Always fighting the world', was a comment he made about himself; certainly he had a capacity to develop personal antagonisms and become involved in disputes. His successor at Johns Hopkins summed him up as follows: 'Sylvester was quick-tempered and impatient, but generous, charitable and tender-hearted. He was always extremely appreciative of the work of others and gave the warmest recognition to any talent or ability displayed by his pupils. He was capable of flying into a passion at the slightest provocation, but he did not harbour resentment, and was always glad to forget the cause of the quarrel at the first opportunity.' Klein wrote that 'as a personality Sylvester was lively, witty and sparkling, he was a splendid speaker who often distinguished himself with his striking and clever versifying, and in the brilliance and versatility of his spirit he was a true representative of his race.'

The mathematical papers of Sylvester run to four large volumes of nearly three thousand pages altogether, spanning nearly sixty years of creative activity. Some of his major contributions amount to monographs on the subjects they deal with. The insular nature of much British mathematical research in the Victorian era cannot be denied. On the Continent Abel, Cauchy, Jacobi, Poincaré, Riemann, Weierstrass, and others had revolutionized the subject. Although Sylvester was in touch with the continental mathematicians, especially the French, he did not absorb the new ideas to any great extent. A notable example of this is his theory of cyclotomic functions, which he had published in several foreign journals, only to find that he had been greatly anticipated by Ernst Kummer. 'It was manifest', one critic pointed out, 'that the professor had not read Kummer's elementary results in the theory of ideal primes, yet Henry Smith's report on the theory of numbers, which contained a full synopsis of Kummer's theory, was professor Sylvester's constant companion.' On one occasion he submitted a paper for publication to the London Mathematical Society accompanied by a note saying it was the best thing he had done for ten years, only to have it returned with a note saying that the society had already published it.

After his death Max Noether (1898) wrote a very full appreciation of Sylvester's achievements for *Mathematische Annalen*, observing that:

> The enthusiasm of Sylvester for his own work indicates one of his characteristic properties: a high degree of subjectivity in his productions and publications. Sylvester was so fully possessed by the matter which for the time engaged his attention, that it appeared to him and was designated by him as the summit of all that is important, remarkable and full of future promise. It would excite his fantasy and power of imagination in an even greater measure than his power of reflection, so much so that he could never marshal the ability to master his subject matter, much less present it in an orderly manner.

Sylvester never married; he was turned down by a young lady in New York and, back in London, made overtures to the philo-Semitic

Barbara Leigh Smith but without success, as we shall learn later in this chapter. However, his elder sister Fanny married the son of her father's business partner and their family of children, grandchildren, and great-grandchildren contains some remarkably gifted people, descendants of Joseph and Miriam. Other Jewish mathematicians and physicists who worked in Britain were mainly immigrants. One exception was the experimental physicist Hertha Ayrton, who was born thirty years after Sylvester. By the time she grew up the legal disabilities Jews shared with other non-Anglicans had been removed, although those suffered by women still remained. She is profiled later in this chapter.

Child of Misfortune
Gotthold Eisenstein (1823–1852)

We now return to Prussia. According to Gauss, who was surely exaggerating, the talents of Ferdinand Gotthold Eisenstein were such as nature bestows on only a few in each century, comparable to the talents of Archimedes or Newton. Yet although Eisenstein was endowed with genius, his life was short and unhappy, as we shall see. The mathematician's father, Johann Konstantin Eisenstein, and his mother, the former Helene Pollack, had converted from Judaism to Protestantism before their son was born in Berlin on 16 April 1823. His father, who had served eight years in the Prussian army, tried his hand at various commercial enterprises, including manufacturing, without financial success. Not until late in life did he begin to make a reasonable livelihood. Eisenstein's younger brothers and sisters died in childhood, nearly all of meningitis, which he also contracted. His interest in mathematics, awakened and encouraged by a family acquaintance, began when he was about six. 'As a boy of six I could

understand the proof of a mathematical theorem more easily than that
meat has to be cut with one's knife not one's fork.' His mother's favourite
child, the boy showed musical inclinations that continued throughout his
life and found expression when playing the piano and composing.

Unfortunately the boy's poor health led his parents to send him for
a time to board in a quasi-military school outside the city. The effects on
him of its Spartan pedagogical methods were manifested in frequent, often
feverish, illness and depression. By 1840 he lost the last of his siblings, a
beloved small sister, who died at the age of seven. From September 1837
to July 1842 Eisenstein attended schools in Berlin, but in addition he
went to hear Dirichlet and others lecture at the university. In his youthful
autobiography he wrote:

> What attracted me so strongly and exclusively to mathematics, apart from
> its actual content, was especially the specific nature of the mental operation
> by which mathematical things are dealt with. This way of deducing and
> discovering new truths from old ones, and the extraordinary clarity and self-
> evidence of the theories and the ingeniousness of the ideas had an irresistible
> fascination for me. Starting from the individual theorems, I soon became
> accustomed to pierce more into their relationships and to grasp more theories
> as a single entity. That is how I conceived the idea of mathematical beauty ...
> and there is such a thing as a mathematical sense or an instinct that enables
> one to tell immediately whether an investigation will bear fruit and to direct
> one's thoughts and efforts accordingly.

At the gymnasium Eisenstein found teachers who understood and
encouraged him to study the works of Euler, Lagrange, and Gauss—
especially the last. In the summer of 1842, before completing school,
Eisenstein accompanied his mother to England to join his father, who
had gone there two years earlier in search of a better livelihood than he
could find in Germany. Still searching, but without success, he took his
family across to Ireland, where Eisenstein used the time to steep himself
in Gauss's masterpiece *Disquisitiones Arithmeticae* and started on his own
study of forms of the third degree and the theory of elliptic functions. In
Dublin in 1843 he visited Hamilton, to whom he had written to enquire

about possible teaching positions in Ireland. Nothing came of this but Hamilton gave him a copy of a paper he had written for presentation to the Berlin Academy.

By around mid June 1843 Eisenstein and his mother were back in Berlin. His parents were now living apart, and from then until his death Eisenstein was alienated from his father and stayed with his mother only briefly from time to time. In August 1843 he applied (aged twenty) to the gymnasium for permission, as a non-student, to take the *Abitur*, so that he could enter a university. Eisenstein passed the examination successfully; his perceptive mathematics teacher reported 'his knowledge of mathematics goes far beyond the scope of the secondary school curriculum. His talent and zeal lead one to expect that some day he will make an important contribution to the development and expansion of the subject.'

Eisenstein was now qualified to enrol at the University of Berlin. In January 1844 he delivered to the Berlin Academy the paper that Hamilton had given him, using the occasion to submit for publication a monograph of his own on ternary forms in two variables. The academy's referee was August Leopold Crelle, who became Eisenstein's patron. Crelle was a successful civil engineer by profession. In 1826 he had founded the *Journal für die reine und angewandte Mathematik* (Journal for pure and applied mathematics), commonly known as Crelle's journal, which rapidly became the leading German mathematical periodical and helped to establish Berlin as an important centre for mathematics.

On the recommendation of Crelle himself, Eisenstein's work was accepted for publication in his journal. Crelle went on to assist the young scholar by introducing him to Alexander von Humboldt, who immediately took an interest in Eisenstein and, as well as trying to obtain financial support for him from official sources, often helped him out of his own pocket, making it clear that he valued Eisenstein not only as a mathematician but also as a human being. The young man longed for companionship, since he did not get on well with his parents. One of his mathematical friends was a Harvard graduate, who was studying in Berlin at the time. However his closest friend and support in the troubles which lay ahead was the Jewish mathematician Moritz Stern, a brief account of whose life has been given in Chapter 2.

The parts of Crelle's journal published in 1844 contained no fewer than twenty-five contributions from Eisenstein, which made him famous throughout the mathematical world. They dealt primarily with quadratic and cubic forms, the reciprocity theorem for cubic residues, cyclotomy and forms of the third degree, plus some notes on elliptic and Abelian transcendental integrals. He sent some of his work to Gauss, who praised it very highly and encouraged Eisenstein to pay him a visit. So Eisenstein went to Göttingen for two weeks, armed with a glowing letter of recommendation from Humboldt, and won high praise from one of the hardest men to please in the mathematical world.

However, on his return to Berlin Eisenstein succumbed to another bout of depression. Even the sensational recognition that came to him when he was still only a third-semester student failed to brighten his spirits more than fleetingly. It is thought that his friend and patron von Humboldt was behind a most unusual award of an honorary doctorate of philosophy by the University of Breslau in 1845, which qualified Eisenstein for entry into the academic profession. The next year found Eisenstein involved in an unpleasant priority dispute with an enraged Carl Jacobi, who accused him of plagiarism and misrepresentation of known results in a wholly unfair footnote in Crelle's journal. Jacobi, previously a supporter of Eisenstein, charged him with scientific frivolity and with appropriating as his own the ideas imparted to him by others. He maintained that Eisenstein had no original achievements to his credit, but had merely cleverly proved certain theorems stated by others and carried out ideas conceived by others. Writing to Stern in 1846, Eisenstein explained that 'the whole trouble is that when I learned of his work on cyclotomy, I did not immediately and publicly acknowledge him as the instigator, while I have frequently done this in the case of Gauss. That I omitted to do so in this instance is merely the fault of my naive innocence.'

In 1846 and 1847 Eisenstein published various papers, mainly on the theory of elliptic functions. Humboldt, who had tried in vain to draw Eisenstein to the attention of Crown Prince Maximilian of Bavaria, early in 1847 recommended him for a professorship in Heidelberg—even before he had reached the status of *Privatdozent* in Berlin—but without success. Eisenstein's lectures were attended by more than half the Berlin students of mathematics, which was the more remarkable since he was competing with such luminaries as Dirichlet and Jacobi. During the summer of 1847 the young Riemann was among those who attended Eisenstein's course on elliptic functions. Eisenstein felt a mission to bring home to his audience the most recent results of research.

Eisenstein, like Carl Jacobi, attended some political meetings that took place in 1848 where republican ideas were discussed. Although he took no active part in the accompanying violence in the streets, when some shots were fired from a house he was inside, he was forcibly removed with other prisoners to the citadel in Spandau, suffering severe maltreatment en route. Although he was released the following day, the experience gravely affected his health and he published nothing for the next two years. Moreover when word spread around that he had republican leanings, financial support for him dwindled, and it took von Humboldt's most strenuous efforts to keep it from drying up altogether. Eisenstein's situation rapidly worsened. While they were in regular correspondence on scientific matters, even Stern proved unable to dispel the depression that increasingly held Eisenstein in its grip.

Eisenstein was a hypochondriac who often cancelled lectures because he did not feel well enough to give them. Sometimes he delivered lectures from his bed. Yet all this time he was publishing one masterly paper after another in Crelle's journal, especially on the quadratic partition of prime numbers, on reciprocity laws, and on the theory of forms. In 1847 Gauss wrote a highly flattering foreword to a collection of Eisenstein's publications. In 1851, on the recommendation of Gauss, he was elected a corresponding member of the prestigious Göttingen Society, and the next year Dirichlet, with Jacobi's concurrence, proposed him for membership of the Berlin Academy. Eventually, when still under twenty-nine years of age, he was elected to the place made vacant by Jacobi's death. In late July of that same year Eisenstein suffered a severe haemorrhage caused by pulmonary tuberculosis. Funds raised by von Humboldt so that he could go to Sicily to recover arrived too late. He died on 11 October 1852; the eighty-three-year-old von Humboldt accompanied the coffin to the graveside. It was not until the 150th anniversary of Eisenstein's death that his collected works were published.

Cleverness and Tenacity
Leopold Kronecker (1823–1891)

Most of the subjects of these profiles needed to earn a living, usually through teaching or other professional work, and often their early years were by no means easy. Only a few were born into wealthy families, were provided with a good education and had no need to earn their living afterwards. For them research and teaching provided a sense of purpose in life and although they had no material need to compete with others, they still tended to do so.

The first of these to be profiled here is Leopold Kronecker, who was born on 7 December 1823, the same year as Eisenstein, in the important Silesian city of Liegnitz, now in Poland, then in Prussia. His father Isidore was a successful businessman, and his mother Johanna (née Prausnitzer) was independently wealthy. They took great care over their son's education, since he was obviously gifted. He took music lessons and became an accomplished pianist and vocalist. At the local gymnasium he was fortunate to have Kummer as his mathematics teacher. Although the boy was good at mathematics he was, all his life, interested in other subjects, including philosophy, history, and classics. An able gymnast and an expert swimmer, he was also one of the pioneers of mountaineering.

In 1841 Kronecker began studying at the University of Berlin. In those days students at German universities were encouraged to spend a semester or two studying elsewhere. Kronecker spent one at Breslau, the university to which his former teacher Kummer had moved, and another at Bonn, where he founded a *Burschenschaft* (a nationalistic student association). At the age of twenty-two Kronecker graduated from Berlin with a thesis on the complex roots of unity. In his report Dirichlet, later one of Kronecker's closest friends, wrote that he demonstrated unusual penetration, great assiduity, and an exact knowledge of the present state of mathematics.

Kronecker's mother had a wealthy brother in banking, who controlled extensive farming enterprises. When the uncle died his estate was placed in his nephew's hands for administration. The young man, who had just taken his degree, returned to Silesia to wind up the banking business and manage the agricultural property, which he did with notable success. Evidently he was also thinking about mathematics during this period, which lasted eight years, since he conducted a lively correspondence with Kummer. When he finally began to publish his research ideas, fourteen years after leaving Berlin, few people could understand them. Two years later Kronecker concluded his business affairs and returned to Berlin. Seven years earlier he had married Fanny Prausnitzer, his late uncle's daughter; they raised a family of six children. Dirichlet had introduced him to Berlin notables, including his brother-in-law the composer Felix Mendelssohn and the scientist Alexander von Humboldt. The Kroneckers enjoyed great wealth, mixed with the elite of Berlin society, and travelled widely.

Meanwhile, Kummer had succeeded Dirichlet at the university, where he had been joined by Weierstrass. Kronecker had been elected to the Berlin Academy in 1861; later he nominated a number of foreign mathematicians for membership. Kronecker in turn was elected to the Paris Academy in 1868 and to the Royal Society of London in 1884. He was often consulted about appointments outside Germany and his advice carried considerable weight. He also had some influence on the way the teaching of mathematics was being organized at universities in the United States. As an academician he had the right to lecture at the university, and he did so regularly, with Kummer's encouragement. The triumvirate of Kummer, Weierstrass, and Kronecker made Berlin the leading university of the mathematical world for the latter part of the nineteenth century, much more attractive to aspiring young mathematicians than any other university in Germany. Adolf Hurwitz, of whom more later, was one of these; he came to Berlin mainly to attend Kronecker's lectures on number theory and like others found Kronecker's personality much less appealing than his mathematics.

When Riemann died in 1866, Kronecker was offered his chair in
Göttingen but turned it down because he preferred to remain in Berlin
as an academician. It was not until 1883, when Kummer decided to retire,
that Kronecker became a professor at the University of Berlin in his place.
His wife Fanny died in 1891 and Kronecker himself, shattered by her death,
followed her on 29 December of that year, shortly after his sixty-ninth
birthday. In the last year of his life he converted to Christianity. Kronecker
was preparing to make Eisenstein's work the theme of the address he was
to give at the inaugural meeting of the German Mathematical Society but
he had to cancel the lecture when his wife died, and Kronecker himself
died before he could write down what he planned to say.

Kronecker had decided views about the philosophy of mathematics,
and these have been the subject of much controversy. His opinions were
unorthodox, one might even say heretical, and have been misrepresented.
Unfortunately he published very little about them so that most of what
we know is at second-hand, coming from people who disagreed strongly
with his opinions. However the following quotation from the preface to
Kronecker's lectures on number theory, written by one of his disciples,
must give a fair statement of his views:

> I must also point out a requirement that Kronecker consciously imposed
> on the definitions and proofs of general arithmetic, the strict observance
> of which distinguishes his treatment of number theory and algebra from
> almost all the others. He believed that one could, and that one must, in these
> parts of mathematics frame each definition in such a way that one can test
> in a finite number of steps whether it applies to any given quantity. In the
> same way, a proof of the existence of a quantity can only be regarded as fully
> rigorous when it contains a method by which the quantity whose existence
> is to be proved can actually be found. Kronecker was far from wanting to
> discard completely a definition or proof which failed to meet this highest
> demand, but he felt that in such situations something was lacking, and that
> to supply the deficiency was an important problem, through which our
> knowledge of an essential point could be extended. Moreover he believed
> that a formulation which was rigorous in this respect would in general take
> a simpler form than another which did not fulfill these requirements, and
> in his lectures he gave ample demonstration of this in many cases.

Kronecker is often quoted as saying, 'God Himself made the integers—everything else is the work of man.' There is some doubt as to what his true position was. Klein particularly disliked his purism, saying that 'he worked principally with arithmetic and algebra, which he raised in later years to a definite intellectual norm for all mathematical work. With Kronecker, who for philosophical reasons recognized the existence of only integers or at most rational numbers, and wished to banish irrational numbers entirely, a new direction in mathematics arose that regarded the foundations of Weierstrassian function theory as unsatisfactory.' Later, in his account of the development of mathematics in the nineteenth century, Klein gave a more positive assessment:

> That Kronecker, even in the last years of his life, was able to bring new ideas to our science with such youthful ambition, and thereby to uphold Berlin's old fame as a centre for mathematical research in a new form, that is an accomplishment one can only admire without reservation. My critique only concerns the one-sidedness with which Kronecker, from a philosophical standpoint, fought against various scientific directions that were remote from his own. This one-sidedness was probably less grounded in Kronecker's original talents than it was in the disposition of his character. Unconditional mastery, if possible over the whole of German mathematics, became more and more of the goal which he pursued with all the cleverness and tenacity he could muster.

Kronecker specifically criticized the kind of mathematics practised by his colleague Weierstrass. The disagreement between these two men had unfortunate consequences for their personal relations. In their early years together they were close friends but became estranged to the point of enmity later. Weierstrass wrote that 'Kronecker ... acquaints himself very quickly with everything new; his ability to grasp ideas easily makes him capable of doing that. However, he does not do it in a penetrating fashion—he does not have the gift of involving himself with a good piece of unfamiliar work with the same scientific interest as with one of his own investigations.'

According to Georg Frobenius, Kronecker was not the equal of the greatest mathematicians in the individual fields he pursued. That may be so, and yet his place among the most original mathematicians of the nineteenth century seems assured. Perhaps his rather too dogmatic opinions have caused his merits to be undervalued. Since electronic computers became available, there has been renewed interest in some of the questions about which Kronecker felt so passionately.

Kronecker was fascinated by the properties of complex multiplication for elliptic functions. He conjectured that the elliptic functions for which such a multiplication exists would perform for imaginary complex number fields what the circular functions do for the rational field, namely generate all the Abelian extensions. Although he published a number of papers on elliptic functions which might have been relevant, death overtook him before he could achieve a proof of the conjecture, which he called '*meinen liebsten Jugendtraum*' (the dearest dream of my youth). It was demonstrated by the Japanese mathematician Takeo Takagi around the time of the First World War.

Philosopher of the Infinite
Georg Cantor (1845–1918)

By the second half of the nineteenth century a great deal of thought was being given to the foundations of mathematics, especially in Germany. Georg Cantor, the founder of transfinite set theory, revolutionized mathematical thinking in this area. The full impact of his ideas was not felt until well into the twentieth century; in his lifetime they were regarded as highly controversial. The future mathematician was raised in an intensely religious atmosphere by his Danish parents; his mother was a Roman Catholic but his father had been brought up in a Lutheran mission and was a staunch Protestant. Cantor himself was born and bred a Lutheran and remained a devout Christian his entire life. Although Bell (1937) states that Cantor was of pure Jewish descent on both sides, he does not provide any evidence for his assertion. Cantor himself makes a reference in one of his letters to his *israelitsche* grandparents, apparently on his father's side, and it has been claimed that the paternal line originated in a Sephardic family. People who were partly Jewish, in this sense, are included in this book. However his most recent biographer Dauben (1979) is not convinced. Although his status is debatable, I have followed his earlier biographer Fraenkel (1930) and included him here.

Cantor's father Georg Woldemar Cantor was a native of Copenhagen but in his youth had moved to cosmopolitan St Petersburg, where he became a successful wholesale trader. His wife Maria Anna (née Bohm) came of a particularly musical family. Their son Georg Ferdinand Ludwig Philipp was born in the Russian capital on 3 March 1845, the first of six children. On the occasion of his son's confirmation his father, a sensitive and gifted man, wrote a letter to him that Cantor would never forget. It foreshadowed much that was to happen to him in later years.

> No-one knows beforehand into what unbelievably difficult conditions and occupational circumstances he will fall by chance, against what unforeseen and unforeseeable calamities and difficulties he will have to fight in the various situations of life. How often the most promising individuals are defeated after a tenuous, weak resistance in their first serious struggle following their entry into practical affairs. Their courage broken, they atrophy completely thereafter, and even in the best case they will still be nothing more than a ruined genius. But they lacked the steady heart, upon which everything depends! Now, my dear son! Believe me, your sincerest, truest and most experienced friend—this sure heart, which must live in us, is a truly religious spirit.
>
> But in order to avoid as well all those other hardships and difficulties which inevitably rise against us through the jealousy of and slander by open or secret enemies in our eager aspiration for success in the activity of our own speciality or business; in order to combat these with success one needs above all to acquire and to appropriate the greatest amount possible of the most basic, diverse technical knowledge and skills. Nowadays these are an

absolute necessity if the industrious and ambitious man does not want to see himself pushed aside by his enemies and forced to stand in the second or third rank.

In 1856, when young Cantor was eleven, the family moved from Russia to Germany. They lived in Wiesbaden to start with, and from the age of fifteen he attended the gymnasium there. He showed all-round ability, with mathematics and science his strongest subjects, and his father decided he should train as an engineer. With this end in view Cantor began his higher education at the Swiss Federal Polytechnic in Zurich, but then his father agreed to let him transfer to the University of Berlin and study mathematics instead of engineering, where he proved to be a good but not exceptional student.

Cantor spent one semester at the Georgia Augusta before presenting his dissertation *De aequationibus secundi gradus indeterminatis* (On indeterminate equations of the second degree). By then twenty-two, he was already beginning to suffer from episodes of depression, which were to become increasingly serious later in his life. After obtaining his doctorate in 1867, he became a schoolteacher for a short while and then *Privatdozent* at the University of Halle, not far from Leipzig. It was five years before he became *Extra-Ordinarius*, and another seven before he was promoted to *Ordinarius*. Cantor hoped to move to a wealthier and more prestigious university but for the rest of his entire career he remained at Halle.

Normally a cheerful man, with kindly ways, Cantor described himself as 'rather artistically inclined', and at times he appeared regretful that his father had not let him become a violinist. He married Vally Guttman, a Berlin Jewish friend of his sister's, in 1874. During their honeymoon in the Harz mountains the couple happened to meet Richard Dedekind, from then on a close friend and mathematical confidante of Cantor's. After his wealthy father died they were able to purchase a fine new house where they raised their six children.

In Berlin Cantor had become interested in number theory and came to the notice of Kronecker. However, after settling down at Halle he turned to the theory of trigonometric series, especially the question of uniqueness for the Fourier representation of a given function. This led him to think deeply about the difference between denumerably infinite sets like the rationals, and continuous sets like the reals. At this stage Cantor's ideas had much in common with those of Dedekind. At that time it was not yet known whether or not the set of real numbers was countable. By December 1873 Cantor was able to write to Dedekind that he could show that they were not. This major discovery was followed by another. The idea of physical space being three-dimensional, an old and well-accepted notion, was relatively uncontentious. While metaphysical questions concerning the meaning of four- and higher-dimensional 'hyperspaces' were raised, geometers accepted the notion of dimension on an intuitive basis. Cantor showed that this was not good enough by constructing a map of a square onto a line segment, using a continuous one-to-one function, with similar results in higher dimensions. Cantor himself was very surprised by this: 'I see it but I don't believe it!' he exclaimed. The conclusion seemed to undermine the whole intuitive concept of dimension, on which much depended.

Cantor went on to develop his increasingly revolutionary ideas in a series of papers published between 1879 and 1884 on what we now call transfinite set theory. Hilbert described it as one of the greatest achievements of the human spirit. It is in the fifth of these papers, published as a separate booklet known as the *Grundlagen,* that concepts of a topological nature start to appear. The definitions of dense subset, the idea of closure, and so on, originate with Cantor. Later on these were to play an important part in Frechet's memoir on abstract spaces of 1906 and then in Hausdorff's classic *Grundzüge der Mengenlehre* (Principles of set theory) of 1914.

When they first appeared, Cantor's revolutionary theories were generally received with scepticism, often hostility, particularly from Kronecker, who tried to prevent or at least delay publication of Cantor's work. Cantor would have liked to return to the more mathematically stimulating environment of Berlin, but Kronecker ensured that he did not. Other influential mathematicians such as Klein and Poincaré were also unsympathetic, but there were exceptions. One was the Swedish mathematician Gösta Mittag-Leffler, who had founded the journal *Acta Mathematica,* and was willing to publish Cantor's new work when other journals would not.

Several of his major papers, originally published in German, were translated into French and republished in 1883 in the *Acta*. As Cantor found when he visited Paris in 1884, the leading French mathematicians were more favourably disposed towards his work than his German colleagues, although it was criticized by some as having form without substance.

Mittag-Leffler was not prepared to publish Cantor's more philosophical writings, and began to hesitate about some of his mathematical work as well. In 1885 Cantor wanted to publish two short articles in the *Acta* containing some new ideas about ordinal numbers, but Mittag-Leffler politely advised him against it:

> I am convinced that the publication of your new work, before you have been able to explain positive new results, will greatly damage your reputation among mathematicians. I know very well that basically this is all the same to you. But if your theory is once discredited in this way, it will be a long time before it will again command the attention of the mathematical world. It may well be that you and your theory will never be given the justice you deserve in your lifetime. Then the theory will be rediscovered in a hundred years or so by someone else, and it will be subsequently found out that you had it all. Then, at least, you will be given justice. But in this way (by publishing the article) you will exercise no significant influence, which you naturally desire as does everyone who carries out scientific research.

There is an amusing letter to Mittag-Leffler from the Russian mathematician Sonya Kovalevskaya which describes what happened when Cantor tried giving a course on the philosophy of Leibniz: 'In the beginning he had 25 students, but then little by little, melted together first to 4, then to 3, then to 2, finally to a single one. Cantor held out nevertheless and continued to lecture. But alas! One fine day came the last of the Mohicans, somewhat troubled, and thanked the professor very much but explained he had so many other things to do that he could not manage to follow the professor's lectures. Then Cantor, to his wife's unspeakable joy, gave a solemn promise never to lecture on philosophy again!'

When Cantor returned to mathematics it was with another major work, the *Beiträge zur Begründung der transfiniten Mengenlehre* (Contributions to the foundation of transfinite set theory). The first part of this, on simply ordered sets, was published in 1895 while the second, on well-ordered sets, did not appear until two years later, although apparently they were written at the same time. In these works he considered questions, such as the axiom of choice and the continuum hypothesis, which defeated his best efforts to prove them. Of course nowadays the logical position is much better understood, but students of mathematics still feel uneasy when they meet, for the first time, the ideas which were so controversial when Cantor introduced them.

There were many, including Poincaré, who were happy enough with point-set theory but had strong reservations about the full generality of Cantor's transfinite numbers. For ten years following the publication of the *Grundlagen* Cantor, discouraged by the generally hostile reception of his theories, turned away from mathematics. He published in philosophical journals, and his correspondence reveals a preoccupation with matters like Rosicrucianism and Freemasonry and with literary questions such as the Bacon–Shakespeare controversy.

After publication of the synoptic *Beiträge* and its translation into French and Italian almost immediately, Cantor's ideas became widely known and circulated among mathematicians the world over. The value of his transfinite set theory was quickly recognized, and soon Cantor's ideas were stimulating heated polemics between widely divided camps of mathematical opinion. Partly to try and secure a fairer hearing for his controversial ideas Cantor was instrumental in the foundation of the German Mathematical Society in 1889. By this time other mathematicians were taking up Cantor's ideas and, in the hands of Frege, and later Gödel, the implications of the deep questions he raised became better understood.

In the words of Dauben, although Cantor never seemed able to avoid controversy and division over the nature of his work, after 1895 his theories were increasingly defended by younger and more energetic mathematicians. No longer was he left to face the opposition alone. Although Kronecker's dissent was kept alive by critics of a similar persuasion, Cantor could begin to count an impressive and growing array of mathematicians ready to support transfinite set theory. For him, the crusade was nearly over, and though the theoretical difficulties were by no means satisfactorily resolved, recognition that Cantor had contributed something of lasting significance to the world of mathematics had been achieved.

The second half of Cantor's life was marred by recurrent episodes of mental illness. Like many exceptionally gifted people he suffered from bipolar disorder. In those days it was the manic phase, rather than the depression, which aroused most concern. The first serious episode occurred in 1884, after he returned to Halle from Paris. As soon as he recovered he made an attempt, quite cordially received, to achieve a reconciliation with Kronecker. In 1899 another breakdown occurred and this was followed by the news that his youngest son, a gifted youth approaching his thirteenth birthday, had died unexpectedly, plunging the family into lasting grief. At increasingly frequent intervals from 1904 onwards Cantor was under treatment in sanatoria. He died at the psychiatric hospital in Halle on 6 January 1918 at the age of seventy-three.

Artist in Science
Albert Michelson (1852–1931)

The first five subjects were all mathematicians. We now turn to physics. Moritz Jacobi, Peter Riess, and Benjamin Goldschmidt were mentioned as precursors; after them there is a long gap. The study of physics was slow to develop in the New World. There were notable individuals from time to time such as Benjamin Franklin, Joseph Henry, and Willard Gibbs. Touring lecturers from Europe, such as John Tyndall, attracted large and enthusiastic audiences. Ambitious young Americans went abroad to study, but it was only towards the end of the nineteenth century that research in the field began to be carried out in America. One of the pioneers came to the United States from Posen with his parents as a small child, and after a lifetime of achievement in experimental physics became in 1907 the first American Nobel laureate, awarded the prize for his accomplishments in the study of optics.

Albert Abraham Michelson was born on 19 December 1852 in the small Polish town of Strelno, which had been in Prussia since the partition of 1772 and was not returned to Poland until after the First World War. When he was two years old his parents Samuel Michelson and Rosalie (née Przlubska) emigrated like many others to the United States, first to unhealthy New York, then via Panama to San Francisco where an aunt of his had settled earlier. His father, a retailer, opened a small store in the Sierras of California, supplying gold-miners with 'dry goods'. His mother, the daughter of a Jewish physician, had ambitions for their talented son, who spent much of his time reading and playing the violin. When the family moved to Virginia City, Nevada, then a boom town, the boy was sent to board first with relatives in San Francisco and then with Theodore Bradley, headmaster of the Boys' High School in the city. Bradley seems to have aroused young Michelson's interest in science and to have recognized and rewarded his talents in the laboratory. By then Rosalie had given birth to nine children, of whom six survived, and there was another on the way, so it was clear that he would have to fend for himself. At Bradley's suggestion Michelson competed for a state appointment to the United States Naval Academy in Annapolis. Three boys were ranked equal in the competition for the appointment. When Michelson was not chosen he decided to take his case to the White House. President Ulysses S. Grant interviewed him and provided him with a place at the academy; it was said that he wished to please Jewish voters.

At Annapolis Michelson excelled at boxing and physics, but he was not an outstanding cadet in other ways. He is described as a man of medium size, rugged physique, and black hair and hazel eyes. After graduating with the class of 1873 Michelson went to sea, first as a midshipman and then as an ensign, on a series of cruises, returning to be instructor in physics and chemistry two years later. Apparently he was not greatly interested in science before he received this appointment. In 1877 he married Margaret Hemingway, daughter of a wealthy New York stockbroker and lawyer. This marriage lasted twenty years and produced two sons and a daughter. In 1899 Michelson remarried, his first marriage having ended in divorce; he took as his second wife Edna Stanton, of Lake Forest, Illinois, who bore him three daughters.

While teaching physics in 1878 Michelson found a way of improving Foucault's method for measuring the speed of light terrestrially by using revolving mirrors. Simon Newcomb, superintendent of the National Nautical Almanac office, became interested in his work. His first scientific papers were published and he began to collaborate with Newcomb on a government-sponsored project to refine further the determination of the speed of light. In 1879 he spent a year in Washington working with Newcomb. He then travelled to Europe to spend the next two years visiting scientists in Paris, Heidelberg, and Berlin, where he worked in the laboratory of Helmholtz, the leading German scientist of the day. In the middle of this European tour Michelson decided to resign from active duty in the Navy and devote himself to research in physics. The next year he joined the faculty of the new Case Institute of Applied Science in Cleveland, Ohio. As a lecturer he was admirably clear and soon he was to be recognized as the leading experimentalist in the United States. It was in Cleveland that he first met Edward Morley, then on the faculty of Western Reserve College. Together they began a classic series of experiments designed to detect the movement of light through the 'luminiferous ether'.

The success of Johns Hopkins had inspired a wealthy American businessman named Clark to found another such institution in Worcester, Massachusetts. Michelson moved to Clark University in 1887, after seven years at Case, but then moved again after six years to become the head of the department of physics at the new University of Chicago, founded by John D. Rockefeller. At American universities both sides of the subject were usually combined in a single physics department.

Unlike the Ivy League colleges, but like Johns Hopkins, Chicago was influenced in many respects by the German university model. After three years building up his department Michelson recruited the young Robert Andrews Millikan, then studying in Europe, to join him. While Michelson pursued the experimental research which would make him famous, he left Millikan to take responsibility for the department's graduate school. Throughout the twenty-five years they were together Michelson always treated Millikan with the utmost courtesy and consideration.

When Einstein's famous three papers of 1905 appeared, one of which inaugurated the special theory of relativity by dispensing with the idea of an ether and by elevating the velocity of light into an absolute constant, Michelson was much too busy with administrative duties and with receiving honours to pay much heed. From 1901 to 1903 he served as president of the American Physical Society, in 1910–1911 as president of the American Association for the Advancement of Science, and from 1923 to 1927 as president of the United States National Academy of Sciences. He was elected a foreign member of the Royal Society of London in 1902 and awarded its prestigious Copley Medal five years later, when he was also awarded a Nobel Prize for 'his precision optical instruments and the spectroscopic and metrological investigations conducted therewith'.

The undulatory theory of light as generally accepted in the 1880s simply assumed a luminiferous medium. This ether, it was argued, must pervade intermolecular space, as well as interstellar space. Hence it should be at rest in the universe and therefore provide a reference frame against which to measure the earth's velocity. Michelson boldly denied the validity of this hypothesis of the stationary ether but he always maintained the need for some kind of ether to explain why no ether-wind or relative motion appeared to be detectable. The relation between Michelson's experimental work and Einstein's theories of relativity is complex and historically indirect. Einstein said that the Michelson–Morley experiment was not a considerable influence on his thinking about relativity: 'I even do not remember if I knew of it at all when I wrote my first paper on the subject.' Although scholars continue to debate the role of his classic ether-drift experiment, Michelson himself in his last years spoke of 'the beloved old ether which is now abandoned, though I personally still cling a little to it'. In his last book, *Studies in Optics*, published in 1927, he advised that relativity theory be afforded a 'generous acceptance', although he remained personally sceptical.

During the First World War he returned to the Navy as a reserve officer, at the age of sixty-five. In the early 1920s he began to spend more time at Mount Wilson, site of the famous astronomical observatory, and in nearby Pasadena, where the California Institute of Technology had recently been established, with Millikan in charge. Leading physicists came to lecture from all over the world, including Max Born, Albert Einstein, Werner Heisenberg, and Erwin Schrödinger. Michelson could hear about their revolutionary ideas, could work in well-equipped laboratories, and could enjoy his favourite recreations: he was an excellent tennis player, a good violinist, and a fine billiards player, and also enjoyed bridge, chess, and watercolour painting. He was described as a quiet, withdrawn man, unhurried and unfretful, who pursued his modest, serene way along the frontiers of science, entering new pathways and ascending to unattained heights as leisurely and as easily as though he was taking an evening stroll. He died on 9 May 1931 at the age of seventy-nine, after suffering a series of strokes. Einstein once described Michelson as an artist in science: 'his greatest joy seemed to come from the beauty of the experiment itself, and the elegance of the method employed.'

First Jewish Woman of Science
Hertha Ayrton (1854–1923)

We now return to England, and the first of our three Jewish women. Until the end of the nineteenth century and even beyond there were all kinds of obstacles which made it difficult for a woman to become a scientist. Phoebe Sarah Marks, afterwards to make her name as Hertha Ayrton, was born on 28 April 1854 in Portsea, near Portsmouth on the English Channel. Her parents Alice Theresa and Levi Marks were then living in the old Sussex town of Petworth, but it seems her mother returned to the home of her own parents to give birth to this, the third of her eight children. Her father, the son of a Polish innkeeper, had fled to England to escape the persecutions of the Jews under the tsarist regime. His health, probably undermined by these youthful experiences, was never good. He traded as a clockmaker and jeweller from a shop in Petworth, until his last year when he took out a licence to hawk his wares as a pedlar. An unworldly man, he was unsuccessful in business and when he died in 1861 his family was left in poverty.

Thus Sarah, as she was known as a child, was mainly brought up by her mother Alice, whose parents were also Polish refugees. Alice was a remarkable woman, who brought with her the strict and narrow Judaism of her Polish forebears. Sarah's education began at a dame school in Portsea, to which her widowed mother had moved. When her exceptional ability began to show itself she was sent to continue her education at a private school in northwest London kept by her maternal aunt Miriam and her husband Alphonse Hartog, through whom she got to know some remarkably gifted cousins. Among them was the brilliant mathematician Numa Hartog, who after obtaining a London BSc 'with honours entirely without precedent', in 1869 became the first Jew to be classed as Senior Wrangler in the Cambridge Tripos. Since he refused to make the statutory declaration 'on the true faith of a Christian' he was granted his degree by special grace of the University Senate. He had just embarked on a career in the law when he died from smallpox in 1871, just three days before the act of parliament abolishing the remaining religious tests received royal assent.

At school Sarah learnt fluent French from her uncle Alphonse, among other subjects. After school hours she gave private tuition to earn some money to send home to help her impoverished mother, who was struggling to raise her other children. Sarah, who was short in stature, had penetrating grey-green eyes and raven-black hair. Like her father she was good-looking but took no trouble over her personal appearance. Fiercely independent, free-thinking, and stubborn, on one occasion when she felt unjustly accused of some misdemeanour Sarah went on hunger-strike for several days. At the age of sixteen she told everyone that in future she wished to be known as Hertha, the earth goddess in one of Swinburne's poems.

In London Hertha's social circle began to widen. The most important of her friends was Barbara Leigh Smith (1827–1891), a first cousin of Florence Nightingale, who was an outspoken feminist and a prominent figure in the movement for women's emancipation, a cause dear to Hertha's own heart. After Barbara married a French-born physician named Eugene Bodichon she was generally known as Madame. Madame introduced Hertha to various liberal-minded people, including the writer George Eliot, whose novel *Daniel Deronda*, dealing with the place and problems of Jews in Victorian society, features a character, Mirah, said to exhibit some of Hertha's personal characteristics. Hertha also met Sylvester, another member of Madame's social circle who believed in higher education for women. He already knew the Leigh Smiths when Madame was still single; possibly he also coached her brother when he was an undergraduate at Cambridge. Sylvester became very fond of Barbara and seems to have contemplated matrimony. She rejected his overtures but remained his friend and correspondent.

Madame was one of the founders of Girton College, Cambridge and she encouraged Hertha to try for a college scholarship there. Although Hertha was not awarded this she was nevertheless admitted to the college in 1876, supported by a loan from Madame Bodichon and her friends. She was prominent in the Choral Society and helped to form the famous Girton Fire Brigade, which is still going strong. After her first term she became ill and left Cambridge for the rest of the year to convalesce. At this time women were only permitted by the university to sit the Tripos examination in college, rather than in the Senate House with the other candidates, and they could not proceed to take their degree. When the time came Hertha did not do at all well; she was only fifteenth in the third class. The university never granted her a degree, but she remained attached to the college until the end of her life. Cambridge did not grant degrees to women until 1948, when it was the last British university to do so.

After leaving Cambridge, Hertha and a college friend gave private tuition at their flat in London. In her spare time she took lessons in Hebrew; she loved to sing Hebrew hymns she had learnt from her mother as a child. She also invented a device designed to divide a line into any number of equal parts. Based on an idea of one of her cousins, this was accorded a favourable reception by architects, artists, and engineers. After two years of preparing candidates for university entrance she decided that she wanted to study applied physics and took a course at the Finsbury

Technical College under William Edward Ayrton, a pioneer in physics education and electrical engineering. The son of a barrister, he had studied mathematics at University College London and electricity at Glasgow under William Thomson, later Lord Kelvin. For some years he had worked abroad, in India and Japan. After he returned to London he was appointed lecturer at several of the technical colleges, of which Finsbury was one.

After the death of his first wife, who had just qualified as a doctor, he married Hertha in 1885; they raised two children, one daughter from each of his two marriages. Thanks to a legacy from Madame, Hertha was able to employ a housekeeper which enabled her to start assisting her husband with his experiments on the electric arc. The arc, which is produced when an electric current flows between two electrodes, had been discovered in 1820 by Humphry Davy but by this time it was in regular use when a very bright source of light or very high temperature was required. Soon she was conducting her own experiments at home while her husband looked after their daughter, and these led her to make some important discoveries.

Hertha began to lecture on her research, at home and abroad, and wrote a useful book, *The Electric Arc*, which was published in 1902. Her book was a practical treatment as well as theoretical; later it was partly superseded by technical developments in the practice of welding, but for arcs between carbon electrodes it remained the standard work. It was the only complete history of the subject. She worked on the design of electric searchlights for the Admiralty between 1904 and 1908.

Her husband had been elected a Fellow of the Royal Society in 1881 and was awarded a Royal Medal twenty years later. Efforts were made to get Hertha elected to the Royal Society as well but although she had strong support the statutes in force at that time blocked the nomination of women, and the attempt was not repeated even after the statutes had been changed. The argument was that a woman's person was, in common law, covered by that of her father or husband; no woman was elected until 1945. However her work was recognized in 1906 by the award of the society's Hughes Medal for an original discovery in the physical sciences, especially in the field of electricity and magnetism or their applications, for which her research on the electric arc qualified her admirably. The previous year she had been admitted a full member of the Institution of Electrical Engineers.

Hertha had studied French under Alphonse Hartog and with the help of Eugene Bodichon became fluent. She gave an invited address in that language on the electric arc at the International Electric Congress of 1900, held in Paris. She returned to Paris in 1911 to lecture, also in French, to the Société de Physique on her new research into the formation of ripples in sand under standing waves in the water. When the Curies came to London to report on their discovery of radium she found a kindred spirit in Marie Curie. Whenever she was in Paris she would visit Madame Curie who, on her own in 1912 and with her daughters in 1913, came to stay with her in England.

When poison gas was used in the First World War she succeeded, not without difficulty, in persuading the War Office to make use of a simple invention of hers which could disperse clouds of gas when used in a certain way, based on her understanding of the reasons for the formation of sand ripples. Over 100,000 of these Ayrton fans, which also had other applications, were used on the Western Front.

Always left-wing in her political views, Hertha joined the new Labour Party when it was formed. She had always been a staunch supporter of women's rights, as was her husband. In 1899 she presided over the science section of the second meeting of the International Congress of Women. She played a leading part in the suffragette movement, especially after the war, and was proud that her daughter became an even more militant suffragette. Being Jewish was never a problem for her; by the time she grew up British Jews had won full rights of citizenship. Devoutly religious in her youth, she became more sceptical of organized religion later but never renounced Judaism and until her marriage always went home for the Passover rituals. She was always deeply proud of her Jewish heritage. In 1898 her mother died; her husband died ten years later. She herself died on 26 August 1923, at the age of sixty-nine, famous as the first Jewish woman to make a name for herself in scientific research.

5

Years of Success

The birth-dates of the subjects of the second group of profiles span the two decades from 1857 to 1877. For those who lived in Germany unification brought a period of stability; in many respects it was a golden age, in which Jews could prosper. In most branches of science Germany captured the lead from France. Of course there were other centres of excellence but Berlin became the most exciting place for physicists, Göttingen for mathematicians. Scientific activity continued to thrive until the Weimar Republic collapsed and the anti-intellectual and anti-Semitic National Socialists took control, with disastrous results. German Jews, and Jews who were working in Germany, began to leave. Of course there were also outstanding scientists in other countries—Britain and France, for example—but at this stage the United States was still heavily dependent on European immigrants.

Discoverer of Radio Waves
Heinrich Hertz (1857–1894)

We now return to Germany, where Heinrich Rudolph Hertz, the discoverer of radio waves, was born in the free city of Hamburg on 22 February 1857, and grew up in a prosperous and cultured Hanseatic family. His father, Gustav, was a barrister and later a judge of appeal, with a seat in the Senate; his mother was Anna Elizabeth (née Pfefferkorn). He had three younger brothers and one younger sister. Hertz was a Lutheran, although his father's family were Jewish. Thus Hertz was half-Jewish, according to the Nazis, who believed his more important 'pragmatic' experimental work was due to his Aryan side, his 'dogmatic' theoretical work to his Jewish inheritance. At the age of six Hertz entered a strict private school where his 'benign and understanding' mother watched over his progress; he was always first in his class. He had an uncommon gift for languages both modern and ancient. He left the private school at fifteen to enter the Johanneum Gymnasium, where he was first of his class in Greek; at the same time he took private lessons in Arabic. Very early Hertz showed a practical bent; at the age of twelve he had a workbench and woodworking tools. Later he acquired a lathe and with it made spectral and other physical apparatus. On Sundays he attended trade school for lessons in mechanical drawing. His skill in sketching and painting marked the limit of his artistic talent; he was totally unmusical.

After taking his *Abitur* in 1875 Hertz went to Frankfurt to prepare for a career in structural engineering. He gained some experience in a temporary job with a civil engineering firm in Frankfurt. After a brief spell in 1876 in the Dresden Polytechnic he put in his year of military service, serving with the railway regiment in Berlin. He then moved to Munich in 1877 with the intention of studying further at the technical university there. Since his schooldays he had had conflicting leanings toward natural science and engineering. While preparing for engineering he had regularly studied mathematics and natural science on the side. With his father's approval and promise of continued financial support he enrolled at the University of Munich rather than the Technical University. The latter institution had a more vocational emphasis but its facilities included a good physics laboratory. The university by contrast promised a life of study and research, one that suited Hertz's scholarly, idealistic tastes. He was relieved at having decided on an academic and scientific career after long vacillation and was confident that he had decided rightly.

Hertz spent his first semester at the University of Munich studying mathematics. Following the advice of the experimental physicist Philipp von Jolly he read the works of the French masters, learning mathematics and mechanics in their historical development and deepening his identification with investigators of the past. Elliptic functions and the other parts of the newer mathematics he found too abstract, unlikely to be any use in physics. Although Hertz thought that, when properly grasped, everything in nature is mathematical, he was in his student days and throughout his career interested primarily in physical and only indirectly in mathematical problems. It was expected at this time that an intending physicist should have a grounding in experimental practice as well as in mathematics. Accordingly, Hertz spent his second semester at Munich in Jolly's laboratory in the university and the third at the Technical University. He found this practical experience immensely satisfying, especially after intensive mathematical studies; throughout his life he alternated between predominantly experimental and predominantly mathematical studies.

After a year in Munich Hertz was eager to make the customary student migration. After consultation he decided in favour of Berlin, where he was attracted by the fame of Helmholtz and Kirchhoff. Soon after arriving in the Prussian capital in 1878 Hertz became the disciple of Helmholtz. The research environment in Berlin was highly competitive, especially in physics. Hertz found that a prize was being offered by the Berlin philosophical faculty for the solution of an experimental problem concerning electrical inertia. Although only in his second year of university study he was anxious to begin original research and try for the prize. Helmholtz, who had proposed the problem in question and had great interest in its solution, provided Hertz with a room in his new Physics Institute, directed him to the relevant literature, and paid daily attention to his progress. Helmholtz saw the two sides of physics as complementary, so that an experimentalist needed to have a good grasp of theory, and vice versa. Hertz showed himself to be an extremely persistent and self-disciplined researcher.

Outside the laboratory Hertz attended Kirchhoff's lectures on theoretical physics but found little new in them. He wrote home that his greatest satisfaction lay in seeking and communicating new truths about nature. His belief in the conformity of the laws of nature to the laws of human logic was so strong that to discover a case of apparent non-conformity would make him highly uncomfortable; he would spend hours closed off from the world pursuing the disagreement until he found the error. He won the Philosophical Faculty prize in 1879 earning a medal, a first publication in *Annalen der Physic* in 1880, and the deepening respect of Helmholtz.

Helmholtz encouraged Hertz to compete for another, much more prestigious and valuable prize which was being offered by the Berlin Academy. The subject was to test experimentally the critical assumptions of Clerk Maxwell's theory of electromagnetism. Hertz decided against doing so, feeling that the project might take him three years to complete and that the outcome was uncertain in any case. Instead he wrote a doctoral dissertation on electromagnetic induction in rotating conductors, a purely theoretical work that took him only three months. It was a thorough study of a problem that had been partially treated by many others, from Arago to Faraday to Emil Jochmann and Clerk Maxwell. He submitted his dissertation in January 1880 and took his doctoral examination the following month, earning a *magna cum laude*, a distinction rarely awarded in Berlin.

The same year Hertz began as a salaried assistant to Helmholtz in the practical work of the Berlin Physics Institute, a position he held for three years. He got to know Helmholtz and his second wife Anna well; they entertained in great style, bringing together intellectuals, scientists, artists, and leaders of both government and industry. His duties left him time to complete the research for fifteen publications and with them to begin establishing a reputation. This work in his Berlin period is difficult to summarize because of its diversity, but it was mainly concerned with electricity.

Helmholtz was a poor lecturer, who simply read out verbatim passages from the books he had written in a halting and ponderous voice, but for Hertz what mattered was to be working under Germany's greatest physicist and enjoying the use of country's finest research facilities. When the Berlin Physical Society began meeting in the Physics Institute he attended regularly, enjoying the sense of being at the centre of German physics. However it was time for him to advance to a regular faculty appointment, and for this the first step was to serve as a *Privatdozent*. It was at this time that mathematical physics began to be recognized as a separate subdiscipline in Germany; Hertz's opportunity came when the University of Kiel requested a *Privatdozent* for the subject and Kirchhoff recommended Hertz for the post. So in 1883 Hertz moved to Kiel, where he discovered that he was a success as a lecturer; by the second semester he drew an audience of fifty students, an impressive number for a small university. The drawback was that Kiel lacked a physics laboratory, so that he could not carry out much experimental work. Instead he returned to theoretical physics and wrote a deep study of Clerk Maxwell's theory of electromagnetism. When Kiel offered to promote him to the rank of *Extra-Ordinarius* he declined because he did not want to be a purely theoretical physicist. When this became known the Technical University at Karlsruhe offered him the position of *Ordinarius* in physics, and once he had inspected their physical laboratory he accepted.

Hertz spent four fruitful years at Karlsruhe, from 1885 to 1889. His stay began inauspiciously: for a time he was lonely and uncertain about what research to undertake next. In July 1886, after a three-month courtship, he married Elizabeth Doll, the daughter of a colleague. A few months later he began the experimental studies that were to make him world-famous. He began by settling the problem proposed for the Berlin Academy Prize. Then he confirmed the existence of the electromagnetic radiation predicted by Clerk Maxwell which extended the visible spectrum of light into what we now call the radio spectrum. He not only showed that electromagnetic waves exist but that they can be propagated in free space. The nine papers he published on these researches at Karlsruhe won him immediate international recognition.

With his experiments Hertz had gone far towards his goal of testing Clerk Maxwell's theory decisively. Helmholtz informed the Berlin Physical Society of Hertz's demonstration of the existence of these 'electric waves' in these words: 'Gentlemen, I have to communicate to you today the most important discovery of the century.' In summing up the significance of Hertz's experiments Helmholtz said that they showed that light and electricity are very closely connected. Hertz was asked to lecture and repeat his experiments in Berlin and elsewhere. Hertz took no interest in the commercial applications made possible by his revolutionary discovery, which had to wait for the development of wireless telegraphy by Marconi and others after his death.

In September 1888 the University of Giessen tried to recruit Hertz, while the Ministry pressed him to consider Berlin instead. At thirty-one he thought he was too young for a major position in German physics, which would draw him away from research. In any case Berlin wanted a mathematical physicist. In 1889 Clark University tried to recruit him to join Michelson at its new physical institute, planned to be as splendid as Berlin's, and then Graz tried to secure him as Ludwig Boltzmann's successor, but without success. Finally, when he was offered the physics chair at the Rhenish University of Bonn he accepted, more because of Bonn's attractive location than its scientific reputation.

So Hertz moved to Bonn in the spring of 1889, succeeding the great thermodynamicist Rudolf Clausius. He and his wife moved into the house that Clausius had lived in for fifteen years; the historical connection mattered a lot to him. He found the Bonn Physical Institute cramped, the apparatus a jumble which he had to put in order. Hermann Minkowski, then a *Privatdozent* in mathematics, joined him in research into electro-magnetism. He also had his one and only assistant in Philip Lenard, later to win a Nobel Prize for physics but notorious in Hitler's Germany as a fervent Nazi. According to Max Born, Lenard, at a conference in 1920, directed 'sharp, malicious attacks against Einstein, with an unconcealed anti-Semitic bias'.

Hertz's research on electromagnetism not only facilitated the acceptance of Clerk Maxwell's theory among German physicists; it taught them the value of a good theoretical basis for experimental work. Hertz himself, once he had finished arranging his laboratory at Bonn, returned to experimental research, but grew tired of repeated failures. He published two more classic papers in the *Annalen* on Clerk Maxwell's theory, and then turned to something quite different.

The principle of least action has a long history in mechanics and physics. Helmholtz had been studying it afresh and Hertz decided to follow his example by writing a purely theoretical study of the principles of mechanics. While Helmholtz and others looked on his work in this field with respect they suspended judgement, and Hertz's theories have never been generally accepted, although Ludwig Wittgenstein believed in them. Meanwhile Hertz was starting to suffer from ill-health. The decline began at Karlsruhe with toothache, and all his teeth were extracted. Then his nose and throat became so painful that he had to stop work. The cause was diagnosed as a malignant bone condition that his physicians could not treat. He had several surgical operations but to no avail and he died from blood-poisoning on New Year's Day 1894 at the age of thirty-six, almost the same life-span as Mozart. His wife and two daughters emigrated to England from Nazi Germany in 1937 and settled in Cambridge.

After his early death his mother wrote a most interesting account of his childhood. Hertz himself kept a diary, in which he recorded the events of his everyday life. With other material, including a short biography by Max von Laue, these memoirs have been published in English as Hertz (1977). McCormmack (1982) has given a vivid picture of what it was like in nineteenth-century Prussia to be a classical physicist, partly based on this first-hand account, in which people whose names are familiar to us from histories of the subject come to life. We learn how the autocratic Friedrich Althoff, who advised the minister of culture on faculty appointments, used to treat people who came to see him. We begin to appreciate how Klein, who knew Althoff from the time they were comrades in the army, came to have so much influence that people said that he could make or break the career of a young mathematician.

Appleyard (1930) concludes his admirable outline of Hertz's life and work by saying:

> Among those who knew him best, the remembrance that remains of him is of a man of amiable disposition, social, genial, a good lecturer, possessed of singular modesty, who gave himself no airs as of a great professor, and who, when speaking of his own discoveries, never mentioned himself. When the

Royal Society presented him with the Rumford medal, he silently disappeared from Bonn for a few days—none knew why—and he returned as silently. The habit he formed early in his life of solving difficulties for himself continued with him; he preferred, upon occasion, to puzzle things out in loneliness in the laboratory. His decision to follow pure science instead of a technical career was faithfully kept, and yet the importance of the part he played in the ultimate technical advance in electrical science is important beyond measure.

Zealous Promoter of Science
Vito Volterra (1860–1940)

The Enlightenment was slow to reach Italy. Reforms introduced by Bonaparte, which benefited the Jews, were reversed after the Congress of Vienna. Austria gained control of much of the north, while the south continued to endure Bourbon mis-rule. Jews played an active role in the Risorgimento, and after 1870 were able to participate fully in the political and intellectual life of the unified country. A close-knit circle of distinguished mathematicians emerged soon afterwards and the majority were Jewish. Their leader was the mathematical physicist Vito Volterra, whose life is the subject of this profile.

(Samuel Giuseppe) Vito Volterra was the only child of Abramo Volterra, a cloth merchant, and his wife Angelica (née Almagià). Most of his early ancestors were citizens of Bologna, but at the beginning of the fifteenth century one of them had moved to the ancient city of Volterra, hence the name of that branch of the family (in northern Italy, patronymics taken from names of towns were normally Jewish names). In 1459 the Volterras opened a bank in Florence; they became known as writers, travellers, and collectors of books and ancient codices. In the following centuries members of the family could be found in various Italian cities including Ancona, where the future scientist was born on 8 May 1860, at the height of the revolutionary wars. When he was only three months old, a bomb destroyed his cradle during a siege of the city; fortunately he was not in it at the time.

Volterra's father died when he was two years old. His mother was left almost destitute but a brother of hers, who worked for the Banca Nazionale, came to the rescue. Eventually she and her son settled in Florence, where he attended the excellent Scuola Tecnica Dante Alighieri and Istituto Tecnico Galileo Galilei. Volterra considered himself virtually a Florentine. He was a precocious child, with an aggressive curiosity and an early passion for science, especially mathematics. At the age of eleven he began to study Bertrand's *Arithmetic* and Legendre's *Geometry*, and then progressed to Bertrand's *Differential Calculus*. He discovered for himself that certain types of problem could be solved mathematically by means of an operation (integration) which was the reverse of differentiation.

When Volterra was about to leave school his mother, still living in poverty, wanted him to start earning his living. In this she was supported by her brother; they appealed to a distant cousin, Edouardo Almagià, hoping that he would persuade the boy to agree. Instead the cousin, a celebrated civil engineer, was so impressed by the boy's ability, determination, and sincerity that he convinced them to let him pursue his interest in science. Furthermore, his former physics teacher from the Istituto Tecnico, having learnt that his most able student was being urged to become a bank clerk, managed to get him work as a paid assistant in the university physics laboratory. The outcome was that when Volterra graduated from high school in 1878 he became a student in the department of natural sciences at the University of Florence.

Two years later he won a competition to become a resident student at the Scuola Normale Superiore in Pisa, originally an offshoot of the French École Normale Supérieure. He had already changed universities from Florence to Pisa. In the course of the next three years he attended courses given by Enrico Betti and Ulisse Dini, among others. It was the lectures of Betti which interested Volterra most of all, and under Betti's influence his studies began to turn more and more towards mathematical physics and mechanics.

After Volterra graduated in 1882 he was promptly appointed Betti's assistant. The following year, at twenty-three, he was chosen to be *professore straordinario* of mechanics at the University of Pisa; three years later he was promoted to *professore ordinario*. Someone who heard him lectured at this time said that he did so with his eyes shut, speaking in a rather high-pitched voice. Volterra shared the mathematics prize of the Lincei with his near-contemporary the geometer Corrado Segre, who also had a Jewish ancestry, and was elected to membership of that ancient academy. In 1892, the year in which Betti died, Volterra left Pisa to become professor of mechanics at the University of Turin; two years later he succeeded Eugenio Beltrami in the chair of mathematical physics in Rome, and was ready to get married.

His bride was the capable and intellectual Virginia Almagià, one of the daughters of the distinguished and wealthy relative who had first made it possible for him to follow a scientific career. She had inherited business sense from her father, who gave her a good education, and musical and other gifts from her mother, Eleonora. Although both their mothers observed Jewish practices, neither Virginia nor Vito did so. She took upon herself all the cares which might have distracted him from his scientific work, undertaking the education of their children and the administration of all their possessions. Four of their six children would survive to maturity; all of them attended the University of Rome. Eduardo became the first Jewish judge on the Italian Constitutional Court, Luisa was a biologist, Enrico migrated to the United States after the Second World War and ended up as professor of aerospace engineering at the University of Texas, while Gustavo practised law in Rome.

By this time Volterra had become well known outside Italy. At the 1900 International Congress of Mathematicians in Paris he gave a plenary address which began: 'The scientific existence of Italy as a nation dates from the journey which Betti, Brioschi and Casorati took together in the autumn of 1858, with the object of entering into relations with the foremost mathematicians of France and Germany. It is to the teaching, labours, and devotion of these three, to their influence in the organization

of advanced studies, to the friendly scientific relations that they instituted between Italy and foreign countries, that the existence of a school
of analysts in Italy is due.' He then went on to say something about all
three of the young Italian mathematicians, particularly his own teacher
Betti, who had met Riemann in Göttingen and looked after him when
he came to Pisa.

Volterra was well known in Paris; Hadamard was a particularly close
friend. In a course of lectures given at the Sorbonne, Volterra described his
method of studying a natural phenomenon by dividing into small intervals
the time over which it occurs, and investigating the phenomenon in each
such interval by regarding the causes that produce it as constant. He
explained how this idea first occurred to him at the age of thirteen, when
he was working on problems of ballistics. After reading the novel *From the
Earth to the Moon,* by Jules Verne, he tried to determine the trajectory of a
projectile subject to the combined gravitational field of the Earth and the
Moon—a special case of the three-body problem. In his solution, time is
apportioned into small intervals, for each of which the force is regarded
as a constant, and the trajectory is given as a succession of small parabolic
arcs. Later he applied the same method to many other kinds of problems
involving linear differential equations and linear substitutions, and more
generally in the theory of functionals.

In 1905 Volterra was appointed chairman of the Turin Polytechnic
until two years later he moved to Rome to be dean of the university's
science faculty. As president of the Italian physical society he helped
to revitalize the somewhat moribund organization, which was slow to
respond to the revolutionary new ideas coming out of Germany. At this
period, mathematicians outnumbered physicists four to one at Italian
universities, but Volterra and his younger colleagues spent as much time
at meetings of physicists as those of mathematicians. In Italy at this time
there were no posts in theoretical physics as such, although Max Abraham,
who had gained a reputation in theoretical physics at Berlin and Göttingen,
was *professore straordinario* of rational mechanics at the Milan Institute
of Technology. The leading Italian physicists were experimentalists who
turned to their mathematical colleagues when a theoretical question
arose.

Volterra was a close friend of many prominent scientific, political, literary, and artistic figures of his day. When still only forty-five he was made a Senator of the Kingdom of Italy in recognition of his scientific distinction. The fact that he was Jewish was commented on in the press, although he was not the first Jew to be made Senator. He was an effective speaker, usually on university affairs. Internationally recognized as the spokesman for Italian science, he worked tirelessly to bring about reforms and to ensure that young talent received due recognition. He thought that Italy could learn from the German model and consulted Felix Klein in Göttingen as to how to modernize scientific education. Virginia complained that he was away so much; when the children were grown she often accompanied him on his travels.

In 1914, when the First World War broke out, Volterra actively supported those who believed that Italy should enter the war on the side of the Allies. When that view prevailed, Volterra, although already fifty-five years old, enlisted as an officer in the army corps of engineers, joining the branch concerned with aerial warfare. He was the first to propose the use of helium as a substitute for the more dangerous hydrogen gas in airships, and the first to fire a gun from an airship. He also experimented with early designs of aircraft and published papers on the mathematical theory of flight. For these accomplishments he was mentioned in dispatches and decorated with the Croce di Guerra.

At the beginning of 1917 Volterra established the Italian Office of War Inventions and became its chairman. In the process of promoting scientific and technical collaboration among the Allies he made frequent journeys to England and France. When in 1917 some parliamentarians—especially the socialists—wanted Italy to make a separate peace, he strenuously opposed their proposals and after the disaster of Caporetto helped to create the parliamentary bloc which convinced the government to continue until final victory. In the postwar settlement Italy gained territory at the expense of Austria but the subsequent economic collapse led to social unrest with disastrous consequences.

In October 1922 the fascists seized power in Italy, and Volterra was one of the few to understand from the beginning the resultant threat to the country's democratic institutions. He was one of the principal signatories of the 'Declaration of Intellectuals' against fascism, an action he took while president of the Lincei. When the proposed 'laws of national security' were debated in the Italian Senate, Volterra joined Benedetto Croce in leading a small group of senators to oppose the proposals, at considerable personal risk, but without success. After 1930 Volterra never attended the Senate again. Under Mussolini, as in Germany later, anti-Semitic policies began to be put into effect. University professors who refused to swear fidelity to the fascist regime were dismissed from their posts; Volterra was the sole mathematician among the thirteen who refused to take the oath. The ancient Lincei and other scientific academies were suppressed and a new academy formed, excluding those, like Volterra, who did not support the regime. In the autumn of 1938, under German pressure, the Italian government promulgated further racial laws. All naturalizations after 1919 were annulled. Foreign and denaturalized Jews were ordered to leave the country without delay, and the majority did so.

In the period between the wars the scope of Volterra's scientific research had broadened; his interests began to include economics and ecology, where he introduced the well-known predator–prey model. During these years he lived a peripatetic existence, only returning to Italy for brief visits to Rome and to his country house at Ariccia in the Alban Hills near Rome. Much of his time was spent in Paris, where he gave lectures and was able to renew his friendship with Hadamard and other French mathematicians. He also lectured in Romania, in Spain, in Belgium, in Czechoslovakia, and in Switzerland. He liked visiting America and crossed the Atlantic several times, although never with his wife.

Volterra was just under five and a half feet tall and strongly built, but inclined to work himself too hard. In later years he steadily put on weight and became decidedly corpulent. He suffered from heart trouble. When he was seventy-eight he was advised not to travel so much, but his intellectual energy was undiminished and he continued his passionate pursuit of science until his death in Rome on 11 October 1940 at the age of eighty. In accordance with his wishes he was buried in the town graveyard of Ariccia, the country retreat he loved so well. After twenty-eight years of widowhood Virginia died at the age of ninety-three.

Volterra received numerous honours, was a member of almost every major scientific academy, and was awarded honorary doctorates by many universities. He was appointed a Grand Officer of the French Legion of Honour. In 1921 he received an honorary knighthood from King George V for his services during the war. In 1936, on the nomination of Pope Pius XI, he was elected a foundation member of the Pontifical Academy of Sciences, members of which had to be not only scientists of world renown but 'men of irreproachable civic and moral conduct who had always assumed a respectful attitude to religion, without allowing a humanistic evaluation of strictly scientific results to lead to conclusions opposed to the faith'.

Gift from Heaven
Hermann Minkowski (1864–1909)

The future mathematician Hermann Minkowski was born to Jewish parents on 22 June 1864, in the Russian city of Alexotas, near Kaunas, now part of Lithuania. His elder brother Oskar was to become famous as the physiologist who discovered the link between diabetes and the pancreas gland. Both their father Lewin Minkowski and mother Rachel (née Raubmann) were of German nationality, although Lewin's antecedents were Russian, but Hermann is generally regarded as a Lithuanian mathematician. In 1872 the Minkowskis moved from Alexotas to Königsberg, where they had resided some time previously. The future mathematician spent the rest of his childhood there and attended the Altstadter Gymnasium, where one of his schoolfriends was the future physicist Arnold Sommerfeld. Minkowski was an avid reader of Shakespeare, Schiller, and Goethe; he could recite most of *Faust* by heart. Then, apart from three semesters at the University of Berlin, he studied at the Albertina, where he showed unusual ability in mathematics. The child prodigy turned into a brash young man, whose sharp wit was matched by his fellow student David Hilbert.

The *Extra-Ordinarius* at this time was Adolf Hurwitz, a charming, modest, and very warm individual, with the emaciated face of an ascetic and unusually large eyes. He became the mentor and friend of Hilbert and Minkowski, who used to accompany him on his daily constitutional; they were totally overwhelmed by his mathematical knowledge. Perhaps a few words about this exceptionally gifted Jewish mathematician could be inserted here since he provides a good example of someone who grew up in the relatively liberal period when Prussia was enjoying the fruits of its recent victory over France. Hurwitz was born in 1859 at Hildesheim, between Hanover and Göttingen, where he attended the local gymnasium. His mathematics teacher was Hannibal Schubert, inventor of the enumerative calculus in geometry, who recommended the boy to Klein, then at the University of Munich. So Hurwitz became Klein's protégé, following him from Munich to Leipzig, and broadening his experience by studying in Berlin and Paris as well. He was appointed *Privatdozent* at Göttingen, where he worked with Moritz Stern and Wilhelm Weber, and now, at Königsberg, was at the height of his powers. We shall meet him again in the profile of Pólya.

In 1883, when he was nineteen, Minkowski entered for the Grand Prize of the Paris Academy for the solution to the problem of finding a formula for the number of ways of expressing an integer as the sum of five squares. Eisenstein had already published such a formula but without proof. Unknown to the mathematicians of Paris, the number-theorist Henry Smith, Sylvester's predecessor as Savilian professor of geometry at Oxford, had published the outline of a proof of Eisenstein's formula in 1867. Smith heard of the prize competition by chance and entered for it by submitting full details of his proof. Meanwhile Minkowski, apparently without knowledge of previous work, reconstructed the entire theory of integral quadratic forms in any number of variables and gave an even better formulation than Smith, because he used a more general definition of the genus of a form. Minkowski was accused of plagiarism, and there was a good deal of ill-feeling. In the end Minkowski shared the prize with Smith, although by then the Oxford mathematician had died.

After obtaining his doctorate from Königsberg in 1885, Minkowski habilitated at Bonn two years later and as we know served as *Privatdozent* there for the next five years, working alongside Hertz. He was promoted to *Extra-Ordinarius* in 1894 but two years later succeeded Hilbert at the Albertina. In 1894 he became *Ordinarius* at the Swiss Federal Polytechnic in Zurich, where his former mentor Hurwitz had succeeded Frobenius a few years previously. The polytechnic, founded in 1853, was adjacent to the university, with which it enjoyed lively professional contacts, for example a common physics colloquium. It was sometimes described as the 'first class waiting room' for ambitious German scientists who used it as a springboard to even more prestigious positions in their homeland. In 1911 it was to be reconstituted as the Eidgenössische Technische Hochschule (ETH).

Hurwitz and Minkowski complemented each other very well. According to Hilbert, Minkowski had more imagination than Hurwitz, but the latter was just as able a mathematician and certainly the better teacher. A talented pianist, he loved to gather with friends and family for music-making. Although Minkowski's speciality was the geometry of numbers, his mathematical interests were very broad, and in Zurich he gave courses on analytical mechanics. As a student, Einstein had attended some of these; one of them an exposition of the kind of mathematical physics that Clerk Maxwell and Helmholtz were developing at that time. Einstein described this as the best lecture he heard in the four years he spent in Zurich.

When Hilbert moved to Göttingen he was able, with Klein's help, to persuade the ministry of culture to create a special position for Minkowski at the Georgia Augusta. So after eight years Minkowski left Zurich to rejoin Hilbert in Göttingen, which was about to rival and then overtake Berlin as the leading German university for mathematics. When Einstein's special theory of relativity was published in 1905, Hilbert and Minkowski were among the first to realize its fundamental importance. The story is told that once, after they had been to an art exhibition, Hilbert's wife asked them how it was. They answered that they didn't know, explaining,

'we were so busy discussing relativity that we never really saw the art.'
Hilbert and Minkowski used to go rambling together in the woods around
the ancient town, when they would discuss not only mathematics but
also philosophical, social, and political problems. Often they would be
accompanied by Hilbert's *Privat-assistent,* an able young physicist named
Max Born, of whom more later.

By 1908 it seemed that Minkowski was about to leave number theory
and make mathematical physics his future field of research. He conducted
a joint seminar with Hilbert on the electrodynamics of moving bodies,
where he described the non-euclidean structure for the space-time
continuum we know as Minkowski space. He persuaded Born, who had
gone home to Breslau, to return to Göttingen and act as his assistant.
However this was not to be, since on 12 January 1909 Minkowski died
unexpectedly as the result of a ruptured appendix. His untimely death,
when he was still only forty-four, came as a great shock to the Göttingen
mathematicians, especially Hilbert who wrote a moving obituary of his
charismatic colleague, in which he described him as a gift from heaven.
Later, Einstein was to adopt Minkowski space as an essential part of his
general theory of relativity, in which gravitational forces arise from the
geometry of space-time.

Insatiable Scientific Curiosity
Jacques Hadamard (1865–1963)

An infatuation with French culture and
an ardent French patriotism characterized
enlightened French Jews of the nineteenth
century. As we have seen, there were already Jewish mathematicians
in France before the Revolution. After the restoration of the monarchy

in 1816 there was rather a long interval before we find others such as Georges Halphen (1844–1889) and Paul Appel (1855–1930) in the histories of mathematics. However, these are overshadowed by Jacques Hadamard, an outstanding all-round mathematician, just as strong in teaching as in research, and extraordinarily versatile. His scientific curiosity was insatiable. During the course of his long life mathematics changed enormously, but he kept abreast of it.

Born in Versailles, near Paris, on 8 December 1865, Jacques-Solomon Hadamard was the son of schoolteachers. His forebears on both sides were mainly intellectuals of Jewish extraction, who had been based in Paris since 1808. His father Amadée taught Latin at the Lycée Charlemagne in Paris; his family came from Lorraine, where fewer restrictions were placed on Jews than in the rest of France. His mother Claude-Marie-Jeanne (née Picard) was a noted teacher of the piano; she taught her son to play the violin at an early age.

In 1871, at the end of the Commune Rising, the Hadamard family found their house had been burnt down and they had lost all their possessions. After they recovered from this setback their son was sent to the lycée where his father taught; he shone in every subject except mathematics, which he did not care for. Although he won prizes in other subjects in the national Concours Généraux, at first he showed no mathematical ability whatsoever. However, in 1875, when his father was transferred to the more prestigious Lycée Louis-le-Grand, the ten-year-old boy went with him and then started to experience mathematics teaching of high quality. When he took the Concours Général in mathematics he was placed second in the whole of France; throughout his life he felt ashamed of his failure to be first.

Entrance to the École Polytechnique and the École Normal Supérieure was highly competitive In a given year there could be a thousand candidates for forty or fifty places. For the École Normale, for example, the first stage of the entrance examinations took place in the candidates' own colleges and lycées on the same two days all over France: first there were six hours of written examinations in mathematics, physics, and philosophy, and on the second day the candidates had four hours of Latin translation. It was on the basis of these examinations that the strongest candidates were then admitted to the final oral and written examinations, which were held in Paris at the École Normale itself. A list of those admitted, in order of merit, was then published.

In 1884, when Hadamard took these examinations at the age of eighteen, he came first in both of them, and was faced with a difficult decision. The quality of the mathematical education at the École Polytechnique had declined somewhat in the second half of the nineteenth century while the prestige of the École Normale Supérieure had risen. After some hesitation he chose the latter, more academic, institution.

On graduating from the École Normale in 1888, Hadamard spent a further year studying in Paris, supported by a sinecure teaching post in Caen. He then taught at the Lycée Buffon for three years. He was not a success as a schoolteacher: 'M. Hadamard believes himself exempted from everything because of his remarkable mathematical abilities,' reported the headmaster to the minister of education. As it happened, the Paris Academy had just announced a prize competition on the theory of the Riemann zeta function; he was awarded the Grand Prize for his entry, the first of a long list of prizes he was to be awarded by the academy. The same year he married Louise-Anna Trenel, a childhood sweetheart with a similar background to his own. A vivacious young woman, she shared his love of music. They had five children, Pierre in 1894, Étienne in 1897, Mathieu in 1899, Cecile in 1901, and Jacqueline in 1902. They were brought up in the belief that they must learn to play at least one musical instrument. At one stage the Hadamards, in collaboration with some other like-minded academics, were educating their children at home.

Hadamard now progressed from school to university teaching. His first such post was at the University of Bordeaux, from 1893 to 1897, and it was there that he proved the theorem which made him famous. His previous work had been on complex analysis, especially the theory of singularities, and he now applied this to number theory. Many mathematicians were trying to find estimates for the density of the set of prime numbers among all the natural numbers. Using the methods of complex analysis he, and independently the Belgian de la Vallée Poussin, arrived at the asymptotic value for the number of primes up to a given integer. This prime number theorem of 1862 resisted all attempts to find an elementary proof until 1949, when one was found which did not involve complex analysis.

Only two years after he arrived in Bordeaux Hadamard was appointed professor of astronomy and rational mechanics. While the Hadamards enjoyed life in Bordeaux, they were hoping to return to Paris. After five years away from the intellectual hub of France Hadamard obtained a position as lecturer at the Sorbonne and as deputy professor at the Collège de France. At the Collège the teaching duties were not onerous but the lectures had to contain new material; not only the content but even the titles of the courses were determined by the lecturers, only subject to formal approval. Hadamard chose to lecture on mathematical physics, in the first year specifically on kinematics. The following year he received the first of many honorary degrees, from the Georgia Augusta.

The thirty-four-year-old Hadamard met the beginning of the twentieth century full of energy and plans. It was about this time that he began research on partial differential equations, arising out of his studies of the dynamics of gases. One of his admirers said that it was in this theory that he gave the most striking proof of his genius. In 1901 he made the first of many visits to America when he represented the Sorbonne at the bicentenary of the foundation of Yale University, during which he was awarded another honorary degree.

In 1904 Hadamard had become involved in the debate on the foundations of mathematics which was raging through the scientific community, revolving around the Axiom of Choice. In 1909 he resigned from the Sorbonne on being appointed professor of mechanics at the Collège de France, where he lectured on complex analysis and its applications to number theory. Two years later when he was invited to lecture at Columbia University in New York, he took as his subject the theory of differential equations, especially the role of topology in the theory as demonstrated by Poincaré, in the course of which he declared:

> Analysis situs is connected ... with every employment of integral calculus. It constitutes a revenge of geometry on analysis. Since Descartes, we have been accustomed to replace each geometric relation by a corresponding relation between numbers, and this has created a sort of predominance of

analysis. Many mathematicians fancy that they escape that predominance and consider themselves as pure geometers in opposition to analysis; but most of them do so in a sense I cannot approve: they simply restrict themselves to treating exclusively by geometry questions which other geometers would treat, in general quite easily, by analytical means; they are, of course, very frequently forced to choose their questions not according to their true scientific interest, but on account of the possibility of such treatment without the intervention of analysis. I am even obliged to add that some of them have dealt with problems totally lacking any interest whatever, this total lack of interest being the sole reason why such problems have been left aside by analysts.

In 1912 Hadamard succeeded Camille Jordan (1838–1922) as professor of analysis at the École Polytechnique. This was the year in which Poincaré died, and Hadamard put everything else aside to write on the life and work of his friend and colleague. Hadamard had been one of Poincaré's greatest admirers; he described him as 'the supreme genius'. The death of Poincaré left a vacancy in the Paris Academy and Hadamard, who had been a candidate several times previously, was finally elected at the age of forty-seven.

There were no offices for professors at the Collège de France and so Hadamard mainly worked at home. Whenever he encountered difficulties he would often resort to the violin. His daughter Jacqueline gave a picture of him at work: 'He practically never wrote a word. He always told me that he thought without words, and that for him the greatest difficulty was to translate his thoughts into words. He only scribbled down equations, not at a table but at a high wooden plinth of the kind that were normally used, at that time, to put a bust on (at my grandmother's it was a bust of Beethoven, of course). In the hall he would write down his mathematical formulas, while walking up and down.'

The Hadamards kept open house for guests. The period before the First World War was an exceptionally happy time for him: new theorems, lectures, a loving wife and children, friends, and a comfortable house filled with the sound of music. They used to collect together a small amateur ensemble; Einstein played in it whenever he was in Paris; the writer Duhamel was the flautist; Hadamard himself played the violin, and his wife rendered other parts on the piano. The sons attended the Lycée Louis-le-Grand, just as their father had done. Pierre, the eldest had just been accepted for the École Polytechnique when the war came, while Étienne, the second oldest was accepted for the École Normale two years later. Both were killed in action on the western front. Towards the end of the war the Hadamards' youngest son Mathieu, also destined for the École Polytechnique, was called up but posted to the less dangerous Italian front and survived. Hadamard himself was involved in military research in the Direction des Inventions organized by Emile Borel and Paul Painlevé, while his wife Louise served as a nurse.

In 1920 Hadamard was appointed professor of mathematical analysis at the École Centrale des Arts et Manufactures, where he would remain until he retired at the age of seventy-one, although still retaining his positions at the École Polytechnique and the Collège de France. The following year he inaugurated a seminar which met twice weekly for over twenty years. The only serious window on international mathematics in France during this period, it became famous for embracing practically the whole range of mathematics. The world's leading mathematicians went there to lecture, but it was always Hadamard who had the last word and the surest judgement concerning the significance or the potential of the research presented. At the centenary of Hadamard's birth his protégé Benoit Mandelbrojt recalled what it had been like.

> The sessions on Tuesdays and Fridays were certainly the most intensive that the collective mathematical thinking of France experienced between the two wars. Every mathematician, French or foreign, considered it an honour and an important proof of scientific esteem, to be invited by the illustrious master to speak about his own research or simply to give an account and a comment on newly-published research. Everybody came to Paris for a few days to bring the fresh fruit of their latest researches to the Parisian mathematical public and to other mathematicians passing through, who together made up the seminar audience, and above all to Hadamard who often saw the essence of the subject being considered better than the invited scientist who was,

however, a specialist in that branch of mathematics, compared the results obtained with old results, sometimes seeing connections with a completely different mathematical area.

In 1920 Hadamard was back in America, lecturing about the early work of Poincaré at the newly founded Rice Institute in Houston. Five years later he visited Rice again to speak about Poincaré's later work. He was also greatly in demand as a speaker at conferences and on other occasions, not only in Europe but also further afield: he made quite lengthy visits to China and the Soviet Republic.

The first and second volumes of his *Cours d'Analyse de l'École Poly-technique* appeared in 1927 and 1930 respectively. This was not intended to compete with the classic courses of Camille Jordan and his successors but was meant to cater more for physicists, astronomers, and engineers. Although he never quite equalled the spectacular achievements of his youth, Hadamard remained active in research while putting most of his time and energy into teaching. The seminar continued to flourish until he retired in 1936. Its success was due not only to his exceptional mathematical talents, but also to his cordiality, humanity, and sense of humour. As André Weil wrote: 'All those who were acquainted with Hadamard know that until the end of his very long life, he retained an extraordinary freshness of mind and character: in many respects, his reactions were those of a fourteen-year-old boy. His kindness knew no bounds.'

After the fall of France, in 1940, the Hadamards escaped to the United States where he gave the lectures at Columbia University which were published under the title *The Psychology of Invention in the Mathematical Field,* the fruit of a lifelong interest in trying to understand how mathematicians come up with their ideas. While they were away the Germans had ransacked their apartment and the family's papers were never recovered. After sixty-eight years of marriage Hadamard's wife Louise died in 1960. His own health was already in decline. His hearing became weaker and he experienced difficulty in walking. Hadamard died on 17 October 1963 at the age of ninety-seven, and was buried in the cemetery of Père Lachaise. By that time he had received almost every academic honour

France had to offer, and many foreign honours as well. In the Legion of Honour he had been promoted to the highest rank, the Grand Cross, on the occasion of his ninetieth birthday.

Mathematical work did not absorb all Hadamard's energies. He had an untiring instinct for justice: the notorious Dreyfus affair was an obsession with him, not simply because the victim was a distant relative. It led him to become a communist sympathizer and an avowed pacifist. Hadamard had a lifelong interest in plants, especially fungi and ferns, of which he had an outstanding collection. When he was crossing the Soviet Union on the Trans-Siberian railway he sallied forth at each stop in search of specimens, to the alarm of his wife who feared he would be left behind when the train started moving again. He loved travelling, and hardly a year went by without a visit to another country for one reason or another. He enjoyed mountaineering and was proud of having climbed Mont Blanc when over sixty.

Victim of the Nazis
Felix Hausdorff (1868–1942)

The transition from imperial Germany to Nazi Germany took place within the lifetime of the subject of our next profile. Among the many Jewish mathematicians who were affected by Nazi persecution the first case to be recorded here is one of the saddest. Like many others he misjudged the course of events and remained in his homeland until it was too late. Early in 1939 Hausdorff wrote a 'short but moving' letter to Courant in New York asking about the possibility of a research fellowship in America, but it was too late.

As Sabine Lee (in Peierls 2007) has explained, 'Frequently, the younger generation saw the signs of the times early; they had less to leave behind and were still in a position to start afresh and build a new life outside Germany. In contrast the older generation had a home, friends and material goods to leave behind with less of a chance of starting a new life. By the time older people were ready to face emigration it had become too difficult to carry through, because of the increasingly stringent regulations about transfer abroad of possessions and money.' Loss of pension rights was a strong disincentive; any payments which were made would be into bank accounts from which funds could not be transferred abroad.

Felix Hausdorff was born on 8 November 1868 in Breslau where his father Louis was a merchant dealing in linen, as was his uncle Siegfried. His mother Hedwig, whose maiden name was Tietz, came from the small town of Birnbaum in the then Prussian province of Posen, where the family had been living for over fifty years. So the ancestors of Felix Hausdorff had been Prussian citizens for nearly a century.

Louis Hausdorff and his family moved to Leipzig, where they were joined by Hedwig's sister Natalie, who was married to Siegfried. Louis, who was quite wealthy, published a trade periodical called *The Spinner and the Weaver* (the business was 'Aryanized' in 1935). Felix, the future mathematician, attended the Nicolai Gymnasium in Leipzig where he received a thorough grounding in the classics. He showed such great musical ability as a youth that he wanted to be a composer, and only the persistent pressure of his father made him give up this idea. After taking the *Abitur* in March 1887, he left school to study astronomy and mathematics at the ancient University of Leipzig. As was customary, he spent two of the nine semesters elsewhere, at the universities of Freiburg and Berlin. In addition to mathematics and astronomy, Hausdorff attended lectures on a wide variety of other subjects, such as theology, philosophy, linguistics, literature, music, and social sciences. In 1891 he obtained his doctorate in Leipzig with a thesis *On the theory of astronomical refraction*. Next he served in the infantry for a year, as a volunteer: whatever the new constitution might say, he found that Jews were seldom commissioned in the German army.

Hausdorff continued his scientific work, and in 1895 habilitated with a thesis *On the absorption of light in the atmosphere*. It is perhaps surprising, since Hausdorff became famous for his work in pure mathematics, that both of these efforts were in mathematical astronomy, and Hausdorff's first four research papers dealt with astronomical and optical questions. After six years as *Privatdozent* he was appointed *Extra-Ordinarius* in appreciation of his work, particularly his teaching of the new subject of probability theory. Significantly, one third of the faculty had voted against the appointment specifically because Hausdorff was Jewish, an omen of what was to come.

Thus by 1902 he was comfortably esconced as *Extra-Ordinarius* in his home town of Leipzig. In 1900 Hausdorff had married Charlotte Goldschmidt, one of three daughters of the Jewish physician Sigismund Goldschmidt, who was himself the son of a rabbi of Leipzig. Sigismund had lost his mother at an early age. His stepmother was a very remarkable person, who had done much to promote the education and emancipation of women. Sigismund himself was a successful emancipated Jew who believed in the cultural absorption of the German Jews. His daughters Charlotte and Sitta converted to the Lutheran faith and were baptized as adults; soon after the marriage of Charlotte and Felix their daughter Lenore was born, and she too was baptized. The Hausdorff family could unquestionably be described as 'assimilated', but Hausdorff himself never denied his Jewish descent, nor did he ever opt for baptism.

We have been given a glimpse of life in the Hausdorff household in those years. The evening hours were reserved for family and friends. There would often be music-making; Hausdorff was an excellent pianist and occasionally composed songs. Then he would retire to work in his study, with strong tea and cigars. The study was a sanctum, which hardly anybody was allowed to enter. In the morning his wife would whisper to the children, 'hush, daddy sleeps', and only later would Hausdorff get up and go to the university. He was extremely sensitive, and given to fits of depression. When he was acting as examiner his sarcasm was dreaded by the students.

The friends and acquaintances of the Hausdorff family included a lawyer, an art publisher, a professor of literature, an artist, and a poet (no doubt there were many more). This broad social circle reflects the fact that Hausdorff's first few publications were non-mathematical. They included a satirical play, *The Doctor's Honour,* ridiculing the revival of the custom of defending one's honour by fighting a duel; an obscure philosophical essay,

Chaos in Cosmic Selection; a collection of poems entitled *Ecstasies*; and a book of essays and aphorisms inspired by the philosophy of Nietzsche, in whose ideas Hausdorff was deeply interested. All these works were published under a pseudonym. They are by no means simply amateurish effusions: the play, for example, ran for a hundred performances when it was last performed in Berlin.

As the scion of a wealthy family the young Hausdorff did not have to worry about earning a living; for him, mathematics was more an avocation than anything else. Gradually the youthful litterateur turned into the single-minded mathematician who in his latter years looked back somewhat censoriously on the intellectual efforts of his earlier period. A turning point in Hausdorff's life was when he became acquainted with the new theory of sets created by Cantor, who was teaching at the nearby University of Halle. Hausdorff met Cantor at the regular gatherings of mathematicians from Leipzig, Halle, and Jena. As we know, the new theory met with a lot of resistance from mathematicians and from philosophers. Moreover, contradictions, such as the Russell Paradox, started to appear in the basic notions of the theory. Hausdorff believed, following Nietzsche, that science always stands on shaky foundations.

In 1910 he moved to Bonn as *Extra-Ordinarius* at the university, which, unlike Leipzig, offered him tenure. There he lectured on set theory in 1912 and made decisive progress in defining the basic notions of what was to become set-theoretic topology, with the concept of *neighbourhood* being taken as fundamental. Four years later he was called to the position of *Ordinarius* at the University of Greifswald, on the Baltic. It was there, in the spring of 1914, that he completed his magnum opus *Grundzüge der Mengenlehre* (Principles of set theory), the work which won him world-wide recognition and had a huge impact on the development of many branches of mathematics. The book was studied by the coming generation of young scholars and university students of advanced mathematics in Germany, some other European countries, and the United States. Its publication led to correspondence with mathematicians from all parts of Europe and America, and promising young mathematicians, particularly from eastern Europe, came to study with him. His lectures, according to one devoted pupil, were marvels of artistic form and flawless logic.

A few months after the *Grundzüge* was published, Europe was plunged into war. Large parts of the German intellectual elite, as well as ordinary citizens, were seized with patriotic fervour. However, after the war ended in Germany's defeat, the same elite did not support the new democratic republic. At Greifswald, where the majority of professors had been conservative before the war, few supported the new government. Hausdorff became a member, but not an active member, of the German Democratic Party for three years; this was a liberal party supporting the Weimar Republic, for which many Jews voted. Unfortunately its constituency dwindled as the economic situation worsened.

In 1921 Hausdorff returned to Bonn as *Ordinarius*. Initially the other mathematics chair was held by Eduard Study; when he retired six years later his place was taken by Otto Toeplitz, who was mainly interested in teaching, at both school and university level. Hausdorff got on well with Toeplitz although their personalities and scientific interests were quite different. Both were emancipated Silesian Jews, who had absorbed German culture. The Toeplitz family had relinquished some Jewish traditions, but not all; they were certainly more Jewish than the Hausdorff family. Hausdorff did not seem particularly Jewish to Hilbert who once remarked when names were being considered for a professorial appointment, 'If you want to name a non-Jewish mathematician one might think of Bieberbach, about whom I am not at all enthusiastic, and Hausdorff.' (Bieberbach emerged later as one of the leading Nazi supporters.)

Hausdorff remained at Bonn for the rest of his career. The family lived in a comfortable home on a quiet street then named Hindenburgstrasse, now Hausdorffstrasse. He was an excellent lecturer, regarded as the most capable mathematician at the university. In research the first decade at Bonn was a fruitful one, in which he was mainly publishing papers related to set theory and set-theoretic topology. When, in 1933, the Nazis introduced the racial laws seventeen academics were affected at Bonn. Hausdorff and Toeplitz escaped dismissal at this stage because they had both been in state service before August 1914. Hausdorff concentrated on his teaching and scientiftc work until he almost reached the retirement age of sixty-seven. One day before his sixty-sixth birthday he took the new oath of allegiance to the National Socialist state; even emeritus professors were required to take this. On a civil-service form he had apparently filled out in early 1935, he listed in his distinctive small hand his religion as Israelitsch and his racial status as non-Aryan. He was being forced to retire, just in time to receive the normal pension.

During the first phase of the Nazi regime the life of a retired Jewish professor was 'not completely unbearable', according to Hausdorff. While his attitude was one of resignation, his colleague Toeplitz was more active. For example, he helped to found a private school for Jewish children, needed because of the humiliations they faced in the state schools. Toeplitz watched the situation carefully and realized what might be coming in the next phase. When he was dismissed in 1935 the pension he received was greatly reduced. The American consul was unhelpful when he applied for a visa and so he arranged to emigrate to Palestine where he secured an administrative position at the Hebrew University.

In 1938 the *Kristallnacht* pogrom took place the day after Hausdorff had celebrated his seventieth birthday with family and friends; during the night a mob came to his house shouting, 'There he is, the head rabbi. Just watch out. We are going to send you to Madagascar where you can teach mathematics to the apes.' Hausdorff was deeply shocked. Like other Jewish men, he was required to add a middle name of Israel, so that he became Felix Israel Hausdorff. He continued to work on mathematics, but ceased publishing.

Two years later the wife of a colleague wrote that

> Things go tolerably well with the Hausdorffs, even if they can't escape from the vexation and the agitation over continual new anti-Semitic chicanery. The tax burden and the monetary subtractions that are imposed on them are so high that he can no longer live on his income alone and must use his savings; it's good that he still had these reserves, besides they have been compelled to give up part of their house, whereby their space is very crowded, however I am glad that there are more people who worry about the Hausdorffs, as I occasionally verify when during a visit I meet one or another. Recently, for example, I met a musician who had just played together with Hausdorff. That is really lovely, that in this way some joy will have been brought to them in the house.

I often had great anxiety about the Hausdorffs. Frau Hausdorff was for a long time seriously ill from an old ailment—I don't know what it was. Scarcely was she over the worst than there came the agitation about the intended internment of the Jews here. The procedure was quite mad. In the early part of the year, old nuns were forcibly driven out of a cloister on the Kreuzberg, these poor old women who never harmed anyone and only carried on a retiring life devoted to their pious usages, and who are naturally completely estranged from the machinery of the outside world. Now all the Jews still living in Bonn will be compulsorily interned in this stolen building; they must either auction their belongings or place them for preservation in faithful hands.

For a time the Hausdorffs were allowed to stay in their own home, awaiting their fate, but in January 1942 they were ordered to move to the monastery in the suburb of Endenich, where most of the other Jews in Bonn were already being held prior to their deportation to the Theresienstadt camp in Bohemia. Felix Hausdorff and his wife Charlotte calmly chose death, by taking an overdose of the drug Veronal, on 26 January 1942, when he was seventy-three.

Italian Maestro
Tullio Levi-Civita (1873–1941)

According to Francesco Tricomi, there were no fewer than twenty-nine Jewish Italian mathematicians in the century between 1861 and 1960 (by date of death). The best known are Salvatore Pincherle (1853–1936), Vito Volterra (1860–1940), Corrado Segre (1863–1924), Guido

Castelnuovo (1865–1952), Federigo Enriques (1871–1946), Tullio Levi-Civita (1873–1941), and Guido Fubini (1879–1943). Volterra, of course, has been profiled earlier in this chapter. After him, perhaps the most interesting is Levi-Civita, because of the breadth of his scientific interests, his scruples regarding the fulfilment of his academic responsibilities, and his affection for young people.

Tullio Levi-Civita was born in Padua on 29 March 1873, the son of Giacomo Levi-Civita and his wife Bice (née Lattis). His father, a lawyer, and for many years mayor of Padua, was later to become Senator of the Kingdom of Italy. In childhood Giacomo had moved to Padua from his birthplace of Rovigo and in his youth had fought with Garibaldi in the campaign of 1866. He expected his son Tullio to follow him by studying for the law, but Tullio's interest in the physical and mathematical sciences was apparent even in early childhood, and his father did not stand in his way.

After completing his studies at the Liceo Tito Livio in his native city at the age of seventeen, Tullio Levi-Civita enrolled at the ancient University of Padua as a student of mathematics and four years later took his degree. His teachers at the university included Giuseppe Veronese and Gregorio Ricci-Cubastro (known to the scientific world simply as Ricci), both of whom had considerable influence on the future career of their brilliant pupil. The influence of Ricci is the more obvious, since it developed into active collaboration, but probably Veronese's influence was just as important, since it is largely to him that Levi-Civita owed the remarkable spatial intuition and familiarity with multi-dimensional space which characterized the younger man's own contribution to the subject.

Even before he graduated, Levi-Civita was publishing mathematical research papers, and when he applied for the vacant chair of mechanics at Messina the year after he took his degree, his application was strongly favoured by Vito Volterra and Giacinto Morera, two of the electors. However, the other two electors, with Antonio Cremona, the chairman, preferred another candidate who was considerably senior to Levi-Civita both in years and in experience. Three years later, when one of his former teachers at Padua died, Levi-Civita was elected to the chair of mechanics in his place at the age of twenty-five. For the next twenty fruitful years he occupied this post until in 1918 he was called to the chair of mechanics in Rome.

During his Paduan years Levi-Civita undertook to make Einstein's theory of relativity known in Italy. In 1915 he initiated a brief but intense correspondence with the great physicist, who said that Levi-Civita was one of the few who really understood the implications of the general theory, which was much more mathematical than the earlier special theory. 'I never had a correspondence as interesting as this before', wrote Einstein, 'you should see how I always look forward to your letters.' The two scientists met for the first time in 1921 when Federigo Enriques (sometimes described as the Italian Einstein) brought the great man to Bologna to deliver a series of public lectures on the general theory of relativity, and perhaps for the last time in Princeton in 1936, when Einstein was at the Institute for Advanced Study. When someone asked Einstein what he liked about Italy he replied, 'spaghetti and Levi-Civita.'

Levi-Civita did not cut a very striking figure. He was only about five feet tall and very myopic. In spite of his small stature Levi-Civita was very robust, and he enjoyed excellent health until he was well over sixty. What energy he had to spare from his work was devoted to his three great hobbies: mountaineering, cycling, and foreign travel. As a young man he devoted most of his vacations to climbing in the Dolomites, in spite of his physical handicaps. As he grew older worsening eyesight curtailed his climbing activities, but he was often to be seen on his bicycle in the countryside around Padua. His third passion was foreign travel: he travelled all over the world in order to give lectures. Such visits he enjoyed immensely; he loved to see new places, meet new people, and, thanks to his own personal charm and vivacity, make a host of new friends.

Levi-Civita was also fortunate in his domestic life. In 1914 he married Libera Trevisani, who had been his pupil at the University of Padua and had taken her doctorate in mathematics. She accompanied her husband on his many travels and shared with him the many friendships which he made on these journeys. There were no children to the marriage. There was also a strong bond of affection between him and his parents. While the father was intensely proud of his son's achievements, the son was equally proud of the father's record in the Risorgimento. A visitor to his study would notice that, while three of the walls were lined with bookcases, the fourth remained empty apart from two portraits, one of Garibaldi, the other of his father. Levi-Civita always felt a great tenderness for his mother, and visited her regularly, either at the family home in Padua, or at her villa in Vigodarzere, a nearby village to which she retired after her husband died in 1922. After her own death in 1927 the villa was kept on by her daughter Ida Senigaglia, and Levi-Civita continued to spend a part of each year there.

For Levi-Civita, research and teaching went hand in hand, and he introduced many students to areas of mathematics in which he was a pioneer, such as the absolute differential calculus. His teaching was not circumscribed by any curriculum, as was usual at an Italian university, but was freely given to all who came to consult him. During vacations, either in the Dolomites or at Vigodarzere, his former pupils would come to seek his guidance; nothing gave him more pleasure than to have the opportunity of helping them, and he took pride in presenting their works for publication by one or other of the many learned societies of which he was a member. Indeed, as one of his pupils once remarked, no one ever merited more than he did the title of 'Maestro'.

Many academic and professional honours came to Levi-Civita. He was elected to membership of the academies of Paris and Berlin, also the Royal Society of London, from which he received the Sylvester Medal. In his own country he was a member of the Lincei, until that was suppressed. Unlike Volterra, he was appointed to the new Accademia d'Italia, but they were both foundation members of the Pontificia Accademia delle Scienze.

Though not himself an active politician, Levi-Civita was an outspoken socialist. He was not immediately affected by the rise of fascism in Italy, since his scientific renown helped to shield him from persecution, but when in 1938 the government yielded to German pressure and issued decrees removing from office all professors of Italian universities who were of Jewish origin, and dismissing them from Italian academies, Levi-Civita was included. The first he heard of the decrees was when staying with his sister at Vigodarzere, when someone happened to switch on the radio as they were being announced. His expression did not change, and he went out for his afternoon walk as usual, but the blow soon told on him. Eleven other Jewish mathematicians, including Federigo Enriques, Beppo Levi, and Beniamino Segre, were also forced to leave their university posts, and among the physicists was the Nobel laureate Emilio Segre. Different Italian scientists reacted in different ways to the Mussolini dictatorship. The atomic physicist Enrico Fermi emigrated to the United States; Fermi's wife Laura was Jewish although he was not. Beppo Levi emigrated to Argentina and Beniamino Segre to Britain. Some, such as Federigo Enriques and Guido Castelnuovo, lived through the Nazi occupation, changing hiding-places frequently. A few, such as the geometer Francesco Severi, actively supported the fascist regime. The Italian government remained unresponsive to German demands to deport the remaining Jews until they were forced do so in 1943; as a result about 8000 Italian Jews perished.

Soon Levi-Civita's health began to fail. Severe heart trouble developed, and as he was forbidden by his doctors to take any long journey he could not consider any of the offers of asylum which he received from foreign universities. Soon he was confined to his room and unable to continue his work. He died on 29 December 1941 of a stroke, at the age of sixty-eight. At first the Roman newspapers, except for the Vatican's *Osservatore Romano*, ignored his death, and it was only after the Pontifical Academy had used its influence that the family was able to announce in the newspapers the fact of his death and the arrangements for the funeral.

Struik describes Levi-Civita as combining great personal charm with tremendous will-power and self-discipline. He was one of those persons who in spite of a busy and creative career always seemed to find time for other people. He had unusually extensive knowledge of the literature of pure and applied mathematics, astronomy, and physics, and a passionate interest in all kinds of scientific questions. A born teacher, his scientific papers and specialist textbooks are models of lucidity.

Devotee of Mathematics
Edmund Landau (1877–1938)

We now return to Germany. Edmund Georg Hermann Landau, born in Berlin on 14 February 1877, was the son of a well-to-do gynaecologist. His mother was from the banking family of Jacoby, and Landau grew up in the Jacoby mansion, situated in the most elegant quarter of Berlin, amid other Berlin banking families. His father, although a patriotic German, was politically engaged in Jewish causes. Thus Landau grew up a well-connected and well-to-do person who saw no contradiction between being Jewish and being German. Though not brought up in strict Jewish tradition, Landau was proud of his descent from a brother of the famous eighteenth-century rabbi Jecheskel Landau of Prague, in whose honour he adopted the latter's Hebrew name Jecheskel as his second forename.

Landau not only started life with these advantages, he was also something of a Wunderkind. He graduated from the French lycée in Berlin at the age of sixteen, some two years earlier than normal, and immediately enrolled at the university to study mathematics. He obtained his doctorate in 1899 at the age of twenty-two; the next year he wrote to Hilbert about his ideas for a proof of the prime ideal theorem for algebraic number fields, an oustanding unsolved problem of the time. In 1901 he habilitated at Berlin with a paper on Dirichlet series. Nominally, his adviser throughout was Frobenius, who repeatedly underestimated his gifted student. By 1909 Landau had not only published nearly seventy research papers but also his classic treatise on prime number theory.

In 1905 Landau married Marianne Ehrlich, daughter of the great Paul Ehrlich, who would share the 1908 Nobel Prize in medicine. They were to have a son and two daughters, as well as another son who died young.

In the year of his marriage Landau went directly from *Privatdozent* at Berlin to *Ordinarius* at Göttingen in succession to Minkowski. The story of the appointment of a successor to Minkowski has often been told. All those on the faculty's short-list of three, including Landau, were Jewish. Such an all-Jewish list would not have been acceptable at many other German universities at that time. When the time came, Klein surprised his colleagues by speaking in favour of Landau, who was known as a wealthy, arrogant, and not entirely pleasant man. 'We being such a group as we are here it is better that we have a man who is not easy,' said Klein, whose opinion was, as usual, decisive.

In the obituary they wrote for the London Mathematical Society, Hardy and Heilbronn (1938) commented that 'Landau was certainly one of the hardest workers of our times. His working day often began at 7 a.m. and continued, with short intervals, until midnight. He loved lecturing, more perhaps than he realized himself; and a lecture from Landau was a very serious thing, since he expected his students to work in the spirit in which he worked himself, and would never tolerate the slightest rough edge or the slightest compromise with the truth.' Landau lectured as he wrote his many books, demonstration following assertion in a peculiarly compressed and rigorous style of exposition without a trace of motivation. His speciality was the analytic theory of numbers. In Courant's opinion, both his lectures and his books were sometimes so abstract there was absolutely no relation at all to substance. Landau had no time for the applications of mathematics.

Socially the Landaus were an asset to life in Göttingen. The story is well known that he used to tell people who asked for his address, 'you'll find it easily, it's the finest house in the city.' The Landaus employed a domestic staff of six. Marianne gave parties to which students were invited and took a lively interest in young people and their problems. Landau himself maintained the traditional formal relationship of professors in Wilhelmine Germany towards *Privatdozenten* and students. There were not many observant Jews in German academic life; Landau was one of the few. According to his son Matthias, he was the only member of the Göttingen faculty who observed some Jewish practices and attended a synagogue, possibly the one founded by Moritz Stein.

When officers of the Rockefeller Foundation came to visit Göttingen to discuss various matters they reported back that Landau seemed a rather aggressive person, with a sour outlook on life. When they enquired who might succeed Hilbert as head of department when he retired, it was intimated that it was quite impossible that Landau would be considered. Landau once tried to run the mathematics department of the Hebrew University in Jerusalem but this was not a success, although he retained a strong interest in its development.

In 1934 Bieberbach, *Ordinarius* at the University of Berlin, published two rather similar articles about mathematical creativity which created turmoil in the German mathematical community and caused uproar outside Germany. The main point of these articles was an attempt to distinguish the true German tradition in mathematics, exemplified by Gauss and Klein, where intuition was important, from the more intellectual style of mathematics that Bieberbach particularly associated with the Jews. The Jews, he maintained, attempt to 'create' mathematics while the true German 'discovers' mathematics. He acknowledged that Jews often had good ideas, but it was non-Jews who saw their full potential. The main thrust of Bieberbach's argument was that because Jews thought differently and were 'suited' to do mathematics in a different fashion, they could not be proper instructors of non-Jews. He saw Landau, with whom he already had some mathematical differences, as a convenient archetype for Jewish mathematicians and gave as an example Landau's 'morganic' manner, exemplified in his textbook *Differential and Integral Calculus,* which he characterized as 'foreign from reality and inimical to life'. So Landau was advised not to teach his calculus class himself, but through an assistant. As teaching was so important to Landau he decided to ignore this advice. He was then singled out for student demonstrations, and his lectures were boycotted by the students, led by Emmy Noether's star pupil Oswald Teichmuller, whose death on the eastern front in 1943 was such a loss to mathematics.

In 1935 Landau was compulsorily retired and went back to live in Berlin. 'His enforced retirement must have been a terrible blow to him', wrote Hardy and Heilbronn, 'it was quite pathetic to see his delight when he found himself again in front of a blackboard in Cambridge, and his sorrow when his opportunity came to an end.' In 1938, just after his sixty-first birthday but before the *Kristallnacht* pogrom. Landau died from a heart attack. His disciple Harald Bohr, the younger brother of the physicist Niels Bohr, recalled that 'Landau made a strong impression on everyone who came into contact with him. His baroque sense of humour and his exceptional vitality characterized equally his scientific research and his teaching. His thinking was amazingly quick and sure and his standards for precision and exactitude of exposition were absolute and inexorable. He felt a spontaneous love for mathematics and had a glowing interest in any progress, major or minor, made within the extensive domain of mathematics which he cultivated.' Hardy and Heilbronn concluded their obituary with these words: 'No-one was ever more passionately devoted to mathematics than Landau, and there was something surprisingly impersonal, in a man of such strong personality, in his devotion. Everybody prefers to do things by himself, and Landau was no exception; but most of us are at bottom a little jealous of progress by others, while Landau seemed singularly free of such unworthy emotions. He would insist on his own rights, even a little pedantically, but he would insist in the same spirit and with the same rigour on the rights of others.'

6

Troubled Times

In this chapter the subjects of the profiles were born between 1878 and 1882. After 1882 the oppression and persecution of the Jews who lived in the territories ruled by the anti-Semitic tsar intensified to such an extent that those who could fled to central or western Europe or, increasingly, the United States. It should not be forgotten, however, that others left because they thought the prospects might be better in the west.

In central and western Europe, also, anti-Semitism was becoming more virulent. Far-sighted Jews had already left Germany; now the trickle became a flood which lasted until the outbreak of the Second World War made escape virtually impossible. Nazi persecution extended to Austria, Hungary, Italy, Poland, and other countries which fell under German control; Jews who had not left by then were usually murdered.

Austrian Marie Curie
Lise Meitner (1878–1968)

Throughout Europe the obstacles to higher education for women were breaking down by the end of the nineteenth century, but exceptional determination was still required for a woman to succeed in a scientific career. This profile is of a woman who had that determination but, when her career was at its zenith, it was blighted because of her Jewish ancestry. Lise Meitner's name has become widely known for her part in the discovery of nuclear fission, which made nuclear power possible, as well as the atomic bomb. Although Einstein described her as 'the German Madame Curie', she retained Austrian nationality to the end of her life.

Lise Meitner was born on 7 November 1878 in Vienna, where she was brought up; she remained very much attached to the imperial city, never more splendid than in those last autumn days of its glory. Her free-thinking father Philipp was a respected lawyer and keen chess player. His ancestors came from Moravia, now part of the Czech Republic; the family of her mother Hedwig (née Skovran) was Russian. Being the third of eight children, she was used both to being ruled by her two older sisters and ruling over the four younger children. Although her parents were Jewish, Judaism played no part in her education. Indeed all their children were baptized, and Lise Meitner grew up as a Protestant; in later years her views were very tolerant, except of atheism.

Lise Meitner said she became a physicist because of a burning desire to understand the working of nature, a desire that appears to go back to her childhood. At the end of her school career she first had to pass the state examination in French so that if necessary she would be able to support herself as a teacher; only then did she get permission to sit for the *Matura*, the school-leaving examination, equivalent to the German *Abitur,* that qualified her for university entrance. For two years she worked intensively to prepare herself, coached by Arthur Szarvasy, later professor of physics in Brno. Her sisters used to tease her; she had only to walk across the room for them to predict she would fail because she had interrupted her studies to do so. She was one of only four girls who passed that year, out of fourteen candidates.

Lise Meitner enrolled at the University of Vienna in 1901, when over 30 per cent of the students were Jewish but very few were women. She encountered occasional rudeness on the part of the students (a female student was regarded as a freak) but also much encouragement from her teachers, especially Ludwig Boltzmann, who inspired her with his vision of physics as a search for the ultimate truth—a vision she never lost. She recalled:

Boltzmann had no inhibitions whatsoever about showing his enthusiasm when he spoke, and carried his listeners along naturally. He was fond of introducing remarks of an entirely personal character into his lectures ... His relationship to students was very personal. He not only saw to their knowledge of physics but tried to understand their character. Formalities meant nothing to him, and he had no reservations about expressing his feelings. The few students who took part in the advanced seminar were invited to his house from time to time. There he would play the piano for us—he was a very good pianist—and tell us all sorts of personal experiences.

When she obtained her doctorate in physics in 1905 she became only the second woman in Vienna to have done so. She stayed on at the university for a short while, to clear up a question raised by Lord Rayleigh, and then with her father's approval moved to Berlin to begin advanced study in theoretical physics. She had met Planck briefly when he had visited Vienna in response to an invitation to be Boltzmann's successor, and on arriving in Berlin in 1907 she arranged to attend his lectures.

Although Planck, like so many of his colleagues, did not believe that as a rule women should be permitted to study at universities, he was prepared to make exceptions, and Lise Meitner received his whole-hearted support. After he invited her to his home, she recalled, 'even with my first visit I was very impressed by the refined modesty of the house and entire family.' In her early days in Berlin she found cheerful, informal company and good music in the Grunewald house. 'Planck loved happy, unaffected company, and his home was a focus for social gatherings. Advanced students were regularly invited to his home ... if the invitation fell during the summer semester we played tag in the garden, in which Planck participated with almost childish ambition and great agility. It was almost impossible not to be caught by him.' Later she said that while she had been swept along by Boltzmann's exuberance, she loved and trusted Planck for his depth of character. She often sought his advice in the difficult years ahead. 'He had an unusually pure disposition and inner rectitude,' she said, 'which corresponded to his utter simplicity and lack of pretension.'

At first she had some difficulty in finding anywhere to carry out experimental work. Then she met the young chemist Otto Hahn. He was a frank and informal man of her own age from whom she felt she could learn a great deal. He was looking for a physicist to help him with his own research into radioactivity. One difficulty was that Hahn was to work at the chemical institute under the Nobel laureate Emil Fischer who banned women from his laboratory (they might set fire to their hair); in any case women were not allowed access to laboratories used by male students. However, an old carpenter's workshop was equipped for making radiation measurements, and here Lise Meitner was permitted to work. At that time it was not known for certain whether alpha rays were deflected in passing through matter; she designed and performed one of the first experiments in which some degree of deflection could be observed. Soon she was collaborating with Hahn on research in radioactive substances, taking responsibility for the more physical aspects while Hahn was more concerned with the chemistry. During those years before the First World War, Hahn and Meitner published a large number of joint papers on radioactivity, most of which are no longer of interest. Although she and Hahn became close friends as well as colleagues, except on formal occasions they never had a meal together. She was very reserved, even shy, and had been strictly brought up. When Lord Rutherford and his wife spent a few days in Berlin, he had a valuable scientific discussion with Hahn, while Meitner was insulted by being sent off to help Rutherford's wife, who was no scientist, with her shopping.

The ban which kept her out of the chemical laboratories had been lifted in 1909 when women were at last admitted to higher education in Germany. Three years later she moved to the new Kaiser Wilhelm Institute for chemistry where Hahn was provided with a small independent department. The same year Planck invited Lise Meitner to become his assistant for three years. After the outbreak of war in 1914 Hahn was called up for military service, while Lise Meitner volunteered to serve as an X-ray nurse with the Austrian army. She had a harrowing time, working up to twenty hours a day with inadequate equipment and coping with large numbers of injured Polish soldiers, without knowing their language.

After the war Meitner began to receive recognition for her work. In Hahn's department she was appointed head of physics. She received the *venia legendi* from the university (the subject of her lecture—cosmic physics—was reported as 'cosmetic physics' in the press), and in 1926 she was made titular professor, but never gave any courses of lectures. She regularly attended the Tuesday colloquium of the German Physical Society where some of the greatest physicists discussed the formidable problems presented by the discoveries in atomic physics and Planck's quantum hypothesis.

The discovery of the neutron in 1932, the positron in 1933, and artificial radioactivity in 1934 caused further turmoil in the world of nuclear physics, reflected in a number of short papers in which Lise Meitner and her collaborators tried to keep pace with rapid new developments. In the universities, after Hitler came to power, many 'non-Aryan' scientists lost their posts, but the research institutes of the Kaiser Wilhelm Gesellschaft were less vulnerable, being partly controlled by industrialists. Even so, the Nazis tried to enforce party loyalty by various forms of infiltration, and Hahn and Meitner had to be increasingly cautious to avoid open conflict, and to avoid losing those of their staff who were partly Jewish or who refused to join the Nazi party.

Although the racial laws did not apply to Lise Meitner, at this stage, because of her Austrian nationality, her *venia legendi* was immediately rescinded, she lost her position at the university, she was not allowed to attend meetings or colloquia, and her name was dropped from scientific papers. Her position at the institute was not directly affected but Hahn, pressured by his superiors, asked her not to enter the building any more. She consulted Planck, her most trusted mentor, who advised her to stay in Berlin, as did Hahn. She clung to her research: 'I built it from its very first little stone; it was so to speak my life's work, and it seemed so terribly hard to separate myself from it.' She passed up the offer of a one-year grant at the Niels Bohr Institute in Copenhagen and rejected the possibility of a position at Swarthmore, one of the women's colleges in the neighbourhood of Philadelphia.

The annexation of Austria by Germany in March 1938 created a crisis for Lise Meitner: she was no longer a foreigner protected by her Austrian nationality but had become subject to the racial laws of Nazi Germany. Her honesty did not permit her to conceal her Jewish descent (as some did), and her dismissal could only be a question of time. Her position looked even worse when she heard that in future no technical or academic personnel—whether Jewish or not—would be allowed to leave Germany without special permission. An attempt by Planck to obtain this for her was unsuccessful. There appeared to be a very real risk that she might not only lose her position in Germany but also be prevented from seeking a new one abroad. She decided she must leave without delay, and arrangements were made by sympathizers in the Netherlands for her to escape to their country. On the day of her departure she had just an hour and a half in which to pack her most necessary belongings. In the laboratory no one but Hahn knew she was leaving Germany for good; he gave her a diamond ring to sell in case of need.

The Netherlands has a distinguished tradition in physics but at that time lacked good facilities for nuclear research, and so Lise Meitner quickly moved on to Denmark where for some weeks she enjoyed the hospitality of the Bohrs. The facilities for nuclear research in Copenhagen were excellent, and there were a number of young and active physicists at work. It was probably her own wish not to compete with those younger people that led to her decision not to remain there but instead to accept an invitation to join Manne Siegbahn, head of the new Nobel Institute for physics in Stockholm. In 1924 Siegbahn's researches in the field of X-ray spectroscopy had earned him the Nobel Prize in physics; he and his pupils had created a Swedish tradition in precision physics. She was paid the salary of a junior assistant by the Swedish Academy of Sciences, and was reduced to living in a small hotel room on borrowed funds because her German bank account was frozen.

It was shortly after her arrival in Sweden in 1938 that she made her most spectacular contribution to science. After she had left Germany, Hahn and his assistant Strassmann continued experimental work, as before, until they started discovering barium in the products of uranium bombardment. Hahn wrote to consult Lise Meitner for an explanation of what was happening in physical terms. His letter reached her before the discovery had been published, and thus she became the first scientist outside Germany to learn of this extraordinary phenomenon. The letter arrived during the Christmas vacation when she was visiting friends in a small Swedish village with her young nephew Otto Frisch, the future

Nobel laureate. Lise talked to him about Hahn's letter but at first Frisch did not believe that uranium atoms could split into two almost equal parts. He thought that Hahn and Strassmann must have made a mistake.

In order to talk the matter over at leisure, aunt and nephew took a long walk in the snow. Lise Meitner did most of the talking, urgently, convincingly. At last she persuaded Frisch that Hahn and Strassmann had made no mistake, that uranium atoms underwent fission, and that the energy released in the process was probably very great. Once they felt quite sure, they hastened to Copenhagen to break the news to Bohr. He listened eagerly to what they told him, exclaiming, 'Oh, what idiots we have been. We could have foreseen it all. This is just as it must be.' He suggested an experiment by which they might measure the energy released when uranium atoms split. Bohr was so engrossed in this extraordinary new phenomenon that he almost missed the ship which was about to take him to New York for a meeting of the American Physical Society. When he arrived he told the assembled physicists the news of the sensational discovery of nuclear fission; his gaze, troubled and insecure, moved from person to person but stopped on no one. Those present quickly realized the implications of the discovery and at first it was agreed by all concerned that the news should be kept secret. However, French researchers, headed by Frédéric Joliot-Curie, had made the same discovery and went ahead with publication, forcing others to do likewise. In Berlin Hahn was deeply worried. 'God cannot have intended this,' he is reputed to have said.

The 1945 Nobel Prize for physics went to the theoretician Wolfgang Pauli, whose profile follows later, although there were many who thought that Lise Meitner deserved it more. Bohr nominated Meitner and Frisch for the prize for physics in 1946 and for chemistry later but to no avail. However, her work did not go unrecognized, since later she shared with Hahn the Max Planck Medal of the Society of Physics, and the institute of nuclear research in Berlin was named the Hahn-Meitner Institute. Her relationship with Otto Hahn remained close but he became increasingly inclined to undervalue her contribution to their great discovery. Yet she had been the physicist member of the team for thirty years and Hahn had always deferred to her judgement when it was a question of physics. Later Hahn's assistant Strassmann commented, 'she was the intellectual leader of our team, and therefore she belonged to us—even if she was not present for the discovery of fission.' This close working relationship between the head of a scientific institute in Nazi Germany and an émigrée Jewish scientist was a tribute to Hahn's stability of character and personal loyalty. However it was widely felt that by encouraging her to leave Berlin when she did, he might have saved her life but he had effectively blighted her scientific career.

Lise Meitner remained in Sweden for twenty-two years, during which a cyclotron was constructed in Siegbahn's institute, the first to be built on the mainland of Europe. Her experience was invaluable for making the best use of this new atom-splitting machine and for training students in the required ancillary techniques. She acquired a good knowledge of the Swedish language, built up a small research group of her own, and published a number of short papers, mostly describing the properties of some new radioactive species formed with the help of the cyclotron. Inevitably, she felt cut off at the Nobel Institute since Sweden as a neutral country was isolated during the war; she had few students and lacked the stimulus that Hahn had provided during her years in Berlin. Siegbahn was more interested in his precision physics than in the comparatively crude measurements that were possible in the study of radioactive isotopes. Initially, there had seemed to be a chance that she could go to Britain, which she would have preferred, but the initial response from Cambridge was so lukewarm that she did not think it worth following up. However, in July 1939, just before the war began, Lawrence Bragg invited her to visit the Cavendish. He pressed her to remain on a three-year research contract, but she decided to return to Sweden instead. During the war she contributed to the Allied war effort by helping to provide information about nuclear research in Germany, but she was adamant that she would have nothing to do with the atomic bomb.

In 1946 Lise Meitner spent half the year in the United States as visiting professor at the Catholic University in Washington and was nominated as 'woman of the year' by the American press. In 1947 she retired from the Nobel Institute and accepted an offer from the Swedish atomic energy committee to provide her with a small laboratory at the Royal Institute for Technology. Later she moved to a laboratory of the Royal Academy of

Engineering Sciences where an experimental nuclear reactor was being built deep down in the solid granite on which Stockholm stands. There she remained for the rest of her time in Sweden, first directing the work of a research assistant, later mainly engaged in reading, attending colloquia, and discussing problems with other physicists.

In 1960 she retired to Cambridge where her favourite nephew Otto Frisch, after fleeing from the Nazis, had become Jackson professor of natural philosophy at the Cavendish. After this she led a quiet life, but she still travelled a good deal, to meet friends and give lectures, often about the rightful place of women, and in particular of women scientists. In 1963 she went to Vienna to address a conference on '50 Years of Physics', a talk later published in English. She retained her Austrian nationality, even after she became a Swedish citizen about eight years before her death. She had always taken great pleasure in music, as did all her brothers and sisters (one sister became a concert pianist); she went to concerts as long as she could walk, and tried to follow contemporary trends in music, although hearing loss made this difficult. In old age she still fondly recalled the weekly musical evenings at the home of Planck.

After an exhausting visit to the United States at the end of 1964 Lise Meitner suffered a heart attack which caused her to spend some months in a nursing home, and from which she returned to her flat much enfeebled. Yet her strength only failed slowly, and in 1967 she made a good recovery after a fall in which she broke her hip. After that accident she did not travel any more and gradually gave up all other activity. She died on 27 October 1968, a few days before her ninetieth birthday, having outlived all her brothers and sisters, and was buried in a country churchyard, where her youngest brother had been buried some years previously. The inscription on her headstone, prepared by Frisch, is 'Lise Meitner; a physicist who never lost her humanity.'

In spite of her close friendship with Planck and other great physicists Lise Meitner never quite lost the shyness of her youth, but among her friends she could be lively and cheerful, and was an excellent story-teller. She was interested in almost everything; always ready to learn and ready to admit her ignorance of things outside her own field of study. But within that field she moved with great assurance and was convinced of the power of the human mind to arrive at correct conclusions from the great laws of nature. The advance of knowledge was always her first concern and she felt the delight of every good scientist in an excellent piece of work, whoever it was done by. In her laboratory she kept strict discipline, and it was her justified pride that in a quarter of a century it never became contaminated with radioactivity, despite the large amounts of radioactive elements that were handled in the same building; but while her students feared her strictness they came to her with their personal problems even so, and later her warm, practical humanity was remembered with fondness.

Wise and Humane Teacher
Max Dehn (1878–1952)

Most of these profiles are of mathematician or physicists who were honoured in their lifetime for some bold new theory or spectacular discovery. The next is different. Max Dehn was unusually lacking in personal ambition but through his wisdom and humanity he exercised a profound influence on his students. Although the author of many beautiful and important research papers himself, he was unusually generous with his ideas and content for others to develop them. When he left Germany, under pressure from the Nazis, he found refuge in the United States, but he was not in the first wave of refugees and starting a new life at a relatively advanced age was not easy.

Max Dehn was born on 13 November 1878 in Hamburg, the fourth of eight children of a physician, Maximilian Moses Dehn. The family were secularized Jews, who hardly regarded themselves as Jewish before the Nazis came to power; some of them perished in the Holocaust. Most of the future mathematician's siblings lived in Hamburg until the 1930s, and the Hanseatic city remained the family base, although his own career took him elsewhere. After graduating from the gymnasium in Hamburg, and converting to Protestantism, Dehn studied first at the University of Freiburg, but in 1899 he moved to the Georgia Augusta, where he became a student of Hilbert at a time when the master's main interest was in the foundations of geometry.

Two years later Dehn was appointed *Privatdozent* at the University of Munster, after a year at the Technical University of Karlsruhe. In 1911 he left Munster to spend two years as *Extra-Ordinarius* at the University of Kiel, where he married Toni Landau. From then until 1921 he was *Ordinarius* at the Technical University of Breslau, with an interruption for military service in the First World War. Dehn's last career move in Germany was to the University of Frankfurt, where he succeeded Bieberbach as *Ordinarius* in 1922.

Although Dehn published relatively little mathematical research while he was at Frankfurt, those years were particularly happy and fruitful in other ways. His time was fully occupied by his historical, philosophical, and expository interests and, above all, teaching. Dehn was most effective as a teacher at the graduate level. He was always generous with ideas and concerned with the welfare of his students. He founded a celebrated seminar on the history of mathematics, in which the most important mathematical discoveries of the past were studied in the original texts: Greek mathematics was studied in Greek, and so on. Dehn would never accept the need to learn another language as an excuse for falling back on a mere translation.

In a nostalgic address, his friend and colleague Carl Ludwig Siegel, who presided over the Mathematical Institute, cast his mind back to what in retrospect were some of the happiest days of his life, when the senior members of the institute worked harmoniously together without personal ambition; teachers and students joined in the traditional weekend rambles, and an easy, comradely tone prevailed that was so different from the ritual of authority and infallibility surrounding the traditional German professor. He went on to recall:

Dehn was in a sense our spiritual leader, and we always followed his advice in choosing topics for each semester. As I look back now, those communal hours in the seminar are some of the happiest of my life. Even then I enjoyed the activity which brought us together each Thursday afternoon from four to six. And later, when we had been scattered all over the globe, I learned through disillusioning experiences elsewhere what rare good fortune it is to have academic colleagues working together unselfishly without thought of personal ambition, instead of just issuing directives from their lofty positions.

In the summer of 1935 Dehn, being of Jewish extraction, was compulsorily retired from his university post. He had only been able to keep his position up to that point because of his military service in the First World War. At first he used his forced retirement to write up some of his earlier ideas about combinatorial topology. This paper appeared in 1936, and was followed three years later by his last, and most important, paper on mapping-class groups. Meanwhile Dehn was exploring the possibility of emigrating. In the early 1930s he had sent his daughter Maria to the Herrlingen school, near Ulm. Dehn became involved in the affairs of this school, especially when plans were being made to remove it from Nazi Germany. After much searching for a suitable location, the school was re-established in England. Maria moved there when the New Herrlingen school opened in 1933, and was later joined by her younger sister Eva. Dehn himself taught mathematics there for the spring term of 1938. He sent his son Helmut to the United States, so that all his children were out of reach of the Nazis.

One day in November 1938, after Dehn returned to Germany, he was arrested; it was the morning after the *Kristallnacht* pogrom. His daughter Maria described what happened: 'I was told that when the Nazis came for my father he was very deliberate, insisting on fetching his hat to go out. When they got him down to the police station, they were barked at "We told you not to bring anyone else"—so my father had to go home again! Mother was still standing, clueless, at the top of the stairs (as he had left her), when he came back!' A few days later, Dehn was smuggled onto a train to Hamburg, where Siegel met him, after initially seeking him at home to congratulate him on his sixtieth birthday. After discussing the situation with Siegel and one of the Danish mathematicians, he decided to seek asylum in Scandinavia. Siegel, who was not Jewish, was to follow Dehn's example in March 1940.

So the Dehns left Germany for Copenhagen in January 1939, later moving on the Norwegian port of Trondhjem, where he lectured at the Technical University. Before leaving Germany he was obliged to sell his library and other possessions at a great loss. His pension from Frankfurt was still paid into his German bank account but the money was blocked, so that all he had to live on was the modest income he received from Trondhjem. When Siegel visited him there in March 1940 further trouble was imminent. German ships were loitering in the harbour, claiming engine trouble. In reality they were filled with war material for the German soldiers who suddenly occupied Trondhjem on the day of the invasion of Norway, followed by the Gestapo and Nazi party organizations. The Dehns escaped to a farmer's house, but when no further acts of violence or arrests had occurred they returned to Trondhjem, and started to plan for a move to America. He secured a position at Idaho Southern University (now Idaho State) in Pocatello with the help of a family friend who had fled earlier and found work at the State Hospital South in Blackfoot. The Dehns left Norway in October 1940, and travelled to America via Stockholm, Moscow, Vladivostock, and Japan. After breaking the journey in Japan they went on by ship to San Francisco, arriving on New Year's Day 1941.

They stayed in Pocatello about a year, with Dehn teaching elementary algebra and history of philosophy. Toni Dehn had visited America thirty years earlier, and spoke excellent English, so the culture shock was not as severe as it might otherwise have been. The Dehns were popular at the university, and they appreciated the beautiful scenery nearby, but his post was temporary and not academically challenging. The following year they moved to Chicago, where he taught at the Illinois Institute of Technology, but he disliked the turmoil of the big city. So they moved again, to St John's College in Annapolis, Maryland, but this was not a success either. The school had a pretentious programme of 'great books in ancient languages', which Dehn was required to teach to youngsters who, in some cases, had not even mastered English.

In 1945, at the age of sixty-six, Dehn finally found congenial employment at Black Mountain College in the Blue Ridge Mountains of North Carolina. This celebrated experimental liberal arts college was founded in 1933, with a strong emphasis on the creative arts. Its aim was to combine thinking with doing, strenuous intellectual work-outs with manual labour. The college was so poor that at one time professors received in lieu of salaries free board and accommodation plus five dollars a month pocket money. There were only about a hundred members, including faculty, and Dehn was the sole mathematician, teaching not only mathematics but also Latin, Greek, and philosophy. He described it as 'a wonderful place where I can be together with young people without any institutional impediments. There I can use what little abilities I have to transmit to them what I think is leading most surely onwards towards a happy life. Not to forget the beauty of the surrounding nature which, I think, is of the greatest value to transform young and old people who live in it.' He died there on 27 June 1952, at the age of seventy-three.

Adventurer in Thought
Albert Einstein (1879–1955)

For most of these profiles I have been fortunate if I could find one or two books about the subject, and a few articles. In the case of Einstein there is almost too much material. There are a number of biographies, to start with. There are also books about various aspects of his life and work. His collected works have been published, of course, and much of his extensive correspondence, although important papers have vanished. Some saw him as a secular saint but to others he was a person with faults like anyone else. One of his colleagues commented: 'Einstein was a naturally solitary person who didn't want his weaknesses to show and didn't want to be helped even when they did show.'

Albert Einstein was born in the peaceful old town of Ulm, in the south German state of Wurttemberg, on 14 March 1879. He was the only son of Hermann and Pauline (née Koch); both sides of the family were Swabian Jews. The more dominant parent was his mother, an accomplished pianist with a tendency to melancholia. His father was a kind, inoffensive but somewhat ineffectual person whose brother was a trained electrical engineer. They ran a business designing and manufacturing electrical apparatus, such as dynamos. Not long after Albert was born the family moved to Munich, and a year after that Pauline gave birth to a daughter, Maria. Albert and Maria were fond of each other throughout life.

The future physicist grew up in suburban Munich. Although the family was Jewish he attended a Catholic primary school before proceeding to the Leopold Gymnasium, a conventional school of good repute. His scientific interests were awakened early by a small magnetic compass his father gave him when he was about four, by the algebra he learned from his uncle, and by the books he read, mostly popular science works of the day. A textbook on Euclidean geometry which he studied at the age of twelve made a deep impression. We have an account of his childhood from his son Hans Albert:

> He was a very well-behaved child. He was shy, lonely and withdrawn from the world even then. He was even considered backward by his teachers. He told me that his teachers reported to his father that he was mentally slow, unsociable and adrift forever in his foolish dreams. Very early Einstein set himself the task of establishing himself as an entirely separate entity, influenced as little as possible by other people. In school he did not revolt, he simply ignored authority. His parents, although Jewish, were largely indifferent to religion. Einstein, while still a schoolboy, deliberately emphasized his Jewish origin and went through a period of religious fervour which he later described as his 'first attempt to liberate myself from purely personal links'. At the age of twelve he finally freed himself from conventional religious belief, although

he retained a firm belief in some rather undefined 'cosmic religion', which
was entirely suprapersonal.

Einstein did not learn to talk before he was three, and did not speak
fluently until he was seven. Later in life he was a confusing lecturer, giving
specific examples followed by seemingly unrelated general principles.
Sometimes he would lose his train of thought while writing on the
blackboard. A few minutes later he would emerge as from a trance and
go on to something different. As he explained, 'thoughts do not come in
any verbal formulation. I rarely think in words at all. A thought comes
and I try to explain it in words afterwards.' He did poorly at school, where
so much teaching is verbal rather than visual; he is believed to have been
dyslexic. He was also a loner: 'I'm not much with people,' he would say.
The mature Einstein impressed everyone who met him by his gentleness
and wisdom, but as one of his biographers remarks, 'he has never really
needed human contacts; he deliberately freed himself more and more from
all emotional dependence in order to become entirely self-sufficient.'

When the family business failed in 1894 after an over-ambitious
attempt to compete with much stronger firms, the rest of the family
moved from Munich to Pavia in Lombardy, leaving the fifteen-year-old
Einstein in the care of distant relatives. The intention was to enable him to
continue his education, but he felt abandoned. He found the authoritarian
gymnasium, with its emphasis on classics, increasingly unbearable. He
became ill and before long left, officially on medical grounds but more
probably to avoid liability for military service, and rejoined his parents
in Pavia. One of his first actions was to renounce his German citizenship,
thereby becoming stateless. After spending most of a year enjoying life in
Italy he resumed his education, but the family business was again failing
and he could expect no financial support from his parents. An aunt in
Genoa made him a monthly allowance to see him through school and
university.

Einstein's aim was to enter the Swiss Federal Polytechnic in Zurich, but
to do so he had to pass the entrance examination. After one unsuccessful
attempt, due to a poor performance in non-scientific subjects, he was

advised to complete his school education first. Accordingly, he spent a year at the liberal gymnasium in the Swiss town of Aarau. His teachers thought him lazy and were unimpressed, but he passed the examination. By the time he was admitted to the polytechnic his main interests already centred on theoretical physics, but he had not yet fully realized the creative value of mathematics in physical research. Later he attributed his failure to learn from the lectures of Hurwitz and Minkowski as due to his lack of mathematical instinct. He avoided regular classes and spent most of his time studying the classics of physics, especially what he later called the 'revolutionary' ideas of Clerk Maxwell's field theory of electromagnetism.

At this stage in his life Einstein was about five and a half feet tall, with regular features, warm brown eyes, a mass of jet-black hair, and a slightly raffish moustache. One of his classmates described him as follows:

> Sure of himself, his gray felt hat pushed back on his thick black hair, he strode energetically up and down in a rapid, I would almost say crazy, tempo of a restless spirit which carries a whole world in itself. Nothing escaped the sharp gaze of his bright brown eyes. Whoever approached him immediately came under the spell of his superior personality. A sarcastic curl of his rather full mouth with the protruding lower lip did not encourage philistines to fraternize with him. Unhampered by convention, his attitude towards the world was that of a laughing philosopher, and his witty mockery pitilessly lashed any conceit or pose.

After graduation Einstein became a Swiss citizen; this again made him liable for military service, but he was rejected on medical grounds. For two years he applied for schoolteaching posts but was unable to obtain regular employment. While supporting himself by occasional tutoring and substitute teaching, he published several scientific papers. Then, in 1902, he was appointed an examiner at the Swiss patent office in Berne. The seven years Einstein spent there were the years in which he laid the foundations of large parts of twentieth-century physics. He liked the fact that his official work, which only occupied part of the day, was entirely separate from his scientific work, so that he could pursue this freely and independently, and he often recommended this arrangement to others later on.

In 1903, against strong opposition from his mother (his father had died the previous year), Einstein married Mileva Marić, a Serbian woman who was then studying physics at the university but was five years older than he was. Their two sons were born in Switzerland, Hans Albert in 1904 and Eduard in 1910. A previous child, Lieserl, was born at the home of Mileva's parents and given for adoption; there is no trace of her afterwards. Hans Albert emigrated to the United States before the Second World War and became professor of hydraulic engineering at the University of California; for various reasons he felt bitter towards his father. Eduard was a gifted child who wanted to become a psychiatrist; as a young man his resemblance to his father was said to be 'almost frightening'. After he was institutionalized with paranoid schizophrenia Einstein rarely went to see him but was always delighted to hear from him. Hilbert's only son also suffered from the same affliction and again there was an uncanny resemblance.

The closing decades of the nineteenth century were the period when the long-established goal of physical theory—the explanation of all natural phenomena in terms of mechanics—came under serious scrutiny and was directly challenged. Mechanistic explanation had achieved many successes, particularly in the theory of heat and in various aspects of optics and electromagnetism; but even the successful mechanistic theory of heat had its serious failures and unresolved paradoxes, and physicists had not been able to provide a really satisfactory mechanical foundation for electromagnetic theory. The beginning of the twentieth century, when Einstein started his scientific work, was a time of startling experimental discoveries, but the problems which drew his attention and forced him to produce the boldly original ideas of a new physics had developed gradually and involved the very foundations of the subject.

Einstein realized that each of the separate fields of physics could devour a short working life without having satisfied the hunger for deeper knowledge, but he had an unmatched ability to scent out the paths that led to the depths and to disregard everything else, all the many things that clutter the mind and divert it from the essential. This ability to grasp precisely the particular simple physical situation that could throw light on questions of general principle characterized much of his thinking. In 1905, one marvellous year, Einstein produced three masterly papers on three different subjects which revolutionized the way scientists regarded the nature of space, time, and matter. These papers dealt with the nature of the Brownian motion, the quantum nature of electromagnetic radiation, and the special theory of relativity. Einstein considered the second paper, on the light quantum, or photon, as the most important, and it was for this that he was to be awarded the Nobel Prize, but it was relativity which caught the popular imagination. While Einstein was by no means alone in thinking about relativity—notably, Henri Poincaré and Paul Langevin had been thinking on similar lines—it was only he who understood its revolutionary implications and worked out its consequences. Significantly, his original paper on the subject contained no references and very little mathematics.

It took several years for Einstein's discoveries to receive recognition. When he submitted the relativity paper to support his application to become *Privatdozent* at the University of Berne, it was politely rejected. His academic career did not really get started until three years later when he was appointed *Extra-Ordinarius* at Zurich University; two years after that he became *Ordinarius* at the Charles (German) University in Prague. This was a surprising move since the Czech capital had little reputation for research in physics. He soon realized his mistake, and was pleased to be offered the post of *Ordinarius* at the former Zurich Polytechnic, which in 1911 was reconstituted as the Eidgenössische Technische Hochschule (ETH). So Einstein returned to his alma mater for three more years until in the spring of 1914, he moved to Berlin as a professor of the Academy of Sciences, free to lecture at the university or not as he chose. He was also appointed director of the new Kaiser Wilhelm Institute of physics, which allowed him to pursue his ideas unhampered by teaching and routine work. He had mixed feelings about the move, partly because he disliked the Prussian life-style of Berlin, and partly because in physics he felt he would be expected to produce one sensational new theory after another. As it turned out he found the atmosphere in the German capital very stimulating, and he greatly appreciated having Max Planck, Walter Nernst, and later, Erwin Schrödinger and Max von Laue, as colleagues. Just before Einstein moved to Berlin he spent a week in Leiden, lecturing on his latest ideas and going to see his old friend and mentor Hendrik Lorentz.

Although not in the vanguard of those who accepted Einstein's ideas, in time Planck developed the greatest admiration for what Einstein had achieved. For many years Planck and Einstein were in close contact; their collaboration made Berlin, in the years preceding the First World War, the leading centre for theoretical physics in the world. A friendship developed between them which went far beyond the exchange of scientific ideas. They shared a fascination with the secrets of nature, similar philosophical convictions, and a deep love of music. They often played chamber music together, Planck at the piano and Einstein on the violin. All biographers agree that Einstein had a passion for music, as a way of experiencing and expressing emotion which is impersonal. When he was world-famous as a physicist he is reported to have said that music was as important to him as physics: 'it is a way for me to be independent of people.' On another occasion he described it as the most important thing in his life.

While Einstein's scientific work was flourishing, his private life was not. His marriage had been under strain for some years. He was physically attractive to women and had a number of affairs. His wife Mileva and their two sons followed him to Berlin but before long they returned to Zurich, which remained Mileva's home for the rest of her life. She was a difficult woman, distrustful of other people and liable to depression. Legal separation and finally divorce followed soon after the end of the war. Earlier, when Einstein became ill with a stomach ulcer and was bedridden for some months he was nursed back to health by his cousin and childhood friend Elsa Löwenthal, a widow with two daughters; when the divorce came through, in which violence towards Mileva and adultery with Elsa were cited, they got married. She was three years older than he was, totally ignorant of science, more maternal and protective towards him than Mileva had been. She was not popular with his scientific colleagues. Although it was no more than a marriage of convenience, Einstein wrote to her regularly when he was away lecturing and touring.

Meanwhile Einstein, sustained by food parcels from Zurich to which he was entitled as a Swiss citizen, had been developing the general theory of relativity. A new scientific theory needs to be tested by experiment, and an opportunity for this came in 1919 when the deviation of light passing near the sun, as predicted by the general theory of relativity, was observed during the solar eclipse. Already famous among scientists, Einstein now became a celebrity to the general public. The publicity, even notoriety, which ensued changed the pattern of his life.

He crossed the Atlantic for the first time, in the company of a small party of Zionists headed by Chaim Weizmann, to raise money for the Hebrew University to be built on Mount Scopus in Jerusalem. Thousands of Jews greeted Einstein and his party when they arrived at the Battery in New York; thousands more lined the streets cheering and waving as they drove up the lower East Side, the Jewish quarter of the city. The Jews of Boston met their train with a brass band in the morning, then feted them in the evening with a kosher banquet. On the day they arrived in Cleveland, Jewish merchants closed shop at noon, and what a reporter called a swirl of fighting crowded humanity kept their two-hundred-car motorcade to a slow pace on the way to city hall. Everywhere it was Einstein that was the object of adulation; his humility captivated all the people who met him.

Next, Einstein spent three months in Leiden with Henrik Antoon Lorentz, his scientific father-figure, and then went on a grand tour of China, Japan, Israel, and Spain. When he was awarded the 1921 Nobel Prize in physics for his 1905 paper on photons, the prize money he received went to his former wife Mileva, as part of the divorce settlement, but it lost much of its value through inflation. As usual the prize, to which he attached little importance, was followed by a whole cornucopia of other honours. He was now able to put the prestige of his name behind the causes he believed in while trying not to misuse the status his scientific reputation had given him. In the First World War Einstein had refused to join in the widespread support of the German cause by German intellectuals and urged an immediate end to the war. For a few years he played an active role on the Committee on Intellectual Cooperation of the League of Nations.

Einstein's chief outdoor recreation was sailing a dinghy on the numerous lakes formed by the river Havel around Berlin. He was very skilful at manipulating the little boat, enjoying the gliding motion and the quiet, mind-soothing scenery. He could be seen out sailing almost every day, but he lacked a proper mooring for his boat. As the date of his fiftieth birthday approached the municipality conceived the plan of giving its most distinguished citizen a birthday present: a house beside the lakes, which would give him perfect quiet and direct access to the water. Unfortunately the project became so entangled in politics that Einstein rejected the idea and simply built a lakeside house for himself. It was there that he began meditating on the final goal of his scientific life, the discovery of one unifying theory which would bring together the hitherto separate phenomena of gravitation and the electromagnetic field. With characteristic concentration and obstinacy he advanced numerous ideas on this subject during the rest of his life, but none of them commanded widespread acceptance. His great days of scientific creativity were over.

In Germany, Einstein and his supporters were becoming increasingly the target of the anti-Semitic extreme right. He was viciously attacked in speeches and articles; even his life came under threat. Despite this treatment he remained based in Berlin, declining many offers of positions elsewhere, including one from the Hebrew University in Jerusalem. He still travelled regularly to the Netherlands to visit Lorentz, who had retired and been succeeded by Ehrenfest, as we shall see. In 1931 he spent some time in Oxford as Rhodes Memorial Lecturer, staying at Christ Church, where he accepted a five-year research fellowship, with no duties attached, the only condition being one of residence. Although in the end he did not take this up, he returned to Oxford in 1933 as Herbert Spencer Lecturer. He also visited the California Institute of Technology for three successive winters, and it was on the last of these visits that he finally decided to leave Germany and settle in Princeton.

By this time the Nazis had seized power in Germany and the attacks on him were intensifying. His papers on relativity were publicly burned before the Berlin State Opera House and his property was confiscated. He had been considering an arrangement which would have enabled him to divide his time between the Berlin Academy and the nascent Institute for Advanced Study in Princeton. Such a compromise was clearly no longer viable, and so he simply resigned from the academy and moved to Princeton. With Einstein on the faculty the institute, generously endowed by Jewish philanthropists, was in a strong position to attract other leading scientists. Having automatically become a German citizen again when he was appointed to the Berlin Academy he relinquished this just before the Nazis could deprive him of it. He announced that he would not return to a Germany that was without civil liberty, tolerance, and equality of all citizens before the law and that was ruled by a raw and rabid mob of Nazi militia. Many other Jewish scientists were also leaving Germany, but some stayed behind and ironically a few of them tended to blame Einstein for what befell them. As late as the spring of 1933 Courant at Göttingen was blaming Einstein and other 'agitators' for the anti-Semitic feeling in Germany and distinguishing between 'good' and 'bad' Jews. 'Even though Einstein does not consider himself a German ... he has received so many benefits from Germany that it is no more than his duty to help dispel the disturbance he has caused. Unfortunately, as I see from the papers, a reaction to these events has set in ... I very much hope it will be possible to deter the intended boycott [of Jewish businesses] at the last moment. Otherwise I see the future as very black.' It was.

So the United States became Einstein's homeland for the remaining twenty-two years of his life. He was given a hero's welcome when he first arrived, and deluged with invitations and requests for interviews. The director of the Institute for Advanced Study took it upon himself to deal with this and made Einstein very angry by declining, without consulting him, an invitation from President Roosevelt for the Einsteins to stay at the White House. Fortunately, most of Einstein's scientific correspondence had been saved and brought to America by diplomatic bag. He never returned to Europe; in fact the only time he left America was in 1935 as part of the process of becoming an American citizen. He was noticeably aged; scientifically the Princeton years were much less fruitful than what came before. Although he thought the chances of success were small he continued to seek a unified field theory, and became increasingly isolated from the mainstream of physical research. Princetonians respected his desire for solitude: he was seldom seen in public. He said that really his only friend in Princeton was the mathematical logician Kurt Gödel, who used to call for him every morning at 11 o'clock so that, whatever the weather, they could walk together to Fuld Hall. As he explained:

> I do not socialize because social encounters would distract me from my work and I really only live for that, and it would shorten even further my very limited lifespan. I do not have any close friends here as I had in my youth or later in Berlin with whom I could talk and unburden myself. That may be due to my age. I often have the feeling that God has forgotten me here. Also my standard of decent behaviour has risen as I grew older: I cannot be sociable with people whose fame has gone to their heads.

Einstein was the first of a stream of émigré physicists who left Germany during the 1930s, and who greatly strengthened the physical sciences in the United States. Increasingly preoccupied with Hitler's plans to subjugate Jews and conquer the world, he became convinced that the menace to civilization embodied in Hitler's regime could only be put down by force and renounced his former pacifist stand. When war finally broke out the United States was slow to react. The émigrés were deeply concerned about the Nazi menace, especially the plight of the Jews. The atomic physicists among them knew that a nuclear bomb powered by a fission-based chain reaction was theoretically possible.

To alert the national leadership, the Hungarian physicists Szilard, Teller, and Wigner decided that a letter from Einstein to President Roosevelt would be most effective, describing the potentialities of a nuclear bomb and warning that because fission had first been discovered in Germany, it was most likely that the Germans would be the first to develop it, with devastating consequences. Significantly, they had commandeered all existing stocks of uranium and were able to obtain fresh supplies from Czechoslovakia. Einstein agreed to sign the letter they had drafted and it was sent off. It may have helped to convince Roosevelt of the need for America to take action, but it took two and a half years, from July 1939 until the entry of the United States into the war, for the government finally to make adequate resources available. In later years Einstein said that he regretted sending the letter. 'Had I known that the Germans would not succeed in producing an atomic bomb I would not have lifted a finger.'

Einstein did not participate in the American projects that eventually produced the nuclear reactor and the atomic bomb. After the bomb was used and the war ended, he devoted his energies to the attempt to achieve a world government and to abolish war once and for all. He also spoke out against repression, arguing that intellectuals must be prepared to risk everything to preserve freedom of expression. But despite his concern for world problems and his willingness to use whatever he influence he had towards alleviating them, his ultimate loyalty was to science. As he said once with a sigh to an assistant during a discussion of political activities, 'Yes, time has to be divided this way between politics and our equations. But our equations are much more important to me because politics is for the present but an equation like that is something for eternity.'

After 1936, when his second wife Elsa died, Einstein was looked after by his sister Maria, his stepdaughter Margot, and his secretary-housekeeper Helen Dukas. Maria had come to live with her brother in 1939; she suffered a stroke in 1946, after which she was bedridden, and died in 1951. Einstein had retired from the Institute for Advanced Study in 1945 and was living almost as a recluse, trying to avoid the endless stream of people who wanted to see him about something, or just to see him. He suffered much harassment by press photographers; no other scientist has become so well known to the public in appearance. He was generally quite a merry person, with a strong sense of humour and a loud laugh; on one occasion he put out his tongue to express his annoyance (that photograph has been endlessly reproduced). Around Princeton he could often be seen at the local cinema—he was particularly fond of cowboy films. Although he kept a wardrobe of seven identical suits to wear on formal occasions, his ordinary dress was casual: he favoured sweatshirts, leather jackets, and sandals. He never owned a car or learnt to drive one, but used to sail a dinghy on Lake Carnegie. Otherwise he stayed peacefully at home at 112 Mercer Street, a Colonial-style house no different from others in the neighbourhood. For many years Einstein experienced recurrent health problems, including anaemia and an enlarged heart. He died on 18 April

1955, after a short illness in his seventy-sixth year; the immediate cause was a haemorrhage after the rupture of an aneurysm of the abdominal aorta. One of his last acts was to sign a plea, initiated by Bertrand Russell, for the renunciation of nuclear weapons and the abolition of war as a means of settling disputes between nations.

Einstein never identified with any particular country, living and working in many different places, and although he had quite a few individual collaborators, he never set out to create a research school in any sense. In his own words:

> I have never belonged wholeheartedly to any country or state, to my circle of friends, or even to my own family. These ties have always been accompanied by a vague aloofness, and the wish to withdraw into myself increases with the years. Such isolation is sometimes bitter, but I do not regret being cut off from the understanding and sympathy of other men. I lose something by it, to be sure, but I am compensated for it by being rendered independent of the customs, opinions and prejudices of others, and am not tempted to rest my peace of mind upon such shifting foundations.

As a child Einstein went through a religious phase, when he learnt the basics of Hebrew grammar. His father was proud of the fact that Jewish rites were not practised in his house. Einstein's pride in his ethnic origins emerged more and more strongly as the years went by. He was devoted to the cause of Israel, even though on occasion he was openly critical of its government. He spoke of Israel as 'us' and of the Jews as 'my people'; he believed it was important for a Jew to have Jewish friends. He refused to believe in a personal god but, like the Sephardic philosopher Baruch Spinoza, thought there might have been one who created the universe and the laws of nature.

Best of Teachers
Paul Ehrenfest (1880–1933)

Einstein had a great admiration for Lorentz, a Nobel Laureate, who was professor of theoretical physics at the ancient University of Leiden. When he died Einstein, representing the Berlin Academy at his funeral, said, 'I stand at the grave of the greatest and noblest man of our times. His genius was the torch which lighted the way from the teaching of Clerk Maxwell to the achievements of contemporary physics ... his life was ordered like a work of art down to the smallest detail. His never-failing kindness and magnanimity and his sense of justice, coupled with an intuitive understanding of people and things, made him a leader in any sphere he entered ... His work and his example will live on as an inspiration and guide to future generations.'

The physicist who Lorentz chose to succeed him at Leiden was also a friend of Einstein. Paul Ehrenfest was born in Vienna on 18 January 1880, only two years after Lise Meitner. His parents had moved to the imperial capital about twenty years earlier from Loschwitz, a small Jewish village in Moravia. His father Sigmund worked in a textile mill until he married Johanna Jellinek, the daughter of a merchant in the same village, and set up a grocery shop. The business thrived and by the time their son Paul was born the family was reasonably well off. They had four older sons: Arthur (1862), Emil (1865), Hugo (1870), and Otto (1872); a daughter was lost at birth. As the youngest by eight years, born when his father was forty-two and his mother thirty-eight, Paul was the baby of the family, very much his father's favourite. When he was ten years old his mother died of breast cancer; her place in his upbringing was taken by his widowed maternal grandmother. Paul's older brothers played a major role in his early life.

When Arthur was completing his studies at the Technical University, Emil became his father's right-hand man in the business, while Hugo and Otto were attending secondary school. In due course Paul too passed through the school system, entering the Akademisches Gymnasium in 1890 but transferring in 1897 to the Kaiser Franz-Josef Gymnasium to join his friend Gustav Herglotz for the last two years of school. They were separated again when Paul Ehrenfest enrolled at the Technical University, whereas Herglotz, already recognized as a promising mathematician, was at the University of Vienna.

Ehrenfest listed chemistry as his major field, but also took courses in a wide range of other scientific subjects, including mathematics. When he decided to be a theoretical physicist, it was mainly due to the influence of the charismatic Boltzmann, whose course on the mechanical theory of heat he had been taking. It was Boltzmann who initiated Ehrenfest into both the substance and the spirit of theoretical physics, as he did for so many others, and the Boltzmann influence was to shape Ehrenfest's own teaching and research in the years to come. After Boltzmann left Vienna temporarily for Leipzig in 1900, Ehrenfest stayed on for a second year and then migrated to Göttingen, where he found a much richer scientific culture than he had known in Vienna. He enrolled on no fewer than fifteen courses in the first year, gradually reducing the load as the year went on. While most of these were on physics it was the mathematical lectures which he found most exciting, particularly Hilbert on potential theory and Klein on mechanics.

Among the physics students in Göttingen was a young Russian woman, Tatyana Alexeyenva Afanassjewa, who was accompanied by her aunt Sonya. Her father, the chief engineer of the Imperial Russian Railways, had died when she was still a child, and she went to live with a childless uncle, who was a professor at the Technical University in St Petersburg. During the period leading up to the First World War, St Petersburg (later Petrograd, later still Leningrad) offered special university-level institutions for women which to some extent shadowed the Imperial University (still reserved for men). Tatyana attended first the women's pedagogical school and then the institution which offered women courses in arts, sciences, and law. She shone in mathematics, and went on to study physics at the Georgia Augusta, where she met Paul Ehrenfest. Before long the two young physicists had decided on marriage. Just a few years older than he was, she imposed various conditions: among them he must read all the novels of Tolstoy as soon as possible and was never to smoke tobacco. There was also the problem that Paul was Jewish and Tatyana was Russian Orthodox, and in Austro-Hungary a Jew could not marry a Christian, unless the couple officially declared themselves 'unchurched', and foreswore all religious affiliations.

First Ehrenfest needed to complete his PhD thesis. He decided to study under Lorentz in Leiden, but he was not there a great deal. After a quick trip back to Vienna to see Boltzmann, who had now returned from Leipzig, Ehrenfest spent some time with his fiancée in Göttingen. He then fitted in an Italian tour, spent a year working on his thesis in Vienna, completed it in Dubrovnik, and had it accepted in June 1904. That summer, with his doctorate in hand, Ehrenfest was ready to marry, and Tatyana, who had remained in Göttingen until then, joined him in Vienna. They proceeded to comply with the formalities of renouncing their respective religious affiliations and were married in December that year. He promised her that before long they would move to Russia and settle there.

Fortunately both Paul and Tatyana had inherited small incomes which made it possible for them to continue with scientific work if they lived modestly. To start with, they stayed on in Vienna, where he continued to participate actively in the Boltzmann seminar with Lise Meitner and others, and to devour books at a huge rate. Tatyana suffered from mumps, with high fever and delirium, early that summer. In 1905 their first child was born, a daughter named after her mother. The following spring they left Vienna, never to live there again. After a summer in Switzerland they returned to Göttingen, where Paul was invited by Klein to talk at his seminar about some joint work on statistical thermodynamics that he and Tatyana had just completed.

One of the consequences of her renunciation of the Orthodox faith was that it would be difficult for Tatyana to return to her homeland, since tsarist Russia was reluctant to allow entry to non-believers, but fortunately she was able to persuade the Russian consul in Vienna to grant the necessary visas. There had recently been a revolution, but in the autumn of 1907 they moved to St Petersburg, where Pavel Sigismondovich Ehrenfest, as he was known in Russia, was given a warm welcome by Dimitry Rozhdestwensky and Abram Ioffe, the senior experimental physicists there. During the five years they lived in Russia the Ehrenfests spent their summers at Kanuka, a tiny Estonian village on the Gulf of Finland some ninety or a hundred miles west of St Petersburg. Boltzmann had been writing a review article on statistical mechanics for Klein's encyclopedia of the mathematical sciences, but after Boltzmann's suicide Klein turned to Ehrenfest to replace him. Assisted by Tatyana, he wrote a very original and thorough but also controversial article. At the same time he was trying to qualify for the *Magister,* the essential prerequisite for a faculty position in Russia, his research doctorate being irrelevant. Ehrenfest could speak Russian reasonably well and gave some exemplary lectures on the differential equations of mathematical physics at the Polytechnic Institute. During the five years he was in Russia he introduced several talented students to the new physical theories.

Tatyana published her first paper in theoretical physics in 1905, and went on publishing during these Russian years. In 1910 she gave birth to another daughter, Anna. Meanwhile Ehrenfest was trying again to get his foot on the bottom rung of the academic ladder. Early in 1912 he set out to visit people who might be able to help, calling on Planck in Berlin, on Herglotz in Leipzig, and on Sommerfeld in Munich, but without success. Sommerfeld, for example, consulted his colleague the experimental physicist Wilhelm Röntgen, who replied that from what he had heard, Ehrenfest was fiery, critical, dialectical—in short, a Jewish type. Sommerfeld also asked Peter Debye, who described Ehrenfest as a Jew of the 'high priest' type, who would stifle any fresh ideas and exert an extremely noxious influence in Sommerfeld's institute.

After these rebuffs Ehrenfest returned to Vienna to consult his family and friends. One of his brothers had emigrated to America, and Paul considered following his example. He went to Prague to stay with the Einsteins. Long afterwards Einstein recalled that 'within a few hours we were true friends—as though our dreams and aspirations were meant for each other.' They played the Brahms sonatas for violin and piano together, and Ehrenfest was also a success with their little son, the seven-year-old Hans Albert.

Einstein had just decided to move from Prague back to Zurich, leaving a vacancy which Ehrenfest could fill. However Prague, being in the Austro-Hungarian Empire, required a formal religious affiliation for such an appointment. Although Einstein assured him that this was just a formality, which no one took seriously, Ehrenfest's conscience would not allow him to conceal the renunciation he had made in order to marry Tatyana. When he saw Ehrenfest off at the railway station Einstein said he would try and find an opening for him in Zurich. Meanwhile every effort was being made to persuade Ehrenfest to overcome his scruples and accept the position in Prague.

At this point Ehrenfest received a letter from Lorentz, whom he had not seen for nine years, congratulating him on his encyclopedia article, calling it 'highly interesting' and 'beautiful and profound'. Lorentz went on to say that he had decided to give up his position at the University of Leiden, after thirty years, and retire to nearby Haarlem. He had been hoping to persuade Einstein to succeed him, but Einstein was already committed to the Zurich post. Lorentz then made enquiries about the suitability of Ehrenfest for Leiden. Sommerfeld, who had earlier rejected Ehrenfest's overtures, replied to Lorentz that 'he lectures like a master. I have hardly ever heard a man speak with such fascination and brilliance. Significant phrases, witty points and dialectic are all at his disposal in an extraordinary manner. His way of handling the blackboard is characteristic. The whole disposition of his lecture is noted down on the board for the audience in the most transparent possible way. He knows how to make the most difficult things concrete and intuitively clear. Mathematical arguments are translated by him into easily comprehensible pictures.' Such strong recommendations convinced Lorentz to ask Ehrenfest whether he would be interested in coming to Leiden, while Sommerfeld decided to offer him the position of *Privatdozent* in Munich.

At the time the Ehrenfests were sailing down the river Volga, but on their return to St Petersburg he found the two letters. The proposal from Lorentz was much the more attractive; he replied that only a chair in Switzerland would appeal to him more. Because the appointment had to be made at ministerial level there was some delay until it was confirmed near the end of September, and the Ehrenfests prepared to settle down in Leiden. They arrived with the two daughters. A third child was born in May 1915, a boy named Paul after his father, and then in August 1918 another, Vassily, who suffered from Down's syndrome.

When they arrived in October 1912 they were given a warm reception and Lorentz could not have been more helpful. Once the formalities were over, one of the first actions Ehrenfest took was to attend a special meeting of the Berlin Academy held in Göttingen, where he had the opportunity to meet both the older generation of German physicists and some of the new people, such as Lindemann. Meanwhile Tatyana was planning their new house, with its open plan so different from traditional design. When it was built it proved to be more costly to maintain than they could afford. The hospitable Ehrenfests liked to entertain rather informally; they were vegetarians, offered no alcoholic drinks, and did not permit smoking. He maintained his contacts with Russia, for example by serving as a kind of mentor for Russian scientists, especially physicists and mathematicians, who were applying to the International Education Board for Rockefeller Fellowships.

During the First World War, in which the Netherlands was neutral, Ehrenfest kept trying to get Einstein to visit Leiden again, but there were bureaucratic obstacles. Eventually these were overcome and Ehrenfest was able to bring Einstein and Lorentz together once more. Even more than usual, this particular meeting with Einstein left Ehrenfest inspired and invigorated. They always played violin and piano sonatas when they met. Ehrenfest's favourite composer had been Beethoven. He also played and enjoyed music from Haydn to Brahms, but had never particularly liked the music of Bach. Einstein opened the world of Bach's music to his friend in Leiden, and Ehrenfest was completely captivated. Once the war was over, Ehrenfest made a determined effort to persuade Einstein to move to Leiden from Berlin. Einstein refused a permanent position but agreed to a regular visiting professorship, which enabled him to visit Leiden for three or four weeks annually from 1920 onwards. These visits provided a welcome relief from the personal attacks to which he was subject in Berlin.

However, all was not well with Ehrenfest. He was partially estranged from Tatyana, who had gone back to St Petersburg, and he took very personally the growing threat posed to his fellow scientists by the rise of the Nazi party in Germany. At the same time he seems to have felt overwhelmed and inadequate to deal with the continuing change taking place in theoretical physics during the early 1930s. Niels Bohr reported that 'he is a very clear-sighted man, fertile in ideas, but his temperament is so troubled I have never encountered anything like it.' Increasingly prone to depression and bizarre behaviour, he committed suicide at the age of fifty-three in Amsterdam on 25 September 1933, after shooting and blinding the mentally handicapped Vassily, then aged fourteen.

Afterwards, Einstein wrote of Ehrenfest: 'he was not only the best teacher in our profession I have ever known; he was also passionately preoccupied with the development and destiny of men, especially his students. Unfortunately the accolades of his students and colleagues were not enough to overcome his deep-rooted sense of inferiority and insecurity.' Tatyana, 'whom he loved', said Einstein, 'with a passion the likes of which I have not often witnessed in my life,' was in St Petersburg when the tragic events took place. She returned to Leiden, where she lived until her death in 1964. Although she never completed a doctorate nor held a regular university teaching post, her writings substantially enriched the study of physics in the Netherlands. She wrote two major monographs in the 1950s, enlarging her readership by publishing in English as well as Dutch. Her last work, published in 1960 when she was eighty-four, was a treatise on the teaching of mathematics. Her son Paul lost his life in an avalanche while skiing in the French Alps in 1939.

Father of Soviet Science
Abram Ioffe (1880–1960)

As Peter the Great intended, his new capital of St Petersburg was regarded as part of
Europe. Following the reforms he instituted,
Germans had come to occupy central roles in the Russian bureaucracy,
economic life, and professions. For example, the physicist Moritz Jacobi
spent most of his working life at the Imperial Academy of Sciences, as
we have seen. From the late eighteenth to the twentieth century, these
Germans, often from the Baltic states, constituted from 18 to more than
33 per cent of the officer corps, diplomatic service, police, and administration. After the October Revolution they were mainly replaced by
Jews, who rose high in the administrative ranks of the Soviet Republic.
They also played a leading role in Soviet science, particularly mathematics and physics.

There were also temporary residents, such as the Austrian physicist,
Paul Ehrenfest, who spent five important years there, as we know. However
these were foreigners; it is difficult to identify a Jewish mathematician
or physicist who was and remained a subject of the tsars. The situation
changed after the October Revolution, and one of the architects of the
new era in Russian physics was a Ukrainian-born Jew, educated before
the revolution, who became one of the most influential Soviet scientists
of the twentieth century. Abram Fedorovitch Ioffe (or Joffe) shares with
Leonid Mandel'shtam the honour of being called 'the father of Soviet
physics'.

The oldest of five children, Abram was born on 29/30 October 1880
in the small Ukrainian town of Romny. The descendant of a family of
Jewish artisans and craftsmen, he was the son of Fedor Vasil'evich and

Rahel Abramovna (née Veinstein). His father, an employee of a local bank, had received only a limited formal commercial education. Both parents were much interested in intellectual pursuits and undoubtedly greatly encouraged and influenced their son, who showed early signs of exceptional intelligence. After having completed high school in his hometown, he went to St Petersburg to study at the Technical University, where he graduated in 1902 as a technical engineer.

Ioffe's interest in physics prompted him to go to Munich to be trained by Wilhelm Röntgen, who was impressed with his abilities. Initially, the question arose whether Ioffe could be formally admitted as a doctoral candidate because he lacked a proper gymnasium education; eventually his certificate in technical engineering was accepted as an equivalent qualification. In 1905 he obtained his first doctorate, a PhD *summa cum laude*; an abbreviated version of his dissertation was published in the prestigious *Annalen der Physik*. Although Röntgen expected his talented student to continue to work in Munich, Ioffe decided to go back to St Petersburg, where he obtained a position as laboratory assistant at the Polytechnic Institute. There he earned a master's degree with distinction, and won a prize from the Imperial Academy. With Dmitry Rozhdestvensky and Paul Ehrenfest he led a coterie of young scientists who were trying to disseminate the new ideas of quantum mechanics and relativity in Russia. They encountered opposition from the older professors who were devoted to classical physics and reluctant to accept these new ideas. They also fought an uphill struggle against their mathematical colleagues who controlled one of the formal examinations for the university degree in physics, and made it so difficult that even PhDs from top German universities found it an ordeal.

By 1916 Ioffe had become a professor at the Polytechnic Institute, with which he remained associated for the next thirty-five years. After the October Revolution he helped to establish the Röntgenological Radiological Institute and became director of its physical-technical section. The creation of this new centre for physical research must have seemed wildly visionary at the time since, after the chaos of war and the upheaval of the revolution, the economy of the country was in a parlous state. There were great shortages of food and fuel and practically no scientific equipment so that experimental research was only possible on a do-it-yourself basis. A commission of the Soviet Academy of Sciences was set up, at Ioffe's instigation, for renewing scientific relations with other countries. This was liberally provided with foreign currency to purchase equipment abroad. Although foreign travel at that time was complicated because most of the outside world had no diplomatic relations with the Soviet Republic the expedition was successful, although one of its members, Piotr Kapitza, stayed behind, to work in the Cavendish Laboratory under Rutherford.

During these years Ioffe was the moving spirit behind the modernization of Soviet physics, trying to keep abreast of developments in the West. While Ioffe was regarded as the chief spokesman for Soviet physics by officials and the public, younger physicists such as Lev Landau for whom quantum mechanics was part of their youth culture tended to speak of him dismissively because he had not mastered the latest theories. Foreigners were always surprised at the forthright criticism to which the Russians were accustomed when conducting their scientific disputes, without respect for formalities and academic hierarchy.

In the universities of late imperial Russia the priority had usually been excellence in teaching rather than research. Now research-oriented scientists demanded that they should be liberated from teaching entirely and recognized as a separate profession with their own specialized institutes. The Bolsheviks were strongly in favour of this, as it helped them to obtain political control over universities by replacing academics appointed during the tsarist era. Ioffe persuaded the government to establish a network of physical-technical institutes in various cities of the Soviet Union. When the new institutes were set up university staff resented the monopoly on access to scientific journals and other privileges of their employees, such as better food rations in times of shortage.

Between 1928 and 1932 there was tremendous social upheaval in the Soviet Union, involving the collectivization of agriculture and a major drive towards industrialization. Access to education for people of 'bourgeois' origin was restricted. The established leaders of the scientific community found themselves in a difficult position. On the one hand they were exposed to attacks from the security police and the political authorities, and on the other they were vulnerable to attacks from militant junior colleagues below. The political authorities tended to side with the young radicals, especially those who had been educated after the revolution. Eventually radicalism gave way to a renewed emphasis on solid training and disciplined expertise, the marks of the more ordered society of high Stalinism. In higher education, for example, university degrees, which had been abolished after the revolution, were brought back. Unlike most of his colleagues, Ioffe managed to surf the revolutionary wave and turn events to the advantage of his discipline. He succeeded in establishing a laboratory for the practical applications of physics. This eventually became a separate institute, of which he served as director. He was also behind the establishment of several small-scale industrial laboratories in different parts of the Soviet Union. Besides his other duties he became the director of an institute of physical agriculture (agrophysics) that he had helped to establish in 1931.

The Rockefeller Foundation, which played such an important role in fostering scientific research elsewhere in Europe, always had problems in dealing with the Soviet Republic. Official applications for support from scientific institutions were turned down. Rockefeller Fellowships were distributed evenly between the four disciplines of mathematics, physics, biology, and medicine. From his base in Leiden and in consultation with Ioffe in Russia, Ehrenfest mentored likely physics candidates. In 1932 it was stipulated that those intending to hold Rockefeller Fellowships in the United States needed to be interviewed, usually in Paris. This effectively eliminated Soviet candidates because of the difficulties they would face in getting the necessary funds and exit visas from the Soviet authorities. The next year the fellowships entirely ceased to be awarded to Soviet citizens because of the refusal of the authorities to allow them to travel abroad. Nevertheless those who had been able to take advantage of the previous window of opportunity returned to guide Soviet science through the twenty years of almost complete isolation which lay ahead.

By 1938 direct contact between Soviet physicists and their foreign colleagues, especially those in Nazi Germany, had been broken off. Even so, news of the discovery of nuclear fission soon reached the Physical-Technical Institute in Leningrad and funding for the construction of a cyclotron became available. When the Germans invaded Russia in 1941 the energies of Soviet scientists were diverted into more directly useful projects than nuclear physics, such as developing more effective armour-plating and finding methods to demagnetize ships to protect them from magnetic mines. The Germans quickly overran Kiev and Kharkov and were approaching Moscow and Leningrad. The Physical-Technical Institute, which in 1939 had become part of the Soviet Academy of Sciences, was evacuated to Kazan, leaving only a small staff behind in Leningrad, which was soon under siege.

After the war, Ioffe concentrated on the study of semiconductors, whose scientific importance and industrial potential he was one of the first to recognize. He envisaged their widespread use for cooling or heating purposes or conversely as small generators where other power sources were not practical or available. In 1950 Ioffe had been forced to give up the directorship of the Leningrad Physical-Technical Institute because Soviet policy was to concentrate on nuclear physics, to the detriment of other research. Before long he was appointed director of the Semiconductor Institute of the Soviet Academy, the post that he occupied for the rest of his life. Ioffe was not afraid of politial intrigue and controversy. Over the years he had differences with colleagues who objected to his views on modern physics. At one point he complained that some of their criticism of the theory of relativity and quantum mechanics bore a macabre resemblance to what their nationalistic counterparts in Germany were saying at the time.

Persecution of the Russian intelligentsia, in which Jews were strongly represented, followed the German invasion. Another Stalinist campaign was launched after the war, this time directed specifically against the Jews, and this was extended to the Soviet satellites. After Stalin's death the anti-Jewish oppression subsided but discrimination remained. Under American pressure Russian Jews obtained the right to emigrate to Israel, and they did so in large numbers. For most of them Israel was no more than a stage on the way to the United States, which offered generous immigration quotas to Russian Jews. Fewer than a quarter of a million now remain in the former Soviet Union, although some of those who left earlier have returned.

There were other outstanding physicists in the Soviet Republic, and some of them were Jewish, but Ioffe accomplished the transition from young Turk to elder statesman of Soviet physics during a chaotic period in the Soviet Republic. He was the author of numerous papers, textbooks, and monographs on subjects that ranged from theoretical, historical, and philosophical concepts to the practical applications of science to everyday life. Most of his publications are in Russian but some are in German, which he had mastered in his youth, and some were later translated into English. Ioffe's writings contain interesting reminiscences of the famous scientists and other personalities he had met over the years.

János Plesch, the personal physician of Einstein, knew Ioffe well and gave a description in which he described him as kind, cordial, loyal, and modest, endowed with an incisive mind, a man who tended to seek simple solutions to complex problems. He organized his activities with care and had little patience with time-consuming formalities and superfluous paperwork. Instead of writing letters to people he preferred to talk matters over. In spite of all his responsibilities, he never seemed hurried or tired out and always tried to make the best of things. In his research he observed high ethical standards. Though reserved and lacking in humour, Ioffe was courteous and friendly to everybody he met. He read widely and enjoyed walking, playing tennis, and attending theatrical and musical performances. He married twice: first, a dentist named Vera Andeevna Kravtsova, and then, after divorcing her, Anna Vadil'evna Echeistora, a graduate student in physics. He died in Leningrad on 14 October 1960, at the age of eighty. Ioffe received many honours in his own country and abroad. In 1920 he was elected a full member of the Soviet Academy, and in 1929 an honorary member of the American Academy of Arts and Sciences.

Queen of Modern Algebra
Emmy Noether (1882–1935)

In his well-known book *Hereditary Genius*, Francis Galton gave many British examples where exceptional ability seemed to run in families. It is not difficult to find such examples in other countries. The Noether family in Germany might be added to his list. The mathematician Max Noether was the third of five children of Hermann Noether, a wholesaler in the hardware business, and Amalia Würzburger. We are told that his relationship with his mother, who died at the beginning of the 1870s, was particularly close, and that a brother of hers was a merchant who undoubtedly had mathematical talent, although it was not developed. Max Noether attended private schools in Mannheim, his birthplace. He was stricken by polio in his youth, which left him permanently lame. Instruction at home enabled him to complete the gymnasium curriculum and then, unassisted, to study mathematics at university level. After a brief period working at the Mannheim astronomical observatory he went to the University of Heidelberg where he served as *Privatdozent* and then *Extra-Ordinarius*. In 1880 he married Ida Amalia Kaufmann, who came from a wealthy Jewish family in Cologne. There were academics in her family also, as well as successful businessmen. Three of the Noethers' four children were scientists; we will describe the career first of Emmy and then more briefly that of her ill-fated brother Fritz.

Emmy Noether was the first woman mathematician who can unhesitatingly be described as truly great. As Weyl said at her funeral, 'The memory of her work in science and of her personality among her fellows will not soon pass away. She was a great mathematician, the greatest, I firmly believe, her sex has ever produced, and a great woman.' Einstein said, 'in the judgement of most competent mathematicians, Fraulein Noether was the most significant mathematical genius since the higher education of women began.' Sadly, as her friend the Russian mathematician Paul Alexandrov said, 'the greatest woman mathematician who ever lived died at the very height of her creative powers.'

Max Noether had moved in 1875 to Erlangen, where Emmy was born on 23 March 1882. Her father was *Extra-Ordinarius* there, as he had been at Heidelberg, and had to wait thirteen years before becoming *Ordinarius*, although he would have preferred to move to a more prestigious university. His speciality was algebra, in which he was much influenced by the work of Luigi Cremona. It is said that Max Noether strongly influenced the early thinking of his children, and the Noether home was constantly visited by members of a stimulating circle of scholars. Emmy had a conventional upbringing, attending the municipal school for the higher education of daughters until she was eighteen when she was certified as a teacher in French and English at 'institutions for the education and instruction of females'. Women had been allowed to enrol at universities in France since 1861, in England since 1878, and in Italy since 1885. In Germany as late as 1900, this was still not permitted; professors frequently refused permission for women even to attend their lectures, and only very rarely were women allowed to take university examinations. At the University of Erlangen the academic Senate in 1898 passed a resolution declaring that the admission of women students would 'overthrow all academic order'. Prussia delayed female matriculation until 1908.

Emmy Noether was determined to undertake university studies and she was not to be deterred. She succeeded in attending courses in mathematics and other scientific subjects at Erlangen and Göttingen, after which she enrolled at her father's university in 1904, as soon as it was possible for women to do so. Her true abilities were quite slow to show themselves. However, by 1908 she had completed her dissertation 'On Complete Systems of Invariants for Ternary Biquadratic Forms', under her father's (Jewish) colleague Paul Albert Gordan, and was awarded a PhD *summa cum laude*. Later she was quite dismissive of this work.

For the next seven years she remained at Erlangen, without a position, getting a little teaching but mainly engaged in research. During this period she began to work with the algebraist Ernst Fischer, who led her away from the algorithmic methods of Gordan towards the broad theoretical style characteristic of Hilbert. This change of direction led to an invitation from Hilbert and Klein to join them at Göttingen. At that time the new theory of relativity was creating great excitement. Emmy Noether was one of the first to understand its implications and contributed two new results which are important in the general theory. Hilbert tried to secure an academic position for her but there was too much opposition. This provoked his famous outburst at a faculty meeting: 'I do not see that the sex of the candidate is an argument against her admission as *Privatdozent*. After all, we are a university, not a bathing establishment.' She provided a test case of whether women should be allowed to become faculty members at German universities. In 1917, when the mathematical *Ordinarien*, with support from the physicists, petitioned the ministry of culture that she should be granted the *venia legendi*, the reply was that neither she nor any other woman would be allowed to teach at a German university. Although she acted as thesis adviser for a number of Göttingen PhD students, it was not until the reforms of 1919 that she became even a *Privatdozent* at the mature age of thirty-seven. Three years later she received the honorary title of unofficial associate professor, without official responsibilities, and without stipend.

A keen mind and infectious enthusiasm for mathematical research made Emmy Noether an effective teacher, although she could not be described as a good lecturer, as her style was rapid and confusing. Her classroom technique, like her thinking, was strongly conceptual. Rather than simply lecturing, she conducted discussion sessions in which she would explore some topic with her students. She loved to spend free time with them, especially on long walks. Sometimes she would become so engrossed in the conversation that her students would have to remind her to watch for traffic. On one memorable occasion her slip came down when she was lecturing; she bent down, pulled it off, threw it in the corridor, and kept on lecturing. According to Weyl, 'She was heavy of build and loud of voice, and it was not easy for one to get the floor in competition with her. She preached mightily, and not as the scribes. She was a rough and simple soul, but her heart was in the right place. Her frankness was never offensive in the least degree. In everyday life she was most unassuming and utterly unselfish; she had a kind and friendly nature.'

Outstanding mathematicians often make their greatest contributions early in their careers; Emmy Noether was an exception. She began producing her most powerful and creative work around the age of forty. Her change of style started in 1920 with a paper on non-commutative fields (such as Hamilton's quaternions). During the years that followed she developed a very abstract and generalized approach to the axiomatic development of algebra. As Weyl said, she originated above all a new and epoch-making style of thinking about algebra, later written up by her former student Bartel Van der Waerden in his classic textbook on modern algebra.

By this time Emmy Noether was at the height of her powers, and her advanced ideas were winning more and more acceptance. She lectured at the 1928 International Congress of Mathematicians in Bologna, and was a principal speaker at the next congress in Zurich. She gave courses at the University of Moscow and the Soviet Academy in the winter of 1928/9 when, according to Alexandrov, 'she was delighted by Soviet and especially mathematical successes, furthermore her sympathies were always unwaveringly with the Soviet Republic, in which she saw a new era in history.' At the Georgia Augusta she had at last been appointed *Extra-Ordinarius*. She never attained the top rank of *Ordinarius*, although she contributed so much to making Göttingen the premier mathematical centre in Europe, many would say in the world. On her fiftieth birthday her group of algebraists, called the Noether family, held a celebration in her honour.

When the Nazi government enacted the racial laws in 1933 Emmy Noether was one of those immediately affected. The idyllic old town of Göttingen was a hotbed of anti-Semitism. Apparently she had to move out of her rooms in a student boarding house in April 1933 because the other boarders did not want to live with a 'Marxist-leaning Jewess'. For a time Emmy Noether continued to meet informally with students and colleagues, inviting groups to her apartment, while trying, with her despondent colleagues, to decide what to do. She seriously considered moving to Moscow, but Alexandrov was unable to convince the university authorities of the need to act quickly. In the meantime, efforts were being made on her behalf in America, and before the end of 1933 she had arrived there, to take up a temporary position at Bryn Mawr College funded by the Rockefeller Foundation. Normally Rockefeller funding was only intended for cases where there was a definite plan to provide a permanent post (which there was no prospect of Bryn Mawr being able to offer her). However her supporters, including Birkhoff, Lefschetz, and Wiener, succeeded in persuading the foundation to make an exception in her case.

Although Bryn Mawr, a women's college in the neighbourhood of Philadephia, offered graduate fellowships in mathematics there were only five graduate students, none of whom had been exposed to any abstract algebra. She took four of the students under her wing and taught them abstract algebra in a mixture of German and English (she was qualified to teach English but found it hard to lecture in the language). With characteristic curiosity and good nature she settled happily into her new home. She wanted to know how things were done in America, whether it was giving a tea party or taking a PhD, and she attacked each subject with the disarming candour and vigorous attention which won over everyone who knew her. To quote Weyl again: 'Her work was as inevitable and natural as breathing, a background for living taken for granted, but that work was only the core of her relation with her students. She lived with them and for them in a perfectly unselfconscious way. She looked on the world with direct friendliness and unfeigned interest, and she wanted them to do the same, she loved to take walks, and many a Saturday, with five or six students, she tramped the roads around the college with a fine disregard for bad weather.'

From Bryn Mawr she was able to visit other friends and former colleagues from Germany who had also come to America. Ten of these were mathematicians. She gave a course of weekly lectures on algebra at Princeton before a distinguished audience. Olga Taussky, her assistant at Göttingen, had followed her to Bryn Mawr and often accompanied her on these visits to Princeton. She recalled: 'I remember that on one occasion she had to apply the binomial theorem to a very special situation. Although she had enormous insight into difficult abstract structure this computation was a great challenge to her. She did however master it and was very pleased about this. In fact she turned back from the blackboard about three times to smile proudly at us.'

So what was she like personally? 'Warm like a loaf of bread', wrote Weyl,

> there radiated from her a broad, comforting, vital warmth. She was strongly myopic and wore spectacles with thick lenses. She was fat, rough and loud, but so kind that all who knew her loved her. She thought little about what she should wear, what she should eat, and so on. Her intentions could hardly be further removed from the effects which her appearance had, especially on those who did not know her. In particular, there was the handkerchief. She kept it tucked under her blouse. While lecturing she had a way of jerking it out and thrusting it back, very energetically, and this was very noticeable to her audience. During the years before she began keeping her hair cropped short, she wore it up, and little by little, during the excitement of lecturing, it would fall out of place.

At the end of that first year in America she returned briefly to Germany and was appalled to find how much the situation had deteriorated. Towards the end of her second year at Bryn Mawr she went into hospital for surgery. Although the operation was not without risk it was carried out successfully. Unfortunately, while still in hospital, she developed a high fever and died suddenly on 14 April 1935 at the age of fifty-three, apparently from either a post-operative embolism or an infection. Shortly before she died she said that the previous eighteen months had been the very happiest in her whole life, for she was appreciated at Bryn Mawr and Princeton as she had never been appreciated in her own country. After cremation her ashes were interred near the college library. Weyl concluded his eloquent tribute with these words:

> Two traits determined her nature; first the native productive powers of her mathematical genius. She was not clay, pressed by the artistic hands of God into a harmonious form, but rather a chunk of human primary rock into which he had blown his creative breath of life. Secondly her heart knew no malice; she did not believe in evil—indeed it never entered her mind that

it could play a role among men. This was never more forcefully apparent to me than in the last stormy summer, that of 1933, which we spent together at Göttingen. A time of struggle like this one ... draws people together; thus I have a particularly vivid recollection of these months. Emmy Noether, her courage, her frankness, her unconcern about her own fate, her conciliatory spirit, were in the midst of all the hatred and meanness, despair and sorrow surrounding us, a moral solace.

At least Emmy escaped the fate of her younger brother Fritz, well known as an applied mathematician, who in 1933 was teaching at the Technical University in Breslau. He was then forty-eight years old, a wounded veteran of the First World War, who had been awarded the Iron Cross. However, students started to complain that 'his presence on the faculty in large measure contradicts the Aryan principle'. Like his sister, he admired the Soviet Republic and when he was dismissed he made the fateful decision to move to the Kubischev University in Tomsk. The last time his old friends saw him was when he gave a paper at the International Congress of Mathematicians held in Oslo in 1936. In 1937 he was arrested as a German spy and sentenced to twenty-five years in prison, on false evidence; Einstein and Weyl tried in vain to intercede on his behalf. In 1941, while in prison, he was charged with further acts against the Soviet Union, condemned to death, and executed. Over forty years later the Supreme Court of the Soviet Union decided that he had been entirely innocent, and his son was officially informed of his father's complete rehabilitation. With hindsight it is obvious that, having decided to leave Germany, he made a mistake by going east rather than west, but in those days many people, especially intellectuals, had no real understanding of the true character of the Stalinist regime. He could not deny his German origins, in a period when relations between Germany and the Soviet Union rapidly deteriorated, and after the Germans invaded nothing could save him.

Imperturbable Good Nature
James Franck (1882–1964)

Among the contemporaries of Emmy
Noether were two Jewish physicists, James
Franck and Max Born, who were close friends
and colleagues at the Georgia Augusta. After the Nazis came into power,
Born settled in Britain, Franck in America. Although each of them found
good positions without difficulty, their later years were less fruitful than
they might have been, and the pain of leaving their homeland hard to
bear. We discuss the case of Franck first, since he was a few months older
than Born.

James Franck was born in Hamburg on 26 August 1882, the son of Jacob
Franck, a banker, and Rebecca (née Drucker). In the humanist school he
attended, a sound training in classics was regarded as the principal aim
of education, and it was largely due to Franck's lack of interest in ancient
languages that he was considered to be a boy of little promise. At an early
age he earned himself the reputation of being a dreamer on account of
his tendency to become entirely absorbed in the observation of things
around him, and in attempts to understand them. According to his own
report, he only just managed to scrape through the *Abitur*, which enabled
him to enrol at university. His father sent him to Heidelberg to study law
and economics, the normal preparation for a career in business in those
days, hoping that he would later join the family firm.

Franck was never in any doubt that it was physics he wanted to study
but he dutifully attended lectures on law and economics, also physics,
geology, and chemistry. He found the physics lectures at Heidelberg
uninspiring. They reflected the widely held view that nothing fundamental
in the subject remained to be discovered, since everything would ultimately

be reduced to Newtonian mechanics. However, it was at Heidelberg that he first met Max Born, who wrote afterwards that, 'looking back to my Heidelberg semester, it appeared to me that neither the professors nor the romantic atmosphere of that ancient university city were the important things in my life, but the friendship of James Franck was.' Born and other friends supported Franck in his efforts to persuade his parents to agree to a change in his course of studies. It was due to their support as well as to Franck's own stubborn insistence that they finally gave in and allowed him to pursue the study of science.

Franck now wanted to devote himself seriously to physics, and so, in 1902, he went to study in Berlin. Like Lise Meitner and many other young physicists, he found the regular Tuesday physics colloquium an enormously stimulating experience. The informality and intellectual honesty of the discussions made a deep impression on Franck, especially the way that Planck, the great classical physicist, struggled with the revolutionary consequences of his own discoveries, trying hard to preserve as much as possible of the structure of classical concepts, and finally coming to the conviction that quantum concepts would enter all branches of physics.

In 1911 Franck married Ingrid Josephson, a Swedish pianist from Gothenburg, and their two daughters, Dagmar and Lise, were born in Berlin. His own reports, and those of his friends, give the impression of a rich and varied life, with a large circle of friends passionately devoted to physics and spending countless hours in the laboratory with experiments and discussions. Franck was an intense and nervous man, although famously affable in conversation. There were musical evenings in the home of the Francks, where Einstein playing the violin, accompanied by Ingrid Franck on the piano, and Lise Meitner sang Brahms' *Lieder*.

In 1911, the year of his marriage, Franck received the *venia legendi*. The outbreak of war interrupted his scientific career at a critical stage and impeded the exchange of information. Franck joined up and was sent to the front. Though he received a commission and distinguished himself during the war, it was from a sense of duty rather than from conviction that he became a soldier. In fact his war service did not last very long because he became severely ill with dysentery in Russia, and was sent home to recover. In 1916 he was made *Extra-Ordinarius* at the university, and the following year appointed head of a section of the Kaiser Wilhelm Institute for physical chemistry.

When Niels Bohr came to visit Berlin, the younger physicists arranged a discussion meeting at which they could ask him questions without inhibition. Later, Franck recalled Bohr's immense ability to concentrate, in the presence of others, while his face looked completely blank, until the answer was produced. In these talks, Bohr always stressed the provisional nature and philosophical inconsistency of his quantum theory. It was this wisdom and his complete freedom from conceit which created such deep respect and admiration in the young physicists that Franck describes it as bordering on hero-worship. When he responded to Bohr's invitation to visit his institute in Copenhagen they soon became firm friends.

At the Georgia Augusta the departments of experimental and theoretical physics were housed in the same building. In 1921 both chairs were vacant. When Born was offered the theoretical chair he accepted on condition that the experimental chair be offered to Franck. The close cooperation, friendship, and exchange of ideas between Franck and Born were vividly recalled by those who had the good fortune to be there at this time, among them Heisenberg, Pauli, and Wigner. In experimental work Franck collaborated with his younger colleague Gustav Hertz, nephew of Heinrich (a later profile contains a brief sketch of his rather unusual career). Franck and Hertz discovered the laws governing the impact of an electron on an atom, for which they shared the Nobel Prize in physics in 1926.

The physics seminar was an activity which Born and Franck conducted jointly. A student in his last year before beginning research, or a research student, would be given a subject on which to talk at the seminar, where he or she would have to stand up to friendly though quite searching questions. Admission to Franck's laboratory became very competitive, and his choice was mainly based on the performance of the student at these seminars. Once admitted, the research student became not only a pupil of Franck but a member of a community tied together by a common scientific interest and friendship, not least by a feeling of respect and devotion to Franck. He would generally propose the subject of research for the student himself. Twice a week, at a certain time, like a doctor on a hospital ward

round, Franck would troop into the student's room with his assistants
to discuss progress, difficulties, and questions of apparatus; prolonged
discussions with research students and members of staff would take place
either in his office or on a walk in the countryside around Göttingen.
Life in the laboratory was characterized by great informality, allowing
physics and private life to merge pleasantly into one another. He always
treated his assistants and research students as equals—most unusual at
German universities where *Ordinarien* were very rank-conscious. Rather
than through formal lectures he preferred to teach through small group
discussions.

When the Nazi government enacted the racial laws in 1933 Franck
himself, although Jewish, could have remained in office because of his
active service in the war. It would have been easy for him to compromise,
and there were many good and reasonable arguments in favour of such
a course, but Franck saw clearly that this was a fundamental issue, to
be decided by principle rather than expedience. Against the warning of
many well-meaning colleagues, he resigned his chair and published his
statement of resignation and protest in the national press. Neither he nor
anyone else thought that this action would have any effect on the course
of events; for him it was simply the right thing to do and stands out as
one of the few open protests coming from Germany academia against
racial discrimination and the suppression of academic freedom. Planck
advised those who consulted him not to leave. When he tried to persuade
Hitler that the Nazis were ruining German science he achieved nothing.
Fortunately nothing adverse happened to Franck; when he and his family
left Göttingen so many supporters came to the station to see him off that
they almost overflowed the platform, standing in silence as the train drew
out. Within less than a year the laboratory virtually dispersed; most of
the staff members were either dismissed or obliged to leave. Franck was
exceptional in the efforts he made to help them obtain new positions.

Franck made an exploratory visit to Baltimore and other places in
America, looking for a suitable place to continue his research. Then he
spent more than a year in Copenhagen as visiting professor at the Niels
Bohr Institute. In 1935 he and his family finally moved to the United States,
where he had secured a professorship at Johns Hopkins. Unfortunately,

the president of the university at that time was creating problems for Jewish faculty, and so after three years Franck moved to the University of Chicago as professor of physical chemistry, to work on photosynthesis, the process by which green plants manufacture their carbohydrates from atmospheric carbon dioxide and water in the presence of sunlight.

During the Second World War Franck decided to shelve this research and joined the Manhattan project in Chicago, where he was put in charge of the chemistry division. The ultimate aim of this work was repugnant to him, as to many others, but the danger that atomic bombs would first be made by Germany under Hitler was too real to be ignored. The surrender of Germany altered the situation and he, like many scientists involved in the project, became deeply concerned about the consequences of using this new kind of weapon. A committee was formed consisting of three physicists, three chemists, and a biologist under the chairmanship of Franck, to consider the 'social and political implications' of using the bomb. The Franck report which emerged is testimony to the sense of responsibility of the scientists engaged in the project. The dangers of nuclear war, the problem of East–West relations, and all their political implications remained a matter of deep concern to Franck. Although not a member of any of the advisory committees set up by the government after the war, he was occasionally consulted.

After Franck's emigration, if not earlier, the health of his wife gradually deteriorated, and she died in 1942. Their daughters, Dagmar von Heppel and Lisa Lisco, had also settled in America. In 1946 Franck married Hertha Spooner, professor of physics at Duke University, after which he divided his time between Chicago and their home in Durham, North Carolina. She had been his pupil and was an old family friend. The award of the Rumford Medal of the American Academy of Arts and Sciences in 1955 for his work on photosynthesis, was one of many honours he received, apart from the Nobel Prize.

Franck's scientific activity extended over about sixty years, from the beginning of the twentieth century, when the foundations of atomic physics and quantum theory were being laid, to a time when those disciplines had reached a high degree of sophistication. Although primarily a physicist, his work had profound influence on chemistry and on the branch of biology concerned with the fundamental process by which the energy of sunlight is converted into forms of energy that maintain life on earth. In all the varied phenomena that he studied one can recognize a unity of approach in his attempt to understand the processes of the transfer of energy in atomic systems.

The Nazi period cast a deep and lasting shadow over Franck's life, and it was not an easy decision for him to visit Germany again after the war. The welcome he received there convinced him that much had changed, and so he returned several times. In 1951 he was awarded the Max Planck Medal of the German Physical Society, and in 1953 the city of Göttingen conferred its freedom on Franck and Born, along with several others who had left in the 1930s, while Heidelberg and several other German universities awarded him honorary degrees. At the end of his life he was elected a foreign member of the Royal Society. In the postwar years his physical health caused him increasing trouble, but his mind remained clear and active to the last. He died in Göttingen on 21 May 1964 at the age of eighty-two, when on a last visit to old friends in Germany. Otto Frisch described Franck as the most immediately lovable man he ever met.

7

Emigrants and Immigrants

In this chapter the subjects of the profiles were born between 1882 and 1893. The large-scale migrations to the United States from eastern Europe in the nineteenth century included a great many Jews, fleeing tsarist oppression and persecution. This continued into the twentieth century, but it became more a migration of individuals rather than whole populations, and they were usually German or Austrian Jews, rather than Polish or Russian. It has been said that the Weimar culture which flourished in the 1920s did not cease to exist; it went underground and re-emerged in the United States. This was certainly true of mathematics and physics; Princeton, for example, took the place of Göttingen as the most exciting place for mathematicians.

Scientist and Humanist
Max Born (1882–1970)

Thanks to his informative autobiography we know more about the life of the physicist Max Born than many of the others in this book. He was born on 11 December 1882, in Breslau. His father Gustav was an *Ordinarius* in the university whose contributions to embryology anticipated some modern developments in our knowledge of sex hormones. His mother Margarethe (née Kauffmann) came from a wealthy

Silesian family in textile manufacturing. She was an excellent pianist, and it was probably from her that her son inherited his lifelong love of music. Margarethe died when her son was only four years old, after which Max and his younger sister Käthe were placed under the care of governesses. In 1890 their father married again, but although his second wife Bertha (née Lipstein) proved an admirable stepmother, she never quite replaced Margarethe in the affections of her two stepchildren.

The family home, with its atmosphere of scientific and general culture, provided Born with a stimulating environment during his formative years. His schooling at König Wilhelm Gymnasium in Breslau was of the usual humanistic type, with Latin, Greek, and German as the principal objects of study, along with some mathematics, physics, history, and modern languages. His mathematics teacher Heinrich Maschke, who had taken his PhD at Göttingen under Klein, also taught physics. At this time Marconi's experiments on wireless telegraphy were in the news, and Maschke repeated some of them with his pupils.

Shortly before Born graduated from the gymnasium in 1901 his father died, leaving his son plenty of money and good advice. The money was sufficient in normal times to assure his son's independence. The advice was not to specialize too early at university but to sample lectures on a variety of subjects before coming to any decision on his future career. Born enrolled at the University of Breslau and started by attending courses on chemistry, zoology, philosophy, logic, mathematics, and astronomy. Of these he found the last two subjects most interesting, and he considered becoming an astronomer. He spent the summer semester of 1902 at Heidelberg and the summer semester of 1903 in Zurich, enjoying to the full the amenities and cultural opportunities of these cities. It was at Heidelberg that he met his contemporary James Franck, as we have seen; while in Zurich he was introduced to advanced mathematics through Hurwitz's course on elliptic functions. When he was back in Breslau he was able, at the home of friends of his late father, to meet many writers and musicians, including such celebrities as Gerhart Hauptmann, Ferruccio Busoni, Artur Schnabel, Edwin Fischer, and Carl Flesch.

Once he felt ready to do so, Born transferred to the Georgia Augusta, where he began by attending lectures by Hilbert and Minkowski. Before long Hilbert offered him the unpaid post of *Privat-assistent*, his primary duty being to prepare a fair copy of the professor's lecture notes. The main attraction was the privilege of close contact with Hilbert. The joint seminar Hilbert and Minkowski conducted on the electrodynamics of moving bodies introduced Born to Einstein's special theory of relativity, which had just been published. Later on, he wrote a useful elementary introduction to the theory.

Another seminar which Born attended was one on elasticity which Klein conducted jointly with the applied mathematician Carl Runge. Born, who had offended 'the great Felix' by irregular attendance at his lecture course, was called on to give an account of a problem in elastic stability at very short notice due to a fellow student falling sick. Lacking sufficient time to study the literature, he treated the subject *ab initio*; Klein was so impressed by his performance that with Born in mind as a possible competitor he set the same problem for the annual university prize competition. At first Born refused to enter his name, thus giving further offence to Klein, but eventually he capitulated, submitted his entry, and carried off the prize.

When it came to the oral examination for the doctorate, Born deemed it inadvisable to risk having Klein question him on geometry, which he had intended offering as one of his subjects, so he decided to offer astronomy instead. He was accepted into the astrophysical seminar of Schwarzschild, with whom his relations were better than they had been with Klein, and the doctoral examination in January 1907 passed off successfully with Schwarzschild as examiner in place of the formidable Klein. Born's thesis was based on his prize dissertation on elastic stability; for the rest of his life he retained an affection for this, his first scientific offspring, through which he first tasted the joy of independent investigation of a problem and the satisfaction of finding the predicted results in harmony with experiment.

After taking his doctorate, Born would normally have had to undergo a year's military service, but an asthmatic tendency caused him to be released early. The experience, he tells us in his autobiography, confirmed his antipathy to all things military. A visit of six months' duration to Cambridge followed. As an 'advanced student' at Caius College he attended lectures by J. J. Thomson, among others, which he found most stimulating.

Back in Breslau, Born engaged in some experimental work, but soon turned to theory again. Combining Einstein's special theory of relativity with Minkowski's mathematical foundation, he found a new and more rigorous way of calculating the electromagnetic mass of the electron, and sent the manuscript to Minkowski in Göttingen. As a result, Minkowski invited him to return to the Georgia Augusta to assist him with his work on relativity, but as we have seen this plan was aborted through Minkowski's untimely death. In his autobiography Born relates how downcast he felt by the ruin of all his hopes, and how he again fell foul of Klein, but managed through the good offices of Runge to convince Hilbert of the soundness of his ideas. He also attended theoretical and experimental courses under Woldemar Voigt, who offered Born a position as *Privatdozent*. Among his colleagues was the Hungarian von Kármán, with whom he developed the important Born-Kármán theory of the specific heats of solids. This was the beginning of an ambitious programme of research which was to occupy Born and his pupils for many years, namely the explanation of the physical properties of solids—in particular crystals—on the basis of their lattice structure. Although still a mere *Privatdozent*, he received an invitation from Albert Michelson to visit Chicago in 1912.

The next year Born married Hedwig Ehrenburg, the daughter of the professor of jurisprudence at Göttingen; her forebears included the notoriously anti-Semitic Martin Luther, and between them, she and her husband could claim an extended family of great intellectual distinction. They had three spirited and sometimes turbulent children: Irene, who became a well-known singer, Margaret, and Gustav, who became a prominent biologist.

The outbreak of war in August 1914 coincided with the offer of an *Extra-Ordinarius* post at the University of Berlin, where Born would have Planck as a colleague. Arriving in the capital in the spring of 1915, Born was soon drawn into the war effort, but not before he had completed the manuscript of a book on the dynamics of crystal lattices. After a short time as a radio operator in the air force, he was seconded to the artillery with commissioned rank for research on acoustical range-finding. Characteristically, he conceived it to be his duty to have as many as possible of his former colleagues and students recalled from the front line to work in his section. After the war was over, although living conditions in Germany were extremely difficult, Born was able to appreciate the cultural life of Berlin, particularly the scientific life. Among the physicists he particularly enjoyed the friendship of Einstein, with whom he had long been in correspondence but now could know as a colleague and neighbour. Like his mother, Born was an excellent pianist, who often played violin sonatas with Einstein.

In 1919 Max von Laue, at that time *Ordinarius* in Frankfurt, proposed an exchange of chairs with Born in Berlin in order that he could more easily work with his beloved teacher Max Planck. The exchange was agreed by both universities, and as so Born moved to Frankfurt as professor and director of the institute of theoretical physics. Two years later, he transferred to a similar post at Göttingen, where he was joined by James Franck, as we have seen. During the early years of this, his third period in Göttingen, Born and his students carried on with research on lattice dynamics. He also contributed a long survey article to Klein's encyclopedia of the mathematical sciences, later published as a separate book, and helped to edit the collected works of Gauss.

Before long, Born's chief research interest shifted towards quantum theory, where he was particularly fortunate in having as his junior colleagues Heisenberg and Pauli. During the winter of 1925/6 Born was in America again for a lecture tour, including a course on 'Problems of Atomic Dynamics' at the Massachusetts Institute of Technology (MIT). This was written up and became the first book to be published on the new quantum mechanics. He impressed the officers of the International Education Board, when they came to visit Göttingen in 1926, as 'one of the leading men in mathematical physics in the world and probably still coming up'. They commented on his vigour, good judgement, and savoir faire. Three years later he visited the Soviet Union with a party of European scientists. He had been feeling the strain of directing the institute in Göttingen, which had become a place of pilgrimage for large numbers of young theoretical physicists from all over the world, and, although the Russian tour might have provided a respite, instead it triggered a nervous breakdown which forced him to take sick leave for the following year. He maintained that afterwards he never fully recovered his earlier capacity for intensive work. Nevertheless, the publication in 1933 of his classic textbook, *Principles of Optics,* demonstrated his ability to complete a major undertaking on top of his other commitments, even in a field which was not central to his interests.

In May of that same year Born, being Jewish, was effectively deprived of his Göttingen chair and left Germany for a short rest in the Italian Tyrol. At this time Lindemann, as we know, was touring in Europe to find out whether certain physicists who were about to lose their positions in Germany would be interested in moving to Oxford. In Born's own words,

> We spent the summer in Selva, Val Gardena, and there Lindemann appeared with his car and chauffeur to discuss the political situation with me, in particular the fate of the numerous scientists who lost their positions in Germany. He explained to me his plan to improve the situation by inviting displaced physicists to the Clarendon Laboratory. I was not available because Cambridge had already offered me a post. But I was deeply impressed by the idea which was not only generous to the homeless scientists but also clever and far-sighted in regard to the future of Oxford.

Born went back to Cambridge as Stokes Lecturer and Fellow of Caius College. There he collaborated with Leopold Infeld on a non-linear modification of Clerk Maxwell's electromagnetic theory, which they thought might remove the difficulty of the infinite self-energy of the electron, but the results could not be reconciled with quantum theory. Infeld described the atmosphere in the Born household as a combination of high intellectual level with heavy German pedantry. A kindly, even-tempered, but rather formal person, Born could sometimes become surprisingly inflexible in matters of scientific controversy. Infeld noticed that there was something childish and attractive in his eagerness to go ahead quickly, in his restlessness and his moods, which changed suddenly from high enthusiasm to deep depression. In his enthusiastic attitude, in the vividness of his mind, the impulsiveness with which he grasped and rejected ideas, lay his great charm. While in Cambridge, Born wrote his well-known textbook *Atomic Physics*, which went through numerous editions, and a popular work, *The Restless Universe*. Although he had made several visits to America he never seems to have considered starting a second career there, where he might have been able to revive his partnership with Franck. Instead, after Cambridge he made a visit to the Indian Institute of Sciences in Bangalore, which was hoping to recruit some of the displaced German scientists, and then seriously considered the offer of a more permanent post in Moscow, but just at this time the Tait Chair of Natural Philosophy at the University of Edinburgh fell vacant, and in 1936 Born was appointed.

In Edinburgh, Born rapidly established a research school on the continental model, although he was not altogether successful in grafting this onto the undergraduate teaching in his department. A member of the Born school around 1940 described what it was like.

> When Born arrived in the morning he first used to make the round of his research students, asking them whether they had any progress to report and giving them advice, sometimes presenting them with sheets of elaborate calculations concerning their problems which he had done himself the day before. The apparent ease with which he could switch from one subject to another during this inspection tour was truly amazing. Being such an incredibly fast worker himself he could on occasion become quite impatient when he found that a student had not managed to complete the calculations which had been suggested to him only the day before.

During his seventeen-year tenure of the Edinburgh chair Born made many visits, sometimes extended, to conferences and universities at home and abroad, including congresses in Paris, Bordeaux, and the Soviet Union; he also spent a term in Egypt, and gave the Wayneflete Lectures in Oxford. The war years brought little disturbance to his research routine, apart from a temporary decline in the number of his research students. Although a master of atomic physics, he did not contribute to the efforts that went into the development of the atomic bomb.

After the war Born's research school continued to be active but, when he reached the retirement age of seventy in 1953, the Borns decided to return to Germany and settle at a small and secluded spa within easy reach of Göttingen. His confiscated property and pension rights were restored to him, and (along with Courant and Franck) he was made an honorary citizen of Göttingen. He revised several of his books for new editions, and wrote his autobiography, but his scientific career was essentially over. The award of a shared Nobel Prize in physics in 1954, for his fundamental research in quantum mechanics, especially his statistical interpretation of the wave-function, was one of those occasions where the prize was in recognition of work done long before.

In his later years Born became increasingly active in the cause of the social responsibility of scientists, and wrote and lectured indefatigably on what he saw as the appalling dangers inherent in the technological explosion and the concurrent collapse in ethical standards. In 1957, when the nuclear policy of the Federal Republic of Germany was a matter of active debate, Born was one of the leaders of the 'Göttingen Eighteen' who made public their belief that nuclear armament was a suicidal policy and declared that they would refuse categorically to collaborate in any scientific work associated with nuclear weapons (although Born himself was not religious, his wife Hedwig was a Quaker and an absolute pacifist). He died in hospital on 5 January 1970 at the age of eighty-seven, and she survived him by only two years. Today he is remembered both for the scientific discoveries of his youth and middle age and for the humanism of his later years.

Mathematical Harpooner
Solomon Lefschetz (1884–1972)

When they lived in Moscow, Alexander and Verba Lefschetz had taken out Turkish citizenship, one of the devices used by Jews to escape some of the disabilities to which they were otherwise subject in Russia. Their son Solomon, the future mathematician, was born there on 3 September 1884. His father, who dealt in Oriental carpets, needed to spend much time away from home and decided to move his family from Moscow to Paris. There is little on record concerning his son's early life, except that he went to school in Paris, and that his first language was French. At the age of eighteen he enrolled at the École Centrale des Arts et Manufactures, where the lectures on mathematics were given by men of the calibre of Appel and Picard.

It was difficult for a foreigner to obtain employment in France and so, after obtaining the diploma of *Ingenieur des arts et manufactures,* young Lefschetz tried his fortunes in the United States. After serving a short apprenticeship he became an engineer at the Westinghouse Electric and Manufacturing Company of Pittsburgh until he lost both his hands and forearms in the explosion of an electrical transformer. He returned to Westinghouse briefly after a period in hospital, but then decided to change from engineering to mathematics, and with this in view he became a graduate student at Clark University, which still had a good reputation even after losing many of its original faculty due to financial, managerial, and political problems which made it impossible for it to achieve the aspirations of its founder. Although Clark was quite small, it had several distinguished professors of mathematics, and Lefschetz appreciated the education he received from them. 'At Clark', he recalled, 'there was fortunately a well-kept mathematical library with a first-rate librarian. Just the two of us enjoyed it—my fellow graduate student in mathematics and future wife, and myself. I took advantage of the library to learn about a number of highly interesting new fields, notably about the superb Italian school of algebraic geometry.' Thanks to the good foundations laid in Paris he was able to take his PhD in 1911 with a thesis on algebraic geometry after only one year.

Lefschetz became an American citizen in 1912, after seven years in the country, and the following year married Alice Hayes, his fellow student at Clark. She sacrificed her own professional career to provide him with the home he needed, helping him overcome his initial despair and face up to life. Later, when sometimes his exuberance burst all bounds, she was equally successful in calming him down. He was always grateful to the United States for enabling him to follow his deep bent for mathematics.

After leaving Clark, Lefschetz occupied positions of increasing seniority, first at the University of Nebraska until 1913, and then for the next decade at the University of Kansas. It was during those years in the prairies that he came to terms with his disability, rebuilding his self-confidence and laying the foundations of a new career. As he said himself, his mathematical isolation was complete, and this circumstance was most valuable in that it enabled him to develop his ideas in complete mathematical calm, applying topological methods to the theory of algebraic surfaces, especially the work of the Italian school. He arrived in the prairies unknown in the mathematical world and left fourteen years later recognized as one of the outstanding geometers of the day. As he put it, 'the harpoon of algebraic topology was planted in the whale of algebraic geometry.' The major part of Lefschetz's massive contribution to algebraic geometry was completed before he left Kansas.

In 1924 Lefschetz spent a year visiting Princeton University, at the end of which he was recruited to the faculty. At Princeton he found himself for the first time in close contact with a wide circle of able mathematicians, not only the permanent faculty members but also the numerous distinguished visitors. He selected the graduate students and bullied them into becoming real mathematicians. At his lectures there was a great deal of audience participation (which he was entirely happy with), and the details were hammered out democratically. Lefschetz also asked frequent questions, sometimes pretending not to understand and sometimes to illuminate. Loud, rude, and badly dressed, he was given a wide berth on social occasions.

Lefschetz is quoted as saying that 'people first have to make up their minds and then find their reasons.' His assistant, A. L. Tucker, commented,

> That was so typical of Lefschetz himself: he made up his mind very impulsively and then he gathered various arguments. He was very quick and very imaginative. But he had great difficulty making a rigorous argument. I've heard it said that any proof Lefschetz would give would be wrong, but any result he announced would be right. He had a tremendously sound intuition, but he was just so restless and impatient that he wouldn't take the time to make rigorous arguments.
>
> He was very outspoken; indeed, many people found him quite offensive, and sometimes this had unfortunate results: several graduate students left Princeton because of the harsh talkings-to he gave them. He meant well, but he usually spoke really without thinking. People who would give him back as good as he gave impressed him; the people who just curled up under the harsh things that he often said, he had no respect for. Although he was very often right, Lefschetz could make major mistakes … even when he knew he was wrong, he would never admit it, at least not then and there. We had some very fierce arguments and I would go away thinking I hadn't gotten anywhere at all with him. But a day or so later I would find he had accepted the argument I had made and was going ahead with that.

There can be no doubt that some people, notably Birkhoff at Harvard, deeply disliked Lefschetz, and that came to a head in 1934 when he was proposed for election to the presidency of the American Mathematical Society. In the event Lefschetz was duly elected but beforehand Birkhoff wrote to the secretary of the society a private letter which included the passage: 'I have a feeling that Lefschetz will be likely to be less pleasant even than he had been, in that from now on he will try to work strongly and positively for his own race. They are exceedingly confident of their own power and influence in the good old USA ... He will be very cocky, very racial, and use the *Annals* as a good deal of racial perquisite. The racial interests will get deeper as Einstein's and all of them do.'

Nevertheless, Lefschetz did not seem to create many enemies, whatever he might say, because it was felt that there was no trace of malice behind his words. He had an extraordinary capacity to inspire affection, even devotion. According to Tucker, 'He would never refer to his artificial hands. He would never say, "You'll have to do that for me, I can't do it." Instead he made a simple polite request for anything he needed to have done: "please open that door".'

In the mid-1930s the Soviet Academy of Sciences began to sponsor a series of international conferences, of which the first one, held in Moscow in September 1935, was devoted to topology. America was strongly represented by Alexander and Lefschetz from Princeton, Whitney from Harvard, and Zariski from Johns Hopkins. Lefschetz tried to obtain travel grants from the Rockefeller Foundation for some lesser-known American participants, but without success. A second such conference was planned to be held in Warsaw in 1939 but had to be cancelled because of the war.

During the Second World War Lefschetz became a consultant for the United States Navy on guidance systems and the stability of ships. The Navy found that mathematicians could be useful to it, and so in the postwar period an Office of Naval Research was established, which became a valuable source of funding for research in the mathematical sciences. Through it Lefschetz was able to develop at Princeton a major centre for the study of ordinary differential equations, a field hitherto neglected in America, although not in the Soviet Union. Although this activity was wound down after 1953, following his retirement from the university, he was able to re-establish it a few years later within the Research Institute for Advanced Study in Baltimore, funded by industry rather than the federal government. In this form it rapidly gained an international reputation for its work, particularly on the mathematical theory of control and stability. Finally, in 1959, his research group was adopted by Brown University, to form a Center for Dynamical Systems.

Throughout his life Lefschetz loved to travel. In the 1920s and 1930s he made many visits to Europe, especially to France, Italy, and the Soviet Union. During the Second World War, when normal European travel was impossible, Lefschetz devoted his energies to promoting mathematical studies in Mexico. Although he knew no Spanish when he first arrived there, within several weeks he was giving lectures in that language. He went to Mexico City almost every year from 1944 to 1966. In recognition of his achievements in establishing a lively Mexican research school in mathematics, he was awarded the Order of the Aztec Eagle to add to a long list of other distinctions, including the Feltrinelli Prize of the Lincei and the American National Medal of Science. Solomon Lefschetz died in Princeton on 5 October 1972 at the age of eighty-eight.

Gentle Genius
Niels Bohr (1885–1961)

The first of these profiles was of the mathematician Carl Jacobi, younger brother of the physicist Moritz. Now we come to another pair of brothers, the elder Niels a world-famous physicist, the younger Harald an able mathematician, already mentioned in the profile of Landau, but overshadowed by Niels. Inseparable in childhood they remained close throughout life. They had an older sister, Jenny, who studied first history at the University of Copenhagen and then English at Oxford before embarking on a career in schoolteaching, but she later became mentally ill and died at the age of fifty. Their mother Ellen, a generous, intelligent, and liberal woman, came from the wealthy Jewish Adler family, prominent in Danish banking and parliamentary circles. Their father Christian was a university professor, a famous physiologist and lover of science, who was also the founder of the university football club. The three Bohr children were brought up in a patrician home of culture where they were exposed to a world of ideas in animated debates in which conflicting views were examined rationally and in good humour, and they developed a respect for all those who seek deeper knowledge and understanding.

Niels Henrik David, the elder son, was born in Copenhagen on 7 October 1885. At school he was academically successful without being outstanding. Later, looking back, he recalled that 'my interest in the study of physics was awakened while I was still at school, largely owing to the influence of my father.' As well as a growing interest in physics and mathematics, he early displayed an ability to inspire affection in others, forming friendships at school that were to last a lifetime. For a glimpse of him as a schoolboy we have some reminiscences by classmates: 'in those days Niels was tall, rather coarse of limb, and strong as a bear. He was not afraid to use his strength when it came to blows during the break between classes. He seemed to be quite an ordinary boy, gifted but not smug, a promising honours student, but otherwise a young man like the rest of us.'

It was at the University of Copenhagen that Niels Bohr's potential as a scientist was first recognized. In 1907, at the age of twenty, he was awarded the Gold Medal of the Royal Danish Academy of Sciences and Letters for a prize exercise on the measurement of surface tension by the study of vibrating fluid jets. This careful and complete piece of research, both experimental and theoretical, drew upon and extended the work of Lord Rayleigh, and served later on to give Bohr particular insight in his liquid model of the atomic nucleus.

In 1910 Niels Bohr met his future wife Margrethe Nerlund, the daughter of a pharmacist, and they became engaged the following year. Before marriage, he made the first of many visits to Britain, to the Cavendish Laboratory, still presided over by J. J. Thomson. Bohr failed to interest Thomson in the work he had been doing on the theory of metals; instead Thomson suggested some rather routine research project which the young Dane tackled without enthusiasm. Bohr spent his first few months in England feeling fairly frustrated until on a weekend visit to friends in Manchester he met and impressed Rutherford, who had recently devised his new model of the atom.

The association between the exuberant experimenter from New Zealand and the thoughtful young Danish theoretician developed and deepened into a kind of father–son relationship during a quarter-century of friendship and collaboration. Although their personalities were very different, Bohr and Rutherford became close friends. In Manchester Bohr found a stimulating atmosphere and congenial colleagues. It was there, in the spring and early summer of 1912, during a period of almost continuous research, that he made several important contributions to atomic physics.

In August 1912 Niels and Margrethe were married in the town hall of Slagelse, where she had been brought up. They took their honeymoon in Scotland, calling at Cambridge and Manchester en route. During the years leading up to the First World War Bohr held some fairly junior appointments at the University of Copenhagen. It was at this period that Courant first met him; he described Bohr as a somewhat introverted, saintly, extremely friendly, yet also shy young man. Throughout his life Bohr spoke with a quiet voice, hardly above a whisper, and listeners had trouble understanding him in any language. He was always concerned about hurting any person's feelings. Also, he had great difficulty in making definite plans, only too often changing them almost as soon as they had been arranged. An assiduous correspondent, he left a legacy of interesting and apparently spontaneous letters: in fact they were far from spontaneous but, like his scientific papers, only reached their final form after multiple drafts and painstaking revisions. As early as 1911 he began enlisting the aid of an amanuensis—at first his mother and, later on, his sons, his colleagues, or his wife.

Bohr spent the early years of the First World War in Manchester, working with Rutherford, while trying to obtain a more senior post in Copenhagen. In Rutherford's gift, as Langworthy Professor, there was a personally endowed readership in mathematical physics, and he used this to bring Bohr to Manchester. Niels and Margrethe enjoyed the care-free life of Manchester very much: 'we have met with so much kindness and feel so much at ease.' Bohr and Rutherford had much in common scientifically; their collaboration was one of the most brilliant, fertile, and fortunate in the history of science. Both were capable of enormous enthusiasm for a promising idea in physics. Both refused to be deflected by unimportant details, although they could give painstaking attention to detail when it mattered. Both regarded mathematics as an important tool in formulating and applying the laws of physics, but never as an end in itself. Rutherford was fond of making disparaging remarks about theoreticians who were too attached to formal mathematics, so much so that he is sometimes believed to have been opposed to theory altogether. Bohr was too polite for such remarks, but restricted himself to the minimum of mathematics in his own work. Both were untidy lecturers but could fascinate and stimulate an audience.

In 1916 Bohr heard that a new chair in theoretical physics was being created at his *alma mater* and that he was expected to become the first holder. When Rutherford wrote a letter of recommendation for him it was in no uncertain terms: 'in my opinion Dr Bohr is one of the most promising and able of the younger mathematical physicists in Europe today. I think any university would be fortunate who is able to acquire the services of such an original and fruitful investigator.' So in 1916 Bohr returned to Denmark as the first professor of theoretical physics at the University of Copenhagen. As soon as the war was over, young physicists began flocking to the Danish capital, where research could be pursued in an atmosphere free of politics.

Also in 1916, the Bohrs' first child, Christian Alfred, was born. Five more sons followed: Hans Henrik (1918), Erik (1919), Aage Niels (1922), Ernest David (1924), and Harald (1928). Hans, in later life, gave a picture of the family milieu in which he grew up: 'father always took an interest in us and from the beginning tried to teach us something about the things he himself liked best and thought important ... the dinner table was generally a meeting-place at which father was eager to hear what each of us had done, and to relate what he had been doing himself ... he was no doubt not a teacher in the accepted sense of the word, but if you were patient and listened, a wide and rich perspective opened up ... he was nearly always occupied with one problem or another.'

Although still only thirty-one years old when he returned to Copenhagen, Bohr's subsequent influence was exerted not so much through his own original research as through the way he inspired others, for whom he provided an ideal place for scientific work. He began to delve into the logical and philosophical foundations of physics. Even his first papers from Copenhagen are often essays in search of verbal understanding rather than mathematical analyses of crucial problems. His lecturing style was a discursive mumble, but with small groups and especially in one-to-one discussions he was unequalled in his enthusiasm, his empathy, and his contagious love for the subject. He wrote many scientific and other papers in the course of his life, but never a full-scale book. In what he said or wrote he was always conscious of the many limitations and conditions that restrict the validity of any statement; as he liked to express it: 'truth and clarity are complementary.'

Bohr found an invaluable assistant in Hendrik Antonie Kramers, a young physicist who had previously studied with Lorentz and Ehrenfest in Leiden and first came to Copenhagen as a place where science could be pursued in an atmosphere free of politics. The two men worked together, not only collaborating on scientific papers but also on the planning and administration of the new university institute of theoretical physics, later to be named the Niels Bohr Institute. Despite the original name, it was to undertake experimental as well as theoretical research. Within a very few years of its opening in 1921, this unpretentious building in the chief city of a small country was to become one of the best-known centres of physics in the world. The list of visitors over the next two decades—some of whom came for a few weeks, some for months or even years—reads like a roll-call of the founders of quantum mechanics. Small, informal but very intense conferences were often held there. This intensely interactive enterprise, constantly changing in membership but always led and shaped by the mind and personality of Niels Bohr, came to be known as the Copenhagen school of physics. In his forties, the jovial Bohr became a father-figure to scores of young physicists from all over the world. Bohr had enormous charm; people could not resist calling him 'the Great Dane'.

In 1918 Bohr was awarded the Nobel Prize in physics 'for his services in the investigation of the structure of atoms and of the radiation emanating from them'. In his acceptance speech, Bohr surveyed the state of quantum theory and the progress that had been made in applying it to the problems of atomic structure, but he took pains to point out the limitations and weaknesses of the theory. He was more acutely aware of these and more perturbed by them than were others who had accepted his ideas less critically.

After the Nobel Prize Bohr received honours from academies, universities, and other institutions too numerous to mention. In 1921 Planck wrote to him about the possibility of moving to Berlin, and Rutherford sounded him about opportunities in England. But Bohr's attachment to his native land was too great; all he was prepared to do was offer to make visits. In 1923 he went to America for the first time, and while he concluded that he would not like to live there he was happy to make visits to the United States and later on take advantage of American philanthropy.

In 1930 Bohr's mother Ellen died (she had lost her husband in 1911), and further distress was caused in 1934 when the Bohrs' first-born child, Christian, was drowned when sailing out at sea with his father and some friends; he was just seventeen years old, not uninterested in science but more interested in the arts, especially poetry. That year Bohr made his first visit to the Soviet Union, where he was impressed by what he was shown, and three years later he made a world tour including China and Japan as well as Russia. His wife Margrethe generally accompanied him on these longer journeys.

At Carlsberg, near Copenhagen, the Carlsberg Foundation owned a beautiful mansion which was given to be used by 'an outstanding citizen of Denmark, most prominent in science or literature or the arts'. In 1931 it was offered to Bohr for the rest of his life, and the Bohrs moved there the next year from their quarters in the institute, where they had for many years offered hospitality to physicists from all over the world. The mansion, which was ideal for entertaining, became not only a family home for the Bohrs' children and grandchildren, but also a haven for the many young colleagues and visitors who stayed there and a convivial meeting-place for scientists, artists, and politicians from all over the world.

Over the next few years Bohr continued to develop his ideas, both in physics and in epistemology. He published works dealing with the problem of measurement in quantum electrodynamics; an essay entitled 'Light and Life', explaining how the complementarity principle could be applied to biology; and a paper entitled 'Can the quantum-mechanical description of reality be considered complete?', a response to the well-known paper by Einstein and others with the same title. When Bohr and Einstein first met at the Solvay conference of 1920 Einstein presented an extended critique of his interpretation of quantum mechanics. This led to a famous series of discussions which, conducted with mutual pleasure and respect, continued for many years and became part dialogue, part duel, and part crusade. They disagreed on many things, including causality, the meaning of relativity, and the incompleteness of quantum-mechanical descriptions. For nearly twenty-five years each tried to convince the other, by ingenious argument and subtle logic. Eventually Bohr's interpretation of quantum mechanics became the orthodox view. Even today there are deep problems with quantum theory, although it works so remarkably well in practice, and there are many who agree with Einstein that a better theory must be found.

In 1940 Germany occupied Denmark. At first there was a fiction of self-rule, but this did not last. The institute continued to function, but Bohr's own role changed. As a public figure and a focus of national admiration and pride, he felt a responsibility to help maintain Danish science and culture under the prevailing conditions. By August 1943 the position of the Danish Jews had become perilous, and the following month Hitler ordered that they were to be rounded up and deported in two freighters which had docked in Copenhagen. Some were caught, but the great majority were smuggled in fishing-boats across the sound to Sweden in the greatest mass-rescue operation of the war. Bohr himself left Denmark for Sweden in this way, and spent some time there making sure that the refugees would be well treated. Crossing the Kattegat was for him only the first stage in a journey to Britain, arranged by the British government. His son Aage, also a brilliant physicist, followed a few days later, and they went on together to America. In London Bohr was briefed on what was then known as the Directorate of Tube Alloys, the precursor of the Anglo-American Manhattan project, which came as a revelation to him. He was asked if he would work on it, but as he remarked later, 'they did not need my help in making the atom bomb.'

Once in the United States, Bohr ran into security problems because of his firm belief that the Soviet Union should be made aware of what was going on at Los Alamos. Although scientifically interested in the progress being made towards the production of the fission bomb, Bohr turned his attention almost immediately to the political significance of the project and to the need for early and clear recognition of the threat it would pose to postwar stability. Although by no means the only nuclear physicist to do so, he was one of the most active in trying to influence public opinion. In the spring of 1944 Bohr returned to London, in the hope of conveying his concerns to the British prime minister, Winston Churchill. With some misgiving Lindemann, who was now Churchill's scientific adviser, arranged a meeting but Bohr never succeeded in getting his message across. He was more successful later when, on his return to America, he had an audience with President Roosevelt, who was impressed by him at the time but afterwards had second thoughts. A few months later, after Churchill and Roosevelt had met privately at the latter's Hyde Park estate in the Hudson Valley, Churchill sent a note to Lindemann:

> the President and I are much worried about Professor Bohr. How did he come into this business? He is a great advocate of publicity. He says that he is in close correspondence with a Russian professor [Piotr Kapitza], an old friend of his in Russia, to whom he had written about the matter and may be writing still. The Russian professor had urged him to go to Russia in order to discuss matters. What is all this about? It seems to me that Bohr ought to be confined or at any rate made to see he is very near the edge of mortal crimes … I do not like it at all.

In the autumn of 1945 Bohr returned to his family and colleagues and once again took up his role as honoured teacher and stimulating friend of a new generation of physicists. He devoted much time and thought to promoting a sane and realistic policy for nuclear armaments, but his proposals for openness and free exchange of information were never practical politics.

In Denmark, Bohr, as a highly respected elder statesman, was called upon to guide the government's policy on atomic energy. For the next ten years much of his time was given to the detailed planning and completion of the research establishment of the Danish Atomic Energy commission at Risø. In 1955 he reached the mandatory retirement age for a university professor, and was succeeded in his chair by his son Aage, likewise a Nobel laureate, while Niels continued as director of the institute.

At the beginning of the 1960s, Bohr and his colleagues began to plan for a meeting in 1963 to celebrate the fiftieth anniversary of the publication of the original research on atomic structure. They hoped to revive the intimate atmosphere of the interwar Copenhagen meetings by inviting back members of the institute from those years and giving them the opportunity to review the past half-century of progress and to speculate about what the future might hold. But before this could happen Niels Bohr died suddenly in his seventy-seventh year at his Carlsberg home on the afternoon of 18 November 1962; the cause was given as heart failure. Nevertheless, the planned reunion was held, and many of the surviving members of the Copenhagen School returned to exchange their latest opinions and ideas, as he would have wished. Afterwards, at the invitation of Margrethe Bohr and her sons, they gathered once more in the beautiful mansion which they had come to know so well. She survived him by twenty-two years.

Finally, a few words about Harald Bohr, the younger brother of Niels, who was born in Copenhagen in 1887. He was described as an attractive child, full of bubbling life, thoroughly kind and helpful, quick at everything, intelligent, and full of information. He loved to tease those around him, and knew how to be impertinent. At seventeen he enrolled at the University of Copenhagen to study mathematics, and showed such promise that Edmund Landau invited him to come and work on his PhD thesis in Göttingen. The peaceful old town became a second home for Harald, who was fortunate to know it during that glorious period in the history of mathematics which is associated with the name of Hilbert.

There is no room here for a detailed account of Harald's successful but relatively unadventurous career, much of it spent administering the institute for mathematics, funded by the Carlberg Foundation, which was established by the University of Copenhagen adjacent to the one for theoretical physics. When the Nazis forced scientists and other intellectuals to leave Germany, the Bohr brothers became deeply involved with a Danish group that had been formed to offer them support. Their two institutes acted as a temporary haven for many of the refugees, while the brothers dedicated themselves to helping them find suitable positions. Like other Danish Jews, Harald took refuge in Sweden in 1943, where he was able to do much for the welfare of Danish youth in Sweden. After the war he became provost of one of the old student colleges of his *alma mater* and made his home among the students. By this time he was in declining health and at the beginning of 1953 he died in hospital after surgery.

Simple Means, Powerful Results
George Pólya (1887–1985)

Budapest produced an extraordinary constellation of Jewish scholars and scientists between 1890, say, and 1930. The city began to enjoy a renaissance when it became the capital of the separate kingdom of Hungary in 1867. The next year most of the discriminatory laws against the Jews were repealed and as a result the city rapidly acquired a large Jewish population; by the turn of the century close to a quarter of the population of Budapest was Jewish. Initially they came from Austria and Germany, but later more from eastern Europe. Details can be found in McCagg (1972), Dent (1990), and Patai (1996). The business elite became almost entirely Jewish, and as they prospered so did the artistic and intellectual life of the city. Jews also moved into the professions: law, medicine, engineering, the sciences, and teaching. Among them were the mathematicians Artur Erdélyi (1909–1977), Leopold Fejér (1880–1959), Alfred Haar (1885–1933), Georg Pólya (1887–1985), Tibor Radó (1895–1965), Gabor Szegó (1895–1985), Béla von Kerékjártó (1898–1946), and Johann von Neumann (1903–1957). There were also physicists of similar calibre.

Out of this galaxy of talent I choose to profile the mathematician Gyorgy (George) Pólya, who was born in Budapest on 13 December 1887. His Jewish father Jakab practised as a lawyer in an insurance company but also held a position at the university; his mother Anna (née Deutch) was said to be of higher social status than her husband. The couple had six children, of whom one died soon after birth. The eldest son became an eminent surgeon but was murdered by the Nazis towards the end of the Second World War; the youngest, who was also highly gifted, lost his life in the First World War. Both the surviving daughters worked for the same insurance company as their father.

Although some of the best schools in Budapest encouraged scientific talent, the one Pólya attended provided a good general education but was not strong in mathematics. At the university, after trying law, he spent two years mainly studying literature and linguistics. He then tried other subjects; he was not impressed by philosophy, found physics too difficult, and in the end chose mathematics as a compromise. The leading mathematician at the university at that time was Fejér, already an *Ordinarius* at the age of thirty-one. Pólya, who seems to have taken him as a role model, described him as follows: 'He had artistic tastes. He deeply loved music and was a good pianist. He carefully cultivated his talent of raconteur; when he told, with characteristic little gestures, of the little shortcomings of a certain great mathematician, he was irresistible. The hours spent in continental coffee houses with Fejér discussing mathematics and telling stories are a cherished recollection for many of us.'

In 1911 Pólya spent a year at the University of Vienna, which was also enjoying something of a golden age for mathematics led by the geometer Wilhelm Wirtinger, a close friend of Felix Klein. There was a great contrast in atmosphere between the two capitals of the Dual Monarchy. It was not easy to be a Jew in Vienna, especially a Jew with aspirations. The widespread anti-Semitism poisoned student organizations, university politics, and social relationships. Pólya returned to Budapest with relief, although the university was less distinguished. Jews represented one quarter of all university students and nearly half those at the Budapest Technical University. By this time Jews owned 37.5 per cent of the farmland and constituted 51 per cent of all lawyers, 60 per cent of doctors, and

80 per cent of financiers, although they made up only 5 per cent of the Hungarian population.

After graduating Pólya spent two years at the Georgia Augusta, where Hilbert was in his prime. The young Hungarian was able to hear him lecturing on the theory of partial differential equations, on the mathematical foundations of physics, and on the foundations of mathematics. He also heard Toeplitz lecture on invariant theory, Carathéodory on calculus of variations, and Hecke on algebraic number fields. He heard Weyl, at that time a mere *Privatdozent*, lecture on integral equations and their applications in mathematical physics. He heard Landau lecture on infinite series, particularly Fourier series. Landau also gave a course on mathematical problems, the kind of mathematics which before long was to become a speciality of Pólya's. In later years he would often reminisce about his experiences at the Georgia Augusta, where but for an accident he might have been taken on as a *Privatdozent*. One day when he was returning to Göttingen by train after a vacation, Pólya was trying to place his suitcase on the luggage rack when it fell down and hit a German passenger, a university student who proved to have an influential father. Tempers flared and there was talk of a duel. When the university authorities became aware of this Pólya was told he had to leave, so early in 1914 he moved to Paris.

Despite the death of Poincaré, Paris still boasted a constellation of mathematical luminaries comparable with those in Göttingen. Some of the great professors Pólya found intimidating, but not Hadamard, whose famous seminar at the Collège de France he attended. Although Pólya stayed in the city less than a year, at least it gave him time to become reasonably fluent in French and to establish lasting friendships with some of the French mathematicians.

When the ETH offered Pólya the position of *Privatdozent* he accepted it with alacrity; he had been considering moving back to Budapest but Zurich suited him much better. One of the attractions was Hurwitz, who had succeeded Frobenius as *Ordinarius*. He got to know Hurwitz well, and later wrote:

> From the time of my appointment there in 1914 until his death, I was in constant touch with him. We had a special way we worked. I would visit

him and we would sit in his study and talk mathematics—seldom anything else—until he finished his cigar. Then we would go for a walk, continuing the mathematical discussion. His health was not too good so when we walked it had to be on level ground, not always easy in the hilly part of Zurich, and if we went up hill, we walked very slowly. My connection with Hurwitz was deeper and my debt to him greater than to any other colleague.

Göttingen had once tried to recruit Hurwitz, and when he died in 1919 Hilbert wrote his obituary, describing him as a harmonious spirit, a modest, friendly, unassuming, and unambitious man, whose vivid eyes revealed his spirit. Pólya played a leading role in editing his collected works.

After the death of Hurwitz, Pólya began to consider returning to Germany, and when a position at Frankfurt became vacant he applied for it, unsuccessfully. Weyl was asked to comment on the candidates:

> First of all there is Pólya. His way of doing mathematics is completely foreign to me. He is less concerned with knowledge than with the joy of the hunt. However I admire his brilliance. His ideas are certainly not of the type which would cast light on the major relationships of knowledge. His papers are rather single, bold advances toward very specific limited points in an undiscovered land which will remain totally in the dark. But his questions are somewhat unusual. He is full of problems, and is an exceptionally stimulating person in mathematical circles. As an educator he may be somewhat hindered by his anxious desire to temper his investigations to well-defined, precise problems; however he cares about his students in a way that is best described as 'sincere fellowship'. As far as applied mathematics is concerned, he is especially strong on probability theory, and has also published in that field. In addition he is also very knowledgeable in applications (physics, statistics, etc.).

Pólya was afraid that, as a Jew, his appointment might be obstructed by the Weimar authorities, but apparently the main objection was a belief that he was a socialist, that he was a pacifist, and that he had a bad temper. In 1924 Hardy had invited Pólya to spend a year in Oxford; in the end Cambridge was included as well. At the time he and his colleague

Littlewood were trying further to reform the notorious Cambridge Tripos examination. They asked Pólya to take the papers set that year, in the expectation that he would not have much success with such artificial, contrived problems and would thereby strengthen their case for reform, by showing that such a distinguished foreign mathematician would have failed to do well in the Tripos. They were rather disconcerted when Pólya did better than any of the normal candidates. Otherwise the visit was a success, and Hardy and Pólya became firm friends. They wrote several joint papers, but most notably they and Littlewood collaborated on the book *Inequalities,* which appeared in 1934. Later, when Pólya was applying for promotion, Hardy wrote a letter of recommendation that included the following comments:

> I have a very high opinion of Pólya both as a mathematician and as a person, an opinion which was greatly strengthened during his stay here. I feel too that it is very probable that the best has not yet been seen of him; that he has, perhaps, got a little discouraged during recent years; and that the encouragement derived from an improvement in his position would be very likely to stimulate him to even better work. He always seemed to feel that his leisure was scanty, and that he dare not risk squandering any part of it on a difficult problem that might lead nowhere; and of course when a fine mathematician begins to feel like that there is always a serious danger that he may not do justice to his powers.

Shortly before or after arriving in Zurich, Pólya had met his compatriot Gabor Szegö while on a brief visit to Budapest, and became his mentor. Szegö was seven years younger than Pólya. After taking his PhD at the University of Vienna in 1918, following war service, Szegö held a *Privatdozent*ship first at Berlin and then at the Albertina, where he reached professorial rank in 1926. He remained there until the Nazis dismissed Jewish professors eight years later, when he emigrated to the United States, eventually settling down at Stanford University. The two Hungarians shared an interest in posing and solving problems, which led to their classic two-volume *Aufgaben und Lehrsatze aus der Analysis* (Problems and Theorems in Analysis) of 1925.

In 1928 Pólya was appointed *Ordinarius* at the ETH, and soon afterwards completed the lengthy process of becoming a Swiss citizen. By this time he had been married ten years. His Swiss wife, Stella, was the daughter of a professor of physics at the University of Neuchâtel. They acquired a chalet at Engelberg, in the Swiss Alps, where they used to entertain their friends during the 1930s. Although Pólya liked to travel he was afraid to return to Hungary because, in the First World War, he had not served in the army, partly on medical grounds but also because of his pacifist views. He accepted various invitations to spend time as a visiting lecturer, including one in 1929 from Paris and another three years later from Göttingen, just before it was ruined by the Nazis. The most significant of these invitations, as it turned out, was one to spend half of 1933 in the United States, three months at Princeton University followed by three at Stanford.

In 1940 the Pólyas left for America, believing that even Switzerland was not a safe haven for Jews. At first he was offered only temporary appointments, albeit at first-class universities, but by 1942 he had joined his friend Szegö at Stanford University as an assistant professor. Pólya had always been interested in the techniques of problem-solving, especially in heuristical methods, and now he wrote a book about it, entitled *How to Solve It*. He had some trouble finding a publisher, but when it came out in 1945 it proved to be a huge success. After he retired from Stanford in 1953 he followed this up with two more books of general interest: *Mathematics and Plausible Reasoning* (1954) and the two-volume *Mathematical Discovery* (1962, 1964).

By this time Pólya was in his seventies, but still full of energy. He had always been considered an exceptional teacher, and in 1955 he started a series of summer institutes for high school and college teachers, in each of which he played an active part, indeed was the star attraction. Always the showman, he used visual aids as much as possible. His whole approach was the opposite of that of the promoters of the excessively rigorous 'new mathematics'.

Honours descended on Pólya relatively late, presumably because he was so different from the standard model of academic mathematician. In 1947 he became a citizen of the United States and was elected a corresponding member of the Paris Academy. Among other such

memberships, he received that of the United States National Academy
of Sciences in 1976, when he was almost ninety; many felt this honour was
long overdue. Pólya died in Palo Alto on 7 September 1985, aged ninety-
seven, having suffered a stroke shortly before. The first two volumes of
his collected works appeared in 1974, and the remainder ten years later.
In the preface a colleague wrote: 'All his work radiates the cheerfulness
of his personality, wonderful taste, crystal clear methodology, simple
means, powerful results.'

Born to Organize
Richard Courant (1888–1972)

The subject of the next profile is the man
who brought to fulfilment Klein's vision of
a mathematical institute in Göttingen and
then, after the Nazis largely ruined that, started again in the United States
and tried, with considerable success, to develop a similar institution in
New York. Like Klein, Mittag-Leffler, and Veblen, he is an example of the
type of mathematician who, while notable as a teacher and researcher,
is even more remarkable for his ability to lead, influence, and organize.
The mathematical world needs people who can get things done, and few
have achieved as much as Richard Courant.

Richard Courant was born on 17 February 1887 in the small German
(now Polish) town of Lublinitz in Upper Silesia. His parents Siegmund
and Martha lived in a house belonging to Siegmund's father, which was
shared with several other members of the family. A second son, Fritz,
was born in 1888, followed by a third son two years later. By that time
Siegmund had left the family business, in which he had worked from an

early age, and acquired one of his own in the nearby town of Glatz. The family first moved to Glatz and then in 1895 moved again to Breslau, where Richard, having begun his schooling in Glatz, attended the local gymnasium. However, the family business, in which Siegmund was still involved, ran into difficulties, and Siegmund was left bankrupt. From then on Richard's parents, who moved to Berlin, were always in financial straits, and one consequence was that Richard had to start earning his living as a private tutor while still at school.

Courant was already attending lectures at the university, and once he had graduated from school he enrolled as a regular student. Originally, he had intended to specialize in physics, but when he found the teaching old-fashioned and of poor quality he switched to mathematics. There too he found the teaching uninspiring, and after consulting Toeplitz, a former student who was by then a *Privatdozent* at the Georgia Augusta, he resolved to transfer to Göttingen. Before doing so, he spent a semester in Zurich to attend the lectures of Hurwitz, from whom Hilbert had learnt so much. By 1907 Courant was at the Georgia Augusta and quickly fell under Hilbert's spell.

Although Göttingen was an idyllic little town, a medieval poem, beautifully situated on the slopes of the Hainberg, the place reeked of tanning from the local industry. Living conditions for a poor student like Courant were less than idyllic. Rooms were dirty, food poor, washing facilities scanty. 'We used to bathe in the Leine—it was the only effective way to get a bath, and incidentally the Leine was not a particularly clean river,' reported a fellow student. Initially, Courant felt lonely and disappointed in the quality of the lectures. This changed when Hilbert agreed to accept him as a member of his seminar, which was dealing with mathematical physics. That committed Courant into giving a talk on an assigned topic, in his case the theory of electrostatic and related electromagnetic phenomena. His first attempt was not a success, but at least it brought him to the notice of those present. When he tried again the next week his talk was well received and after that he began to feel at home. Hilbert invited him to attend the weekly meetings of the Mathematical Society, much to Klein's disapproval.

The height of Courant's ambition at this stage was to be taken on as Hilbert's *Privat-assistent*, as Max Born had been. When the position became vacant in 1908 there was much competition for this privilege, and Courant was delighted to be chosen. 'My greatest good fortune', he would say afterwards. The course Hilbert was giving at this time was on analysis. Courant was expected to research the literature for the lectures and to write them up afterwards.

Courant's doctoral dissertation was called 'On the applications of Dirichlet's principle to the problems of conformal mapping'. Unfortunately, anything to do with uniformization tended to be taken over by Hilbert's colleague Paul Koebe, who had a reputation for helping himself to other people's ideas. That is what happened in Courant's case, but at least it did not stop him obtaining his degree. Koebe left Göttingen, while Courant prepared for the obligatory year of military service. Rather to his own surprise, Courant found army life to his liking. When the year was over he returned to Göttingen, despite an attractive offer from Marburg, and in 1912 completed a thesis on the calculus of variations, especially the controversial Dirichlet principle, for the habilitation. Shortly afterwards he married a fellow mathematician, Nelly Neumann, two years older than himself and sufficiently well-off to end all his financial worries.

When the First World War broke out Courant found himself back in the army. Like so many of his contemporaries, he was eager to serve and naively expected that the war would end quickly in a German victory. To Jews, especially, it provided an ideal opportunity to demonstrate their loyalty to their adopted country. Twelve months later he had been injured in the fighting and, while convalescing, received a visit from his wife to say that she was seeking a divorce. A few months later he was back on active service, no longer in the infantry, but working on a system of field communication by wireless, which eventually was adopted by the army.

The divorce having gone through, Courant fell in love with Nerina Runge, usually known as Nina, and in 1919 they were married. Her father, the applied mathematician, was rector of the Georgia Augusta at the time. At first Göttingen society disapproved of the marriage because Courant was Jewish and because of the divorce; it was said that he had concluded that the homely Nelly would not be able to further his ambitions. The second marriage proved to be a success, although Courant was something of a womanizer all his life.

Post-war Göttingen had plenty of students, with the men returning from the war, and Courant, by this time a *Privatdozent*, was kept busy. Courant was always interested in politics, especially when they affected science and the university. At Klein's suggestion he stood for election to the town council and was successful. Even before the war was over, he had been in contact with the publishing house of Springer about a series of mathematics books in which the links with physics would be emphasized. This materialized as the famous *Grundlehren der Mathematischen Wissenschaften* (Principles of the Mathematical Sciences), of which Courant was to be editor for many years.

When Klein retired in 1913 his chair was filled first by Constantine Carathéodory and then by Erich Hecke, who moved on to Hamburg in 1919. This left the Göttingen chair vacant again, and both Klein and Hilbert would have liked Courant to be appointed. However, since the ministry of culture would not have approved an internal promotion of this nature, it was settled that Courant would instead move to nearby Münster while waiting until the time was ripe for him to return to Göttingen. In fact this took less than a year; although Klein was old and weary he could still get things done.

Courant soon began to take over from Klein the 'mathematical arrangements', and people began to refer to 'Courant's' mathematical school. He set out not only to attract to the Georgia Augusta exceptionally able young people, such as Emil Artin and Carl Ludwig Siegel, but also to lure back some of those who had left for chairs elsewhere. By common consent, Weyl, then in Zurich, was first priority. Already in 1918 when a vacancy occurred in philosophy Courant tried to get Weyl appointed, without success. However, four years later Courant had negotiated an additional chair in mathematics and it was offered to Weyl. By this time inflation was rampant in Germany and the political situation highly uncertain. Characteristically, Weyl hesitated. After much delay he set out for the telegraph office with his acceptance; by the time he got there he had changed his mind and sent a refusal instead.

While Germany descended deeper into economic and political turmoil Courant was enjoying one of the most fruitful periods of his career. Hurwitz had died at the end of 1919 and Courant, although he had felt Hurwitz's lectures to be too polished to be truly inspiring, strongly believed that they should be made available to a wider audience than just the Zurich students. These lectures were on function theory, in the spirit of Weierstrass; they were straightforward, precise, and remarkable for their clarity and aesthetic qualities. Much as Courant admired them, he felt a need to balance them with the Riemannian approach which was geometrical rather than analytical, intuitive rather than axiomatic. So he added a chapter inspired more by the ideas of physics than those of pure mathematics. One reader said, 'It gives the impression of being the work of a mind endowed with fine intuitive faculties, but lacking in the discipline and critical sense which beget confidence,' but another described it as the most breathtaking thing he had ever read.

Next, Courant completed *Methods of Mathematical Physics,* the book in the *Grundlehren* series which he had proposed in 1918 as a joint work with Hilbert and which became known everywhere as 'Courant and Hilbert'. While Hilbert oversaw the book his colleague was writing he did not participate in any active way; his interests had shifted, with characteristic finality, from physics to the foundations of mathematics. It was based on Courant's own investigations as much as Hilbert's lectures.

Courant's purpose was to produce improved tools for physicists to use in their work. When it was first published, however, the book seemed of more interest to mathematicians than to physicists. The physics with which it dealt seemed, in 1924, to be rather old-fashioned to those who were striving towards some understanding of quantum theory. It brought to mind the definition of applied mathematics as 'those areas of physics in which the physicists are no longer interested'. But Courant was convinced that the book would be important for physicists as well as mathematicians, and he was soon to be proved right. When the Schrödinger theory of wave mechanics appeared in 1926 it turned out that Courant and Hilbert contained, in convenient form, just the kind of mathematics that it required. Although Courant was author or co-author of several other books, Courant and Hilbert is his masterpiece.

Courant was also anxious to do something to improve educational methods. At the Georgia Augusta, as at other German universities at that period, the system was one of lecturing on the part of the professors and note-taking, or just listening, on the part of the students. Textbooks were little used. No examinations or even tests were given until, after several years, the student was faced with either the state examination for teachers or the university examination for a doctorate. Courant introduced the *Anfangerpraktikum* (beginner's practice period), in conjunction with the lecture courses. The students, possibly numbering a hundred or so, received a duplicated sheet of problems, some of them requiring innovative thinking as well as an understanding of the material of the lectures. Next, the professor giving the course conferred with a group of the more senior students, discussing the problems and pointing out different methods of attack. These senior students then went over the problems in the *Praktikum* with the more junior students. Solutions were written up and graded. Collusion was encouraged. Attendance was purely voluntary. Courant's reform made a major improvement in the training of the students.

Klein was second only to Hilbert in Courant's esteem. The Georgia Augusta's mathematical-physical tradition of teaching combined with research had been almost completely Klein's personal creation. Klein had lived long enough to see Göttingen recover its position as the most exciting place for mathematicians after the First World War, but when he died his plan for a mathematical institute at the Georgia Augusta where the mathematicians and the physicists would be in a close proximity was shelved. Unexpectedly, an opportunity arose when the city government wanted to move a secondary school to a new site away from its existing location on land close to the physics institute. The city was willing to build the new institute if the university would provide the site: the city would only let the university take over the old site if it would find the money to build the new school. At this juncture Courant decided to approach the Rockefeller Foundation, which had helped to finance the new Institut Henri Poincaré in Paris. He already had the necessary contacts in New York, since it was his practice to take every opportunity to get to know people who might some day be useful to him. Before long, he heard that a substantial grant had been approved which, when combined with funds from other sources, provided what was needed to enable the project to go ahead, only eighteen months after the death of Klein. The formal dedication of the new institute took place on 2 December 1929. Courant modestly gave the credit to Klein, but Hilbert and others realized that without Courant it might never have happened.

Hilbert retired shortly after the new institute was opened. By that time none of the heroic figures of Courant's student days was left on the active faculty, but their successors were hardly of lesser calibre. Courant himself, in his late thirties, could view his personal situation with satisfaction. He was a university professor, a uniquely comfortable, secure, and respected person in the Germany of the time, especially in a small town like Göttingen. His domestic life was highly satisfactory. Two maids relieved his wife Nina of much of the responsibility for running the house and bringing up the children. She was musically gifted, directed a choir, had an easy mastery of stringed instruments, and was a fine performer of vocal chamber music. Courant himself played the piano, largely by ear. Students were regularly invited to musical evenings at their house. Every year the family went skiing in Switzerland, and often took some of the assistants with them.

Courant felt that many people were what he called 'unfriendly' to him personally. While there may have been some jealousy of his success, he had an irritating way of leaving people in doubt as to what he really meant, by speaking very quietly and obliquely, or by sheer indecision. He was fond of probing, of seeing how people would react to something, even of deliberately creating bad feeling between two people so that he could somehow exploit the situation. On the other hand he would often go out of his way to be helpful, and the loyalty of his supporters was remarkable. He was quite short in stature and, although he might not be in sight himself, it was often possible to tell where he must be by the group of people who followed him around. In publishing, his successful collaboration with the house of Springer continued to flourish. He embarked on a second volume of Courant and Hilbert. He wrote up his lectures on calculus for publication, emphasizing the close connection between analysis and its applications. Here he relied on his assistants to a considerable extent, and there were rumours that he did not have a great deal to do with the undertaking himself.

As it happened, while the physicists were finding a need for the mathematical methods of Courant and Hilbert, Courant himself was engaged in a quite different work which would turn out to be of great practical importance with the development of computing power. The finite difference method had long been used by engineers to find approximate solutions to problems of which the precise solution would involve having to solve difficult partial differential equations. Courant set out to turn this on its head, to refine it until it produced precise solutions, not just approximate solutions, or at least established the existence of precise solutions.

Up to this time Courant had never left Europe, but in 1932 he received an invitation to make an American lecture tour. Americans had been coming to study in Europe for many years, and for mathematicians Göttingen had a special attraction, so that Courant had many contacts in the New World. His tour took him to the Ivy League, the Mid-Western, and the Californian universities, where he met many former Göttingen students and visitors. He took care to renew his contacts with officers of the Rockefeller Foundation as well as getting to know other Americans who might at some future date be useful to him. Courant was also trying to find openings for some of the able young people at Göttingen who needed positions. However, this was 1932, when the economic depression was at its worst. In Germany there was also the worrying political situation; while the Mathematical Institute might be a stronghold of liberal ideas, that was certainly not true of the town of Göttingen or even the university as a whole. Courant tried to distinguish between 'good Jews' and 'bad Jews', saying, 'What hurts me particularly is that the renewed wave of anti-Semitism is ... directed indiscriminately against every person of Jewish ancestry, no matter how truly German he may feel within himself, no matter how he and his family have bled during the war and how much he himself has contributed to the general community. I can't believe that such injustice can prevail much longer—in particular since it depends so much on the leaders, especially Hitler, whose last speech made quite a positive impression on me.'

When the racial laws were promulgated in 1933 Courant's appointment was suspended although, as a war veteran, he was not obliged to retire. This worked to his disadvantage because, by the time he concluded that he, like other Jewish mathematicians, would have to emigrate, most of the more desirable opportunities outside Germany had been taken. He received an offer from Turkey, where Kemel Ataturk was trying to set up a world-class university in Istanbul. He spent a year in England at Cambridge, as a visiting lecturer, but did not much care for the university. Like most of his colleagues he wanted to find a position in America. The best that could be done for him, after much pulling of strings, was a two-year appointment at New York University. Nowadays NYU is a high-ranking centre for excellence, but then it was 'very different from what I had been accustomed to in Germany': as Courant put it, 'there was really nothing scientifically at NYU.'

However, Courant was not a man to be easily discouraged. The very numerous NYU students were mostly Jewish, the sons and daughters of immigrants from eastern Europe. Those who applied to start graduate work he usually found very poorly prepared. Courant nevertheless believed the city of New York contained a great pool of talent and set out to take advantage of this. The chancellor of NYU was supportive of Courant's endeavours and soon made his temporary appointment permanent. Meanwhile the German government, which seemed to have a particular animus against Courant, replaced his suspension from the Georgia Augusta by compulsory retirement. Although urged by friends to get accustomed to American ways before starting to organize everyone, Courant could not resist improving the inadequate mathematics library at NYU. He contributed his own books and, to keep subscriptions to German journals and other serials up to date, arranged that some of the money which emigrants were obliged to leave behind them in Germany could be used for this purpose. He was careful to keep his own name out of it.

By 1936 Courant was presiding over the nucleus of what was to develop into a graduate centre for mathematics at NYU. The International Congress of Mathematicians at Oslo that summer provided him with an opportunity to recruit two exceptionally able young mathematicians. To see old friends he also took the risk of going back to Germany, although not to Göttingen. As the situation worsened, desperate people kept seeking Courant's help, unable to believe that he was no longer in a position to pull strings.

Although the main part of Courant's time and energy went into building up a large and flourishing graduate centre for mathematics he was still writing books. A popular work, *What is Mathematics?*, with Herbert Robbins was a success. When America entered the Second World War such projects had to be put aside. In spite of having fought for Germany in the First World War Courant did not hesitate to serve his adopted country in the second. Classes at NYU dwindled in size but Courant was successful in winning contracts for such war-related work as the mathematics of shock waves. He played a leading part in this research himself but rather at the expense of his teaching.

After the war Courant revisited Germany, making a sentimental journey to Göttingen, where the Georgia Augusta was the first German university to reopen its doors. Before that, his career in America had been crowned by the establishment at NYU of the Institute of Mathematical Sciences, soon to be known throughout the world as the Courant Institute. The dedication of the new institute took place in 1954, a quarter of a century after the dedication of the one at Göttingen. Among those present there were some who could remember Hilbert saying, on that previous occasion, 'there will never be another institute like this! For to have another such institute there would have to be another Courant!'

Courant served as director of the New York institute for five years, the same length of time as he had been able to be director of the Göttingen institute. He rather expected that in 1958, when he reached the retirement age of seventy, a deputation would arrive to beg him to continue; that might not have been possible, but in any case it was time for someone new to take charge. By this time the Courant Institute contained a core of outstanding mathematicians, among them no fewer than nine future members of the United States National Academy of Sciences. Under the new director there was a spectacular expansion in the research and graduate education programme, and in 1965 the institute moved into a new fourteen-storey building (known as the Courant Hilton) close to

Washington Square. By then it had on its staff no fewer than 346 research scientists, administrators, and other employees.

After retirement Courant continued his activities as consultant and author. The second volume of Courant and Hilbert was completed, without the participation of Hilbert, and there were plans for a third. Courant, lacking an outlet for his organizing abilities, had to be discouraged from trying to interfere in the institute's administration. Even in his seventies he regularly went on long excursions on foot or on ski with colleagues and students; in his early eighties he was still worrying about the future of the institute. Courant died at the age of eighty-four on 27 January 1972, following a stroke two months previously. His wife Nina survived him by almost twenty years and was a hundred years old when she died in 1991. In his lifetime Courant received many honours, from the United States, Germany, and elsewhere. He was a member of the United States National Academy of Sciences and a foreign member of many others.

Superb Lecturer and Expositor
Abram Besicovitch (1891–1970)

The Karaites were a breakaway sect of Judaism which originated in Persia and later spread among Jews all over the world, particularly in the Crimea. They accepted the written tradition of Judaism but rejected both rabbinical learning and material enrichment; orthodox Jews considered them heretics. Their language was originally Turkish but is now mostly Russian. The conversion of sects of the Khazars by the Karaite Jews led to their taking of the name Karaims, and the Besicovitch forebears were among them. The Polish mathematician Waclaw Sierpinski (1882–1969) was another Karaite.

Abram Samoilovitch Besicovitch was born at Berdjansk, on the Sea of Azov, on 24 January 1891, the fourth child of the family of four sons and two daughters of Samuel Besicovitch and Eva Ilichna (née Sauskan). His father, a retail jeweller, gave up his shop after losses by theft and took employment as a cashier. He married Eva when she was only fifteen; they had to live frugally to bring up their large family of talented children. The sons enrolled at the University of St Petersburg, the older ones in turn earning money in their spare time by giving private lessons and helping to support the younger. All four gained professional qualifications, one son being the author of a number of mathematical books, and another a doctor of medicine. The daughters attended special university-level institutions for women and had their own careers. In later life the sons and daughters bore witness to the intelligence of their mother and agreed that, if she had not been cut off from higher education by marrying so young and having children, she would have shown conspicuous ability, notably in mathematics.

From an early age Abram had shown extraordinary aptitude for solving mathematical problems. One day he brought a textbook to his father saying, 'I have been able to solve every problem but one in this book.' His father withheld praise for this achievement until his son had successfully solved the remaining problem. Besicovitch graduated in 1912 at the University of St Petersburg, where one of his teachers was the probabilist Andrei Andreevich Markov; his first research paper was on probability theory. Four years later he married another mathematician, Valentina Vitalevna, somewhat older than himself. In 1917 the University of Perm, originally a branch of the University of St Petersburg, became autonomous and recruited a high-powered mathematics staff, including Besicovitch. Mathematics and physics were provided with good accommodation, including a mechanics laboratory, but everything was destroyed during the civil war. However, the resourceful Besicovitch locked the library books away in cellars and succeeded in preserving much of the property of the faculty for use when the university was re-established (its name was later changed to Molotov University).

In 1920 Besicovitch returned to Leningrad as professor at the Pedagogical Institute and lecturer at the university until 1924. Under the new regime the duties of a university teacher were subject to political constraints. Like his colleagues, Besicovitch had to teach classes of workers who entirely lacked the educational background to understand his lectures. He began to seek an opportunity to emigrate, as did several of his contemporaries.

Ehrenfest, as we know, acted as a kind of mentor to Russian applicants for Rockefeller Fellowships (as Volterra did for Italians). 'Besicovitch', he wrote in support of his application, 'is highly talented … the younger Russian generation is full of enthusiasm for science and their spirit of research is wonderful.' When Besicovitch was offered the fellowship he tried in vain to obtain official permission to accept. it. Eventually he decided to leave the country illegally, and with his fellow mathematician Jacob Daniel Tamarkin (1888–1940) he crossed into Latvia under cover of darkness. Besicovitch then made his way to Copenhagen where he was able to spend a year with Harald Bohr, who was developing the theory of almost periodic functions. Tamarkin, after various adventures, emigrated to America, and among other achievements transformed the teaching of pure mathematics at Brown University.

After Landau, Harald Bohr's most important professional contact was with Hardy and his colleague Littlewood, which often brought him to Oxford or Cambridge to collaborate on research. At this stage in his career Hardy was in Oxford, as Savilian Professor of Geometry, the chair previously occupied by Sylvester. He invited Besicovitch to stay in New College, of which he was a fellow, and was greatly impressed by his mathematical calibre. Contrary to their normal policy, the International Education Board renewed Besicovitch's fellowship for a second year, but there was the problem of finding a suitable position for him after that. In fact his irregular departure from Russia had been causing concern to the officers of the board. One wrote to another, 'I had a good talk with our Russian fellow, whose name escapes me. According to Bohr he is very able and I have no doubt of the fact.' Of course Besicovitch had no intention of returning to the Soviet Union, as required by Rockefeller policy, but the policy was about to change.

In the meantime, Hardy renewed his efforts to find Besicovitch at least a holding appointment in England, and he obtained for him a temporary lectureship at Liverpool University, where he proved himself a superb lecturer and expositor. Since Hardy, by then, was expecting to return to Cambridge, his aim was to find an opening for such a fine mathematician there, and the opportunity came in 1927 when a university lecturership became vacant. Besicovitch was appointed to this, and to a college lecturership; three years later he was elected to a fellowship at Trinity College. He lived in college and participated enthusiastically in Cambridge academic and social life, dining at high table and taking brandy in the common room afterwards in the company of Hardy, Littlewood, and other luminaries. He had many research students, whom he would entertain in his rooms with vodka or take walking while developing his ideas. On such walks he would stop to talk with young children they met on the way, or even to talk to the cows in a field. Always deeply suspicious of the Soviet government, he advised his good friend the physicist Kapitza not to keep going back to Russia, but to no avail. On one such visit Kapitza was refused an exit visa and could not return to Cambridge for many years. Besicovitch himself could never risk returning to his homeland because of his illegal departure, but in any case the political self-isolation of the Soviet Union made contact with foreign scientists almost impossible.

Besicovitch's wife had remained behind when he left Russia, and the childless marriage was dissolved in 1926. During his years at Perm he had become friendly with Maria Ivanovna Denisova, the widow of another mathematician, and her two daughters. They used to relate how he kept them from starvation during the years of famine after the First World War by buying half the carcase of a horse, which he buried in a secluded place. Once a week he dug it up and cut off chunks of meat for them. He now brought Maria Denisova and her family to England, and in 1928, when he was nearly forty he married the elder daughter, Valentina Alexandrovna, then aged sixteen.

In 1950, on his fifty-ninth birthday, Besicovitch succeeded Littlewood in the prestigious Rouse Ball chair of mathematics. For many years he was either author or co-author of nearly every published paper on Hausdorff measure. After retirement in 1958 he remained active in teaching and research and spent eight successive years as visiting professor in various universities in the United States, before returning to Trinity. Towards his eightieth year his health began to fail, and he died on 2 November 1970. He had been elected Fellow of the Royal Society in 1934 and awarded the Sylvester Medal in 1952. He won the Adams Prize of the University of Cambridge in 1930 for an essay on almost periodic functions, and in 1958 was awarded the De Morgan Medal of the London Mathematical Society. His intellectual gifts were matched by an outgoing nature which endeared him to pupils, colleagues, and a wide circle of friends, to whom he was affectionately known as Bessy. As he spoke Russian at home, Besicovitch's command of English remained stationary from his early days in Cambridge. For him, as for other Russians, the definite article was superfluous.

At Home in Two Worlds
Franz Simon (1893–1956)

Like James Franck, Franz Simon left Nazi Germany voluntarily, but being at a slightly earlier stage in his career was more successful in making a fresh start. He was born on 2 July 1893 in Berlin, where his father Ernst was a wealthy property developer. His mother Anna was said to be 'artistically inclined'; she was the daughter of a mathematician employed by the Prussian geodetic service, whose ancestry could be traced back to the brother of Moses Mendelssohn. Both parents were of Jewish Silesian stock; he was their only son, but he had both an older and a younger sister. Those who knew Franz Simon in his boyhood remember him as a shy, quiet self-contained child, in no way a prodigy. In 1903 he entered the Kaiser Wilhelm Reform Gymnasium in Berlin. This school had two streams, one classical and the other modern, with the emphasis on modern languages and science. Although the boy was already showing a preference for science he was made to enter the classical stream on the insistence of one of his grandfathers. At school he nevertheless devoted as much time as possible to science and showed particular aptitude for physics and mathematics. He spent several of his school holidays in England and Scotland in order to acquire some English, and spent a little while at a Swiss school to learn some French.

Simon was barely fourteen when an old friend of the family, the distinguished physiological chemist Leonor Michaelis, noticed his unusual talent and encouraged him to consider physics as a profession. Simon accepted this advice with enthusiasm, but there was strong family opposition to overcome, because in Wilhelmine Germany a physicist's career did not appear financially promising or even secure. Michaelis finally said to Simon's father that 'if a man as rich as you would not allow his son to study physics who should?' and that settled the matter. After passing the *Abitur*, Simon enrolled at the University of Munich in the spring of 1912 to study physics, chemistry and mathematics. In physics, Sommerfeld was one of his teachers.

At the end of the year he migrated to Göttingen where he studied under Courant, among others. It was during this period that the quiet, unsociable, scholastically unremarkable boy matured into the good-looking young man with irrepressible curiosity, piquant wit, happy self-confidence, and social ease. In the autumn of 1913 Simon was called up for the compulsory year of military service, during which he was attached to the artillery in Augsburg, and he was still there at the outbreak of hostilities. During the First World War he served in the field artillery with the rank of lieutenant, at a time when it was unusual for a Jew to be commissioned in the German army. He had the misfortune of being one of the earliest poison-gas casualties of the war; later he was twice wounded, the second time only two days before the Armistice and so severely that it was not until the spring of 1919 that he was released from military hospital. He was awarded the Iron Cross (first class), a decoration only given for personal bravery. Simon, usually a most communicative man, hardly ever talked about his war experiences and did not regard his decoration with any particular pride. The war had opened his eyes to the factors which had contributed to his country's downfall—a civilian population distrustful of those in power, especially a bigoted high command whose grandiose dreams ignored the ultimate good of the country.

At Easter 1919, after a break of six years, Simon resumed his studies, having transferred from Munich to Berlin. He attended lectures by Planck, von Laue, Haber, and Nernst among others, and soon, after consulting Michaelis again, he began work on a PhD thesis under Nernst, then director of the physical chemistry institute of the university. His subject was a study of specific heats at temperatures down to the temperature of liquid hydrogen. Judging from the wealth of material contained in the dissertation and the fact that he completed it in only eighteen months he must have been working with extraordinary energy, as if to make up for six lost years. Many of the questions that were to occupy him during the following decade are first considered in his thesis. Simon owed much to Nernst and developed a great admiration and respect for him.

Simon obtained his doctorate at the end of 1921, having offered experimental physics, theoretical physics, and philosophy. In 1922 he was appointed Nernst's assistant, and in the same year he married Charlotte Munchhausen whom he had met two years before. Like him she came of a distinguished Jewish family, still wealthy despite postwar inflation. Accommodation in overcrowded Berlin was very scarce at this time, so for the first eight years of marriage the young couple lived with the Munchhausens, whose huge apartment was right in the centre of the city. Simon's wife was no scientist; he never tried to interest her in his work. On the contrary it was he who found recreation and much-needed relief from exacting scientific work by sharing in her musical and artistic interests. It was a successful marriage and his domestic happiness with his wife and family served as a safe anchor through all the troubles of the years to come.

Simon was expecting to make a career in industry, but Nernst persuaded him to stay on at the institute of physical chemistry, where he became *Privatdozent* in 1924 and *Extra-Ordinarius* three years later. From a scientific point of view, Simon's ten years in Berlin were a most fruitful and successful period. He built up a low-temperature laboratory which, though modest in physical size, was impressive in achievement; by 1929 there were about ten doctoral students and usually one or two assistants working either directly under his supervision or in close co-operation with him. The overcrowded laboratory was always busy, day and night, so that it was almost impossible to keep it neat and tidy, much to Simon's chagrin. He disliked untidiness and always tried to coax his assistants into giving the laboratory a more respectable appearance. It was all done with characteristic good humour.

By the end of the 1920s Simon had become a well-known and respected figure in the world of physics. He regularly attended scientific meetings in Europe and in the summer of 1930, accompanied by his wife, he made his one and only visit to Russia when he went to a conference in Odessa, returning to Berlin via Moscow and Leningrad. Early in 1931 Simon was appointed to the chair of physical chemistry at the Technical University in Breslau. He took with him two promising young physicists from Berlin: his cousin Kurt Mendelssohn, who had been his principal assistant, and the Hungarian Nicholas Kurti, who was just finishing his doctorate. One of the reasons for going to Breslau was the prestige attached to being an *Ordinarius*. Another was the prospect of building up a larger and better-equipped low-temperature laboratory than his Berlin one had been, although in the event that never materialized. Unfortunately, the responsibilities he was presented with in Breslau were not conducive to intense creative scientific work. He was appointed dean of the faculty of chemistry and mining and as such incurred many administrative duties; in addition he had to deal with problems arising out of the merger between the university and the technical university.

Deeply worried as he was about the rise of Nazism and its anti-Semitic policies, the far-sighted Simon was already considering emigration. He spent the spring semester of 1932 at the chemistry department of the University of California at Berkeley, the first of many visits to the United States. While he was away he moved his family to Switzerland for safety. Once Hitler obtained dictatorial powers, Simon realized that he would have to leave Germany for the sake of his family and his career. As a veteran of the First World War, like Richard Courant and James Franck, he was exempt from the original decree dismissing Jews from university posts, so that his own position was not immediately threatened.

In June 1933 Simon sent in his resignation and gladly accepted Lindemann's invitation to move to Oxford, on one of the special research fellowships funded by Imperial Chemical Industries. Other members of his research group soon came to join him, initially supported by funds from the same source. After a brief preliminary reconnaissance in England, Simon, with his family, left Germany, without regret, in August 1933. He said that his chief aim in emigrating was to give his young daughters Kathrin (born 1925) and Dorothee (born 1928) a chance of growing up in peaceful surroundings, away from the hatred and violence of the Third Reich. The Simons bought a house in north Oxford to which they became very attached. Later the Munchhausens, his wife's parents, finally convinced themselves that they could not remain in Berlin any longer, and they also went to live in Oxford, as did Simon's mother. His elder sister studied medicine but gave it up when she married. Her husband became a well-known physician; they settled in London in 1936 and Simon encouraged their younger son became a physicist. Simon's younger sister studied history of art and became curator of the former imperial palaces in Berlin. In 1933 she and her husband emigrated to Palestine where, as keeper of the Rockefeller Museum in Jerusalem, she was engaged in archeological work until her untimely death in 1946.

Under Lindemann, Oxford's Clarendon Laboratory became one of the leading centres of physics in Great Britain, and this was largely due to his success in recruiting Simon and his collaborators, Kurti, Mendelssohn, and others, providing them with decent positions and good working conditions, and, last but not least, encouraging them through a deep understanding of their projects. Although Lindemann essentially gave up research himself he was always amazingly up to date not only about the work being done at the Clarendon but anywhere in the world. When the émigrés arrived they found that the laboratory was housed in a small Venetian Gothic chalet, so that experimental work had to start on a modest scale. To begin with, research funds were so meagre that had Simon not managed to bring out of Germany some of his personal apparatus and equipment, his investigations during the first few years would have been seriously impeded. However, the lack of material facilities was amply compensated for by the friendship and encouragement of his new colleagues.

Although initially Simon had no university position at Oxford, he was given the status of master of arts and membership of the senior common room of Balliol College. Nevertheless, he needed a permanent position. He turned down offers of one in Jerusalem and another in Istanbul, hoping that something suitable would be forthcoming in England. In 1935 Oxford solved the problem by appointing him university reader in thermodynamics, a tenured position similar to associate professor. Still the shortage of laboratory space and lack of research funds were hampering the full development of his scientific potential. However, thanks to Lindemann's negotiating skills, the situation gradually improved, and when a new building for the Clarendon was decided upon Simon made up his mind to stay. Increasingly, Lindemann placed the scientific work of the Clarendon in his capable hands. Under Simon, Oxford became a world centre for low-temperature physics.

With the outbreak of war in 1939, this work at Oxford, as elsewhere, came to a halt. Simon had become a naturalized British subject late in 1938 and eagerly offered his services to contribute to the war effort, but in the early stages of the war there was reluctance to entrust secret scientific work to former aliens. (In a mistaken policy, many of the displaced scientists were arrested, interned on the Isle of Man, and then sent to Canada or Australia to be treated as prisoners-of-war.) With no possibilities of doing official war work, Simon, together with other émigré scientists such as Frisch and Peierls, concentrated on research related to the construction of the atomic bomb, particularly the separation of the rare isotope uranium 235 from ordinary uranium. As in the United States, one of the most vital and most secret war projects was, in the early stages, run primarily by foreign-born scientists (they were barred from other projects, such as radar, which initially had higher priority in both countries).

After the fall of France, a joint invitation was sent by the universities of Yale and Toronto offering hospitality for the duration of the war to the children of senior members of Oxford University. Many accepted this generous offer; the Simons were among the first to do so. In 1941 he was elected Fellow of the Royal Society and in 1945 a Student (i.e. Fellow) of Christ Church. Shortly afterwards, the university, in recognition of Simon's eminence, converted his readership into a personal chair.

During the war, Simon's work brought him into contact with many industrialists, politicians, and civil servants, and as a result he developed a keen interest in the wider political and social aspects of science and technology. The opinions he formed were now expressed freely and often forcibly, in contrast to his reticence in earlier years. When he first came to England he considered himself a guest and tried not to be too critical, especially where the politics of his host country was concerned. From 1948 to 1951 he was science correspondent to the *Financial Times*, and his articles in that newspaper and other publications brought his views before a wide audience. He rapidly became a well-known figure whose advice was often sought but, as he would plaintively remark, not often heeded. He carefully followed postwar developments in German academic circles and came to view the future with grave misgivings. He saw that many of those who, thanks to political opportunism or conviction, had flourished during the Nazi regime were still in important positions and were using their influence to the detriment of their anti-Nazi colleagues. He recognized the same tendencies in politics and feared that the spirit that made the growth of Nazism possible was still alive.

Although Simon spent practically all his professional career as a university teacher, one of the main vehicles for communicating ideas, the lecture course, was not his forte. Public speaking of any kind was irksome to him, and he disliked the detailed preparation that successful lecturing entails. Routine lectures to undergraduates bored him; he became tense and restless, moving chairs, pacing up and down, and so on. However, he could rise to a special occasion, and outside Oxford he began to be in demand as a speaker (notably he gave one of the Friday evening discourses at the Royal Institution in London).

It was in personal talk and discussion and in informal lectures that his breadth of knowledge and vivid understanding were most evident. He had a gift for recognizing the connection between remote facts and for placing small details in the general picture, and he was well known for his ability to clarify issues or to solve controversies by a single apt remark. Although quick in repartee and fluent in expression, his constructions and phraseology were often quaint and he never lost his slight German accent. Simon enjoyed college life, the variety of the conversations and the personalities, the traditions, the stimulus of meeting people who were specialists in subjects other than his own, and the insight into broader worlds beyond the university which distinguished guests helped to provide. It was through common room conversations that his views, many of which were highly controversial, became known. He was mischievous, mercurial, generous, warm-hearted, and impossible to offend.

The war years had strengthened the bonds between Simon and Lindemann. intellectually they had much in common: both possessed extreme clarity of thought and ability to communicate; they shared a passionate conviction of the value of science, not only for what it could achieve but as a mental discipline; equally dear to both of them was the desire to raise the standard of physics in Oxford. During the war each in his own way dedicated himself to winning it; after the war both turned their attention to winning the peace for the United Kingdom, at least in the scientific and technological fields.

Simon was much honoured. In 1946 he was appointed a Commander of the Order of the British Empire, in recognition of his contribution to the war effort; it amused him to think he was probably the only holder of the Iron Cross to be so honoured. In 1955 he was knighted in recognition of both his public service and his scientific achievements, becoming Sir Francis Simon. On the retirement of Lindemann (by then Lord Cherwell) from Dr Lee's professorship of experimental philosophy Sir Francis, at the age of fifty-two, was elected to succeed him in the chair and as head of the Clarendon Laboratory. The prospect of the position which he was about to enter gave him great satisfaction and he looked forward to leading the large and flourishing laboratory, to the growing reputation and success of which he had contributed so much. In the summer of 1956, however, he was taken ill with coronary heart disease, a condition which had first shown itself ten years earlier. During his slow, apparent recovery he was actively planning the future of the Clarendon and, soon after the date of his appointment, began to spend a few hours a day at the laboratory. Then at the end of October he had a sudden relapse and died, aged sixty-three, on 31 October 1956. Lady Simon continued to enjoy life until the end of 1999, when she died at the age of 102.

8

Modern Times

In this final chapter the subjects of the profiles were born between 1894 and 1901. No further historical background is needed beyond that already provided, but the subjects come from a slightly younger age-group. As a result, when they were forced to move to another country, the most important part of their career usually came afterwards, not before. The receiving countries gained what Germany lost; after the Second World War the United States became the world leader in most branches of science. Of course there were also immigrants from eastern Europe, especially Russia after the October Revolution, but Jews were often supporters of the new regime and remained in the Soviet Republic, at least initially.

Gifted Researcher, Excellent Teacher
Heinz Hopf (1894–1971)

Heinz Hopf, the last German to be profiled here, is one of several major Jewish mathematicians and physicists who left Germany to settle in Switzerland. Like Hurwitz, his original intention may have been to return to his homeland when he received a sufficiently attractive call, but once the Nazis came to power there was no possibility of this happening. In any event he was happy to remain in Zurich, as we shall see.

The ancestors of Heinz Hopf belonged to a respected and prosperous family of hop traders in the German city of Nuremberg. His great-grandfather Lob Hopf moved there with his family in 1852 from Uhlfeld, a small town in upper Franconia. He was one of the first Jews to acquire German citizenship. His son Stephan prospered as a wholesaler and was prominent in the local government of Nuremberg as *Kommerzienrat*, *Magistratrat*, and *Landrat*. Stephan's son Wilhelm, the father of the mathematician, trained as a brewer in Flensberg, and then in 1887 moved to Breslau after quarrelling with Stephan. He had his considerable inheritance paid out and with the money became sole owner of Heinrich Kirchner's brewery. Five years later he married Elisabeth, the elder of Kirchner's two daughters, and before long he adopted his wife's Lutheranism. They lived in a villa-like house, with a large garden, in the town of Grabschen near Breslau.

Heinz was born there on 19 November 1894. He started school at the age of seven and, like Max Born, went on to the König Wilhelm Gymnasium in Breslau, where his gift for mathematics was soon recognized. In other subjects his marks were less impressive. Perhaps he neglected his homework at times and preferred doing sports. In childhood his favourite sports were swimming and tennis; later it was swimming, rambling, and mountaineering, in winter often on skis. Short in stature, he was of a tough and strong constitution. An extended daily walk was a necessity for him, as for his father before him.

In April 1913, after passing his *Abitur*, Hopf enrolled to study mathematics at the University of Breslau, where he attended lectures by Adolf Kneser, Erhard Schmidt, and Rudolf Sturm. He also heard Max Dehn and Ernst Steinitz at the Breslau Technical University. Besides mathematics, Hopf also attended lectures in physics, philosophy, and psychology. One year later, the outbreak of the First World War interrupted his education. Hopf, caught up in the patriotic enthusiasm of that time, volunteered for military service. During the next four years he served on the western front as lieutenant in the reserves. He was wounded twice and, like Franz Simon, was awarded the Iron Cross (first class).

After Hopf was demobilized he resumed his interrupted studies at the University of Breslau. The next year he transferred to the University of Heidelberg, perhaps to join his older sister Hedwig who had begun studying law there. In 1920 he moved again, this time to the University of Berlin, where he came under the influence of Erhard Schmidt and Issai Schur. He obtained his degree *summa cum laude* in February 1925 with a masterly dissertation on differential geometry, and a year later habilitated with a thesis on the singularities of vector fields on manifolds, the first of his profound contributions to topology, which Schmidt declared already placed him in the front rank of German mathematicians. Hopf had spent the intervening year at Göttingen, where he was warmly received into the Courant–Hilbert–Noether circle. There he met many famous mathematicians, among them Alexandrov, with whom he established a deep and lasting friendship. In Göttingen they and other mathematicians used to spend their spare time walking in the countryside or swimming at the bathing establishment on the river Leine. In the summer vacations Alexandrov and Hopf used to tour together, often in France. Another regular visitor to Göttingen was the Dutch philosopher and pioneer topologist L. E. J. Brouwer, who invited them to stay at his seaside home near Amsterdam. While they were there Emmy Noether came to join the party with her student Van der Waerden, and showed them how to use algebra in topology.

Alexandrov and Hopf both won Rockefeller Fellowships for the academic year 1927/8 which they spent at Princeton University, getting to know Alexander, Lefschetz, and Veblen, among others. In a draft report for the International Education Board afterwards Hopf praised the exemplary sports facilities at American universities, especially the provision of swimming pools. After they returned to Göttingen Courant suggested that they should write a textbook of topology together; this work took up much of their time for the next seven years, and only one volume had been published when the outbreak of war brought the project to a premature conclusion.

In October 1928 Hopf married Anja von Mickwitz, who came from a German-Baltic family of pastors blessed with many children. She had trained in St Petersburg to become a teacher and after the First World War moved to North Germany and later worked as a private tutor in Berlin. Soon he received several offers of positions, one from Princeton which he turned down, another from the ETH at Zurich, and a third from Freiburg. He decided in favour of the ETH, where in 1931 he became *Ordinarius* in succession to Weyl, who was moving to Göttingen. Hopf quickly settled into work at the ETH. He maintained the highest standards, not only in research, but also in his teaching. Schur described him as an excellent lecturer, a mathematician of strong temperament and strong influence, a leading example in his discipline. Among his research students were Beno Eckmann and Hans Samelson, destined to become major figures in the mathematical world themselves.

Support for the Nazis was by no means unknown in Switzerland in the early 1930s. Heinrich Behnke (1978) recalls in his memoirs that when he travelled to Switzerland in the summer of 1933 'everywhere the children in the streets greeted the car with the raised-hand salute ... and Swiss hurried to express their respect for the new regime.' Hopf wrote to Pólya, 'it is quite unpleasant that now also here in Zurich nationalists and anti-Semites have become powerful,' and to Veblen, 'I am very dismayed that presently there is absolutely no prospect of a German Jew obtaining a position in Switzerland. Professorships are not open, new ones will not be created since there is no money, a large number of good Swiss await for positions as assistant that are becoming open, and besides the tenor among the students is very nationalistic—anti-Semitic.' Hopf would say little about the efforts he made during the Nazi period to help the displaced scholars either financially or by helping them to obtain positions outside Germany. One was his cousin, the mathematician Ludwig Hopf, who was dismissed from the Technical University of Aachen under the racial laws.

The Swiss army was mobilized in case the Germans invaded, which would have been disastrous for any Jews. The endorsement of passports issued to German Jews with the letter J resulted from an agreement in 1938 between Germany and Switzerland to enable the Swiss police, in collaboration with their German counterparts, to exercise complete control over the entry of refugees from Germany. Those who entered the country illegally were transported back to Germany if found within fifty kilometres of the frontier or sent to detention camps if further inside Switzerland. Until 1939 Hopf had been able to visit his parents in

Germany regularly, but when he tried to arrange for them to join him in Switzerland they had trouble obtaining the necessary permits (in fact his father became terminally ill and did not leave Germany, even when the permits had been issued). One refugee was Hopf's old teacher Issai Schur, who passed through Switzerland on his way to Palestine in 1941, after having been strongly advised to leave Germany by the Gestapo. In 1942 another Swiss police regulation denied the status of political refugee to 'persons who became refugees only on racial grounds'. By then Switzerland was surrounded by Axis-dominated countries.

When Lefschetz offered Hopf a position in Princeton in 1941 he declined, saying, 'this is very kind but for reasons of principle we consider it better not to leave the ship as long as, despite the tempest, there is a possibility that it will not sink.' Two years later he was informed that the property he owned in Germany had been confiscated by the authorities. Soon afterwards, the German consul-general in Zurich refused to extend his *Heimatschein*, and he was threatened with the loss of his German citizenship unless he moved back to the area of the Reich. Hopf decided that it would be wise to apply for Swiss citizenship, otherwise he might become stateless. He had considered doing so earlier but felt he should wait until the end of the war in order not to be regarded as an opportunist. Becoming a Swiss citizen is not an easy matter, as Pauli was to find, but Hopf's application was approved without delay.

After the war, Hopf helped to re-establish mathematical activity in the German Bundesrepublik. He made lecture tours in America, where several universities tried to persuade him to stay, but he preferred to remain at the ETH. An esteemed participant at conferences, he served as president of the International Mathematical Union and was awarded many academic and professional honours.

Hopf retired from the ETH in 1964, having reached the age of seventy. Five years earlier he had undergone surgery to remove a stomach ulcer, and needed an extended convalescence: then his wife Anja became seriously ill and died in 1967. Symptoms of a geriatric condition appeared which confined him to his home, and he died in hospital on 3 June 1971 at the age of seventy-seven. Without doubt, Hopf was one of the most distinguished mathematicians of the twentieth century. His work is closely linked with the emergence of algebraic topology as a new and important branch of mathematics. In the words of Henri Cartan, those who knew him will never forget his charm and sweetness, allied with great strength of character.

American Leibniz
Norbert Wiener (1894–1964)

In most profiles we know too little about the parents of the subjects to say much about them. Leo, the father of Norbert Wiener, is an exception. He was born in 1862 in Bialystock, one of the most important cities of the Pale, the centre of a thriving textile industry and of an intellectual elite. He claimed descent from Akiba Eger, the Grand Rabbi of Posen, one of the greatest Talmudic scholars in Germany at the start of the nineteenth century. Leo believed in German *Kultur* and preferred literary German to Polish or Yiddish. He started his education at a Lutheran gymnasium in Minsk, where the teaching was in German, but then moved to one in Warsaw, where Russian was used. He learnt French as the language of educated society, also some Italian, since in eastern Europe, especially in Poland, there were those who adhered to the Renaissance tradition and used Italian as a language of polite conversation. This was in addition to Polish, the vernacular language.

Although Leo had this extraordinary facility for modern languages he also displayed unusual ability in other fields such as Greek, Latin, and mathematics. After leaving school he enrolled at Warsaw University to study medicine. Soon he gave this up and moved to Berlin to study engineering at the *Polytechnikum*, but before long he again became dissatisfied with his studies. He was as annoyed by German philistinism as he had been earlier by Polish inflammability and Russian apathy. The restless youth greatly admired the social ideas of Tolstoy and so, in 1860, at the age of eighteen, he set out to join a group of like-minded people who were going out to Central America to start a pioneer colony in which they hoped to put some of these ideas into practice.

Leo had just enough money to sail steerage to New Orleans, where he found that the hare-brained Belize plan had been abandoned. He decided to stay on in the United States, supporting himself by manual work, particularly in agriculture. Eventually he reached Kansas City where he began his academic career at the high school, teaching Greek, Latin, and mathematics for eight years. This led to his appointment as assistant professor in German and Romance languages at the University of Missouri. During that time he married Bertha Kahn, the daughter of a German-Jewish immigrant who owned a department store. They met at a literary club in Kansas City where the poet Browning was much admired and they named several of their children, including Norbert, after characters in his poem *On a Balcony* (it was not altogether unusual for Jewish parents to name their children after characters in literature).

A few years later Leo lost his job at the university and migrated to Boston, seeking a position at Harvard, where he hoped his gift for languages might be better appreciated. He was taken on first as instructor in Slavic languages and literature in 1896, promoted to assistant professor five years later and to full professor in 1911. He made an English translation of the complete works of Tolstoy which is still recommended. In spite of his strong objections to the quota system then in operation for admitting Jewish students, he remained on the Harvard faculty until retirement in 1930. The Wiener family frequently moved house in the Cambridge urban area until in 1903 they moved out into the countryside.

Let us now turn to the education of the Wieners' eldest son Norbert, born 26 November 1894, before his parents left Missouri. After schools in the Boston area were found wanting, the boy, from the age of seven, was mainly educated by his overbearing father at home. The Wiener household had a fine collection of books, of which the boy took full advantage, despite poor eyesight. Leo was a harsh disciplinarian who exercised an excessively strong influence over the education of his son. He made matters worse by trumpeting his son's intellectual accomplishments in the press. Although the precocious boy was obviously unusually gifted, his father denied this, claiming that any advantage he had gained over other children was due to his better training. As Norbert wrote in his autobiography, 'he would begin the discussion in an easy conversational tone. This lasted until I made the first mathematical mistake. Then the gentle loving father was replaced by the avenger of the blood … father was raging, I was weeping, and my mother did her best to defend me, although hers was a losing battle.' Even so, Norbert greatly admired his father, who used to take him for long walks and encourage him to have interests outside his studies. Norbert was also saddled with the job of bringing up his younger brother, although never allowed to make any decisions about his education, and throughout his life nursed a grievance about this.

Somehow Norbert, although socially inept, managed to get through the crises induced by the high-pressure regime of his early years. His overprotective parents had made it hard for him to become fully independent and strike out on his own. By late adolescence he should perhaps have left his parents' close-knit Jewish household but his mother made it clear that she would never forgive him if he did. Perhaps he suffered from some mild form of autism, as suggested by what he writes in his autobiography.

> I began to discover that I was clumsier than the run of children around me. Some of this clumsiness was genuinely poor muscular coordination, but more of it was based on my defective eyesight. At school they viewed me socially as an undeveloped child, not as an underage adolescent. A further source of my awkwardness was psychic rather than physical. I was socially not yet adjusted to my environment and I was often inconsiderate, largely through an insufficient awareness of the exact consequences of my action. A further psychic hurdle I was to overcome was impatience. This impatience was largely the result of a combination of mental quickness and physical slowness. I had no proper idea of cleanliness and personal neatness, and I never myself knew when I was to blurt out some unpardonable rudeness or double entendre. I was already too much of a lone wolf.

At the age of eleven Norbert Wiener enrolled as a student at Tufts College, with a special interest in science, especially biology, and graduated with a degree in mathematics four years later. After that he sampled zoology at Harvard University and philosophy at Cornell before going back to Harvard to study philosophy and mathematics, receiving his PhD in 1913 at the age of nineteen. The subject of his dissertation was a comparison of the Russell-Whitehead system of mathematical logic with an earlier system created by Ernst Schröder. Throughout this period he seems to have suffered profoundly from adolescent depression. Apparently it was while he was at Harvard that he realized for the first time that he was Jewish, in fact an indirect descendant of the great medieval scholar Moses Maimonides and, although Judaism never meant a great deal to him, he was proud of the outstanding achievements of Jews in mathematics and the other sciences.

Wiener won a Harvard Fellowship which enabled him to study in Europe, free at last from his father's direction. He was at Cambridge University from June 1913 to the following April. 'Like many other adolescents,' he wrote, 'I walked in a dark tunnel of which I could not see the issue, nor did I know whether there was any. I did not emerge from this tunnel until I was nearly nineteen years old and had begun my studies at Cambridge.' Initially, he read mathematical logic with Bertrand Russell, who was not impressed by his understanding of philosophy and advised him to learn more mathematics, particularly mathematical physics, and particularly the new theories of Einstein. Acting on this advice, he attended Hardy's course on analysis. 'In all my years of listening to lectures in mathematics,' he would say later, 'I have never heard the equal of Hardy for clarity, for interest or for intellectual power.' Because Russell was planning to spend the spring semester at Harvard, Wiener then went on to Göttingen and studied briefly under some of the famous mathematicians there. He also went to Paris and described his impressions.

French mathematics, however, has followed a largely official course, and when a professor has retired to his little office and has signed the daybook which gives a record of the lecture he has just finished, it is customary for him to vanish from the lives of his students and younger colleagues. To this withdrawn existence Hadamard forms an exception, for he is genuinely interested in his students and has always been accessible to them. He has considered it an important part of his duty to promote their careers. Under his personal influence, the present generation of French mathematicians, for all the tradition of a barrier between the younger and the older men, has gone far to break down this barrier. I myself benefited from Hadamard's largeness of outlook. There was no reason why Hadamard should have paid any particular attention to a barbarian from across the Atlantic, at the beginning of his career. That is, there was no reason except Hadamard's good nature and his desire to uncover mathematical ability wherever he could find a hint of it.

When the First World War began in 1914, Wiener returned to America, uncertain about the direction his future career should take. He tried a variety of jobs, including one as a newspaper reporter. After spending a few unhappy months at Columbia University studying philosophy under John Dewey, and a short period giving lectures at Harvard, he became an instructor in mathematics at the University of Maine; later he described the experience as a nightmare. Nothing he tried seemed to suit him until the United States entered the war and he joined the group of scientists and engineers working on ballistics at the Aberdeen Proving Ground in Maryland, where he encountered Oswald Veblen and was impressed by his success in producing results which were useful to the military. This experience seems to have decided him to focus his attention on the kind of mathematics which is motivated by potential applications.

Once the war was over, Wiener obtained a position as instructor at MIT, where he climbed the academic ladder until he became full professor and remained there for the rest of his life. Although mathematics was not yet a particularly strong department at MIT there was easy contact with engineers and physicists. Wiener was famous in the MIT community for his eccentricities. He liked to think aloud, even in the swimming pool, and needed listeners to hear what he was thinking. He made a habit of walking around the campus and talking at great length to any colleague or student that he encountered. Those who valued their time learnt to hide when they saw him coming. At the same time he was respected for his achievements and for his encyclopedic knowledge.

In 1926 Wiener had married a former student of his father's named Margaret Engemann, who, after emigrating from Germany with other members of her family at the age of fourteen, had become an assistant professor of modern languages at Juanita College in Huntington, Pennsylvania. They had two daughters, Barbara (born 1928) and Peggy (born 1929). Margaret was a fervent admirer of Adolf Hitler and kept copies of his book *Mein Kampf* prominently displayed in her bedroom, to the intense annoyance of her Jewish husband. He suffered from untreated bipolar disorder: deep depressions that lasted several months were followed by periods of restless and creative activity. The depressions tended to come on more often when he stayed at home, and that was one of the reasons why he spent so much of his time travelling. Away from home, the distractions of public lectures and ceaseless conversations with friends and admirers kept his spirits high. According to Hans Freudenthal, Wiener was a famously bad expositor: 'After proving at length a fact that would be too easy if set as an exercise for an intelligent sophomore, he would assume without proof a profound theorem that was seemingly unrelated to the preceding text, then continue with a proof containing puzzling but irrelevant items, next interrupt it with a totally unrelated historical exposition.'

Between 1922 and 1927 Wiener had visited Europe almost every year, but spent little time in Göttingen, due to friction with Courant. For example, Wiener pointed out that Courant's ideas about the method of finite differences could already be found in a paper he had co-authored. Such things are bound to occur from time to time, but Wiener was so annoyed that he wrote, though did not publish, a novel in which the character of a professor who was unfair to gifted young people by taking over their ideas was rather obviously based on Courant. In 1928 he applied for a position at the University of Melbourne in Australia, but despite the support of Carathéodory, Hardy, Hilbert, and Veblen he failed to get it; nevertheless, this seems to have prompted MIT into granting him tenure, and by 1932 he was full professor. Before that he spent some time back in England, acting as Hardy's deputy at Cambridge.

Wiener made no secret of the fact that he was disappointed not to be a Harvard professor like his father. He was firmly convinced that this was due to the opposition of Birkhoff, whose anti-Semitism was well known. Where appointments to Harvard were concerned Birkhoff was very influential, especially during the period 1935–1939, when he was dean of the faculty of arts and sciences. Like others in his position, he often found himself having to balance the claims of young Americans against those of displaced scholars. At Harvard, the former were usually preferred, leading to accusations of anti-Semitism. On one occasion Birkhoff expressed his views to an officer of the Rockefeller Foundation who noted afterwards, 'B speaks long and earnestly concerning the Jewish question and the importation of Jewish scholars. He has no theoretical prejudice against the race and on the contrary every wish to be absolutely fair and sympathetic. He does however think that we must be more realistic than we are at present concerning the dangers in the situation and he is privately and entirely confidentially more or less sympathetic with the difficulties of Germany. He does not approve of their methods but he is inclined to agree that the results were necessary.'

Wiener was active on the American Emergency Committee in Aid of Displaced German Scholars, set up after the Nazis came into power: the Viennese logician Karl Menger was one of those he was able to assist personally. Wiener was warned of the tactical danger of MIT having too large a proportion of the mathematical staff from the Jewish race: 'Other things being approximately equal it is legitimate to consider the matter of race in case the appointment of another member of the Jewish race would increase the proportion of such men in the department far beyond the proportion of the population.' This referred to a former student of Wiener's then at the Institute for Advanced Study, who mentioned in a letter to Wiener that 'Einstein has been saying around here that Birkhoff is one of the world's greatest anti-Semites.'

When the Second World War broke out Wiener came up with ideas about using computers in the war effort but at the time these were largely ignored as impracticable. After the war was over he decided to have nothing more to do with government or industry and explained his decision in an influential article, 'A Scientist Rebels', in the periodical *Atlantic*

Monthly. Although much of his time and energy were spent in trying to influence public opinion as to the dangers of letting 'irresponsible militarists' take control of scientific discoveries, he continued to think about a variety of subjects, especially statistics, engineering, and biology. He took the idea of feedback from engineering and greatly widened its scope under the name of cybernetics; two of his books on the subject became best-sellers. Wiener has often been described as 'the father of automation'. Some of his ideas were taken up by von Neumann, who made much more effective use of them.

Wiener often pressed his colleagues to confirm that his productivity was not declining. His usual words of greeting were 'Tell me, am I slipping?' The only possible response anyone could make was a strong denial; but even this was usually not enough and it was necessary to affirm in the strongest terms the great excellence of his latest research, whether one knew what he had been doing or not. Pólya recalled that on one occasion Wiener stopped his car in the middle of traffic to ask him, 'Am I really a good mathematician?' As Pólya said later, 'Have you really any choice in what to answer? People were honking all around us.' To quote Freudenthal again: 'in appearance and behaviour, Norbert Wiener was a baroque figure, short, rotund and myopic, combining these and many other qualities in an extreme degree. His conversation was a curious mixture of pomposity and wantonness. He was a poor listener. His self-praise was playful, convincing, and never offensive. He spoke many languages but was not easy to understand in any of them.'

Wiener (1953) wrote a 'most unusual' autobiography, of which Freudenthal remarked, 'although it conveys an extremely egocentric view of the world, I find it an agreeable story and not offensive, because it is naturally frank and there is no pose, least of all that of false modesty. All in all it is abundantly clear that he never had the slightest idea of how he appeared in the eyes of others.' According to someone else who also knew Wiener well, 'He was a man of enormous scientific vitality which the years did not seem to diminish, but this was complemented by extreme sensitivity ... Wiener was a man of many moods, and these were reflected in his lectures, which ranged from among the worst to the very best I have ever heard. Sometimes he would lull his audience to sleep or get lost in his own computations—but on other occasions I have seen him hold a group of colleagues in breathless attention while he set forth his ideas in truly brilliant fashion.'

Much has been written on the psychology of genius, whether it is associated with some degree of insanity or merely eccentricity. Norbert Wiener would make an interesting case study. 'In his reactions like a child, in his judgements like a philosopher,' said Santillana, who knew him well. He had a high opinion of his own abilities, but there he was right: he had such great virtuosity and originality that after his death he was referred to in the press as an American Leibniz. He died on a visit to Stockholm following a heart attack on 18 March 1964 at the age of sixty-nine.

Radical and Nobel Laureate
Igor Evgenievitch Tamm (1895–1971)

We now return to imperial Russia. Igor Evgenievitch Tamm was was born on 8 July 1895 in the port of Vladivostok in the far east of the country, the son of Evgenii Tamm, a civil engineer, and the former Olga Davydova. When he was six years old the family moved to Elizavetgrad (later Kirovograd), a provincial town in Ukraine, where he grew up. Like many gymnasium students of the pre-revolutionary period, Tamm read forbidden political literature voraciously and developed an enthusiasm for politics. He became involved in a Marxist study circle and participated in workers' demonstrations and illegal meetings. These activities worried his parents and so to distract him from politics they sent him to study abroad, choosing the university of tranquil Edinburgh rather than politically active London.

Having spent an uneventful year in the Scottish capital, which left him speaking English with a Scottish accent, Tamm returned home. He was getting bored with dull Edinburgh and wanted to change from mathematics and chemistry to physics and mathematics. In any case, the outbreak of the First World War prevented him from going abroad again. So he transferred to Moscow State University where many faculty members had just resigned in protest after a clash between radical students and police on the university campus. As a result the physics teaching left much to be desired, but even so he chose it as his major field.

At twenty Tamm hoped and feared that he might live the life of a revolutionary, regarding a possible career in science as philistine. In 1915 he joined the Social Democratic Workers Party as a member of its Menshevik faction. During the subsequent years of war and revolution Tamm alternated between Elizavetgrad and Moscow, Kiev and Odessa, between pursuing his academic studies and participating in the turbulent politics of those years. He married Natalya Vasilievna Shuiskaja in 1917; the couple had two children, Irene and Evgenii. After the collapse of the monarchy he turned political agitator and moved to Elizavetgrad to promote revolution there. In April he was elected to the City Soviet of Workers and Soldier Deputies and in June he represented his hometown at the first All-Russian Congress of Soviets in Petrograd (previously St Petersburg, later Leningrad). A leftist among Mensheviks, he shared the Bolsheviks' uncompromising opposition to the 'imperialist war' and voted with them against launching a new offensive on the eastern front.

Unlike the easy overnight coup in Petrograd, the Bolshevik takeover of power in Moscow in November 1917 involved a week of hard fighting. With the start of civil war the following summer, the Bolsheviks declared all other political parties illegal. By that time Tamm was concentrating more on his academic studies. He did not fight in the war, although his sympathies were with the Reds, and managed to graduate in the autumn. The collapse of the *ancien regime* allowed local initiative groups to establish dozens of new universities all over Russia. Tauride University in the Crimea was the first of these post-revolutionary schools. Tamm was spending the academic year 1919/20 there as an assistant lecturer when he met Yakov Frenkel, another political activist, who had already published papers in leading physics journals. They became lifelong friends.

On the day of the Bolshevik coup in Petrograd Frenkel, who had just graduated from the university, was busy taking the *Magister* examination, a formal prerequisite for obtaining the first teaching position in a Russian university. Like Tamm, he secured a junior post at Tauride and moved to the Crimea where he combined university teaching with membership of the governing board of the Commissariat of Enlightenment of the local Soviet. Political power in the south alternated many times in the course of the civil war. When the Whites made the Crimea their stronghold in the summer of 1919 Frenkel was jailed for having worked in the Red administration, and only the fact that he was an academic, a profession somewhat respected by both sides, saved his life.

Tamm also experienced arrest and the fear of execution at least once, in the summer of 1920, when he tried to pass secretly across the front between the Whites and the Reds, from the Crimea to his wife in Elizavetgrad. Caught by the Reds without the necessary papers, he was ordered to be shot as a White spy and escaped death only by explaining that he was a mathematician. To check this, the Red commander, who happened to be a former mathematics student, demanded that Tamm derive the Taylor expansion. After struggling all the night Tamm failed to produce the full derivation, whereupon the Red leader admitted that he too had forgotten most of his college mathematics and postponed the execution.

Some of his best friends and former colleagues-in-arms joined the Bolsheviks, but Tamm remained formally unaffiliated. In 1922 he returned to Moscow and by 1930 he had become professor of theoretical physics and head of department at Moscow State University. He was the first Moscow theoretician to adopt quantum mechanics after Heisenberg invented it around 1925. Ehrenfest invited Tamm to Leiden in 1928, where he met Paul Dirac, the British genius and one of the leaders of the quantum generation. Although generally unsociable, due to Asperger's syndrome, Dirac developed a close friendship with Tamm, Frenkel, and a few other Soviet physicists. For Tamm, he became the main authority in physics, alongside his mentor and revered colleague at Moscow State University,

Leonid Mandel'shtam, who shared with Ioffe the title of father of Soviet physics.

In 1930 Tamm was appointed head of the theoretical physics department at Moscow University, where he revised course materials to include the theory of relativity and quantum mechanics. From 1934 until his death in 1971 he was also head of the theoretical section of the Lebedev Physical Institute of the Soviet Academy of Sciences, after the academy was transferred to Moscow. Some of his younger staff moved to Kharkov, then the capital of the Ukrainian Soviet Republic, where the Physical-Technical Institute, organized by Ioffe, was at first an offshoot of the similar Leningrad institute but rapidly developed into a rival of its parent. Research was mainly carried out by theoretical physicists of the quantum generation led by the brilliant Lev Landau.

In 1922 Lenin had expelled a large number of prominent Russian intellectuals, many of them Jewish, who he suspected were opposed to Bolshevism; they mainly settled in Berlin, Paris, and Prague, awaiting the day when they could return to Russia. Fifteen years later his successor Stalin unleashed the Great Terror nationwide. Every community had to fill a quota for the labour camps. There was also a purge of the academic and administrative elite, in which Jews were well represented; many innocent people were arrested and found guilty. The outspoken Landau thought it prudent to move to the new Institute of Physical Problems in Moscow, directed by Kapitza. All the same he was arrested in 1938 and only Kapitza's influence with high-level politicians saved him from death in prison. The Ukrainian Physical-Technical Institute was never able to recover from the Great Terror.

There had been Soviet research into atomic fission on a small scale during the Second World War and even before that, but once the Americans had shown that thermonuclear weapons were feasible there was an all-out military-industrial effort similar to the Manhattan project in the United States. Andrei Sakharov, the father of the Soviet hydrogen bomb, was one of the leading atomic physicists mobilized to work on the development of the atomic weapons project. Some, like Kapitza, refused to co-operate. Others, like Tamm, regarded it as their patriotic duty to compete with the Americans and their allies. The Russians relied on intelligence work to obtain the technical information from America. Their main informant was Klaus Fuchs, a member of the German communist party, who had emigrated to England when the Nazis came to power and worked with Rudolph Peierls, a former student of Heisenberg and assistant of Pauli who had left Germany in 1929 at the age of thirty-two and after several moves was working in Cambridge. When Peierls was appointed to the physics chair at Birmingham in 1936 he took Fuchs with him, and when Peierls went to Los Alamos, during the war, so did Fuchs. Thanks to a photographic memory, Fuchs was able to tell the Russians all they needed to know about the design of the bomb. There was some delay owing to the small amount of uranium available to the Russians. However a supply could be obtained from occupied Germany after the end of the war in Europe, and in 1949 their first bomb was exploded. By that time Fuchs was back in England, where he was convicted of espionage and sentenced to nine years' imprisonment.

Although some of the German nuclear physicists had already moved or fled to the West some of those that remained agreed to move to the Soviet Union to work on military projects. One of the Germans was Gustav Hertz, the nephew of Heinrich, who has been mentioned earlier, and a few lines about his career will be added at the end of this profile.

For some forty years Igor Tamm was in the vanguard of Soviet nuclear physics, both as a teacher and as a researcher. He maintained the firm conviction that the main thrust of science would soon pass from the physical to the life sciences. His position in the Soviet Union and his international prestige gave him some freedom to criticize bureaucracy constructively. In 1958 the Nobel Prize in physics was shared equally between three Soviet physicists, of whom he was one, for the discovery and interpretation of the Cherenkov effect, which occurs when electrons travel through a substance faster than light would do but more slowly than light travels in a vacuum. Peierls, who knew Tamm quite well, described him as 'modesty incarnate, one of the most charming personalities in physics', adding that he had 'an agile mind, and an equally agile body, and the first impression he gave was of never standing still.' In addition to the Nobel Prize Tamm was awarded the order of Lenin twice and the order of the Red Badge of Labour. He was elected a corresponding member of the Soviet Academy in 1933, a full member twenty years later, and received the academy's highest scientific award, the Lomonosov Medal, in 1968. Peierls tells us that he never took advantage of the special privileges available to academicians, such as better food rations. He died in Moscow on 12 April 1971, at the age of seventy-six.

Finally, a few words about the later career of the Nobel laureate Gustav Hertz, the nephew of Heinrich. Being of Jewish descent, he was forced to leave the Technical University in Berlin-Charlottenburg, where he was *Ordinarius*, after Hitler came to power, but he remained in Germany and became director of an industrial laboratory. After the German collapse, he and other German physicists were drafted by the Russians to work on military projects in a segregated laboratory complex at Sukhumi on the Black Sea coast. By 1955 the task of producing nuclear weapons was complete. When the German scientists returned to their divided country at the end of their ten-year contracts, Hertz became professor and director of the physics institute of the University of Leipzig from 1955 to 1961. Upon retirement he moved to East Berlin, where he died in 1975.

Geometry is the Real Life
Oscar Zariski (1899–1986)

Among the many outstanding mathematicians and physicists from eastern Europe are several who emigrated to the United States at a fairly early stage in their careers. The case of Lefschetz has already been described; another was Zariski. These two mathematicians had much in common but their life-stories were quite different. Zariski was the foremost algebraic geometer of his generation: 'geometry is the real life', he used to say. Oscar Zariski, to use the name by which he was known later, was born on 24 April 1899 in Kobrin, a large town in White Russia (now Belarus), the sixth child and third son of Bezaliel and Hannah Zaritsky, who gave him the first name of Ascher. Under the tsars, Jewish communities had to provide ten military conscripts out of every thousand inhabitants, whereas for other communities it was only seven; moreover Jewish boys were conscripted from the age of twelve, while their years of service were only reckoned after they were twenty-one. Bezaliel, a Talmudic scholar, had ruined his health after taking a poisonous concoction to escape the draft. Hannah was the daughter of the owner of a successful tavern, for whom she acted as landlady. After Bezaliel died in 1901 she opened a general store. A wealthy brother helped support the family, taught Oscar some mathematics, and encouraged him to leave the Pale.

Russian Jews mostly spoke Yiddish, and so Hannah employed a tutor to teach her son the Russian language and arithmetic. He was a quick and eager student. When the quota of Jews allowed to enter high school was doubled, by imperial decree, Zariski gained admission to one which was some distance from Kobrin. At the end of the eight years he spent there his teachers, impressed by his ability, urged him to go on to university, which would mean in practice that he would need to convert to Christianity. This he declined to do because he was by then an atheist and a Marxist; he was never much interested in the Jewish faith and culture.

Zariski decided to move from White Russia to Ukraine. When Russia entered the First World War he went to live in Onenigo for the duration, and then in 1918 enrolled at the University of Kiev, the Ukrainian capital. Since the mathematics faculty there had no room for him he initially studied philosophy, but later was able to transfer to mathematics. During the civil war Zariski wrote for a local Marxist newspaper and on one occasion was wounded in a fracas.

In view of the unsettled conditions in the emerging Soviet Republic, Zariski decided to emigrate, choosing Italy as his destination since the cost of living was low and Italian universities were not charging tuition fees to foreigners. He travelled on a Polish passport, obtained by some judicious bribery, and once in Italy enrolled at the University of Pisa. However, because he found the mathematics courses being given there so inferior to those at Kiev, at the first opportunity he transferred to Rome, at that time one of the leading universities in the world for mathematics, especially algebraic geometry. Castelnuovo became Zariski's official research adviser, but it was the more approachable Enriques, the brother-in-law of Castelnuovo as well as his friend and collaborator, who acted as Zariski's mentor, rather than Castelnuovo himself. Enriques' primary interest at this time was in the philosophy and history of science. Later, Zariski would maintain that Enriques' cavalier attitude to the need for rigorous proofs marked the beginning of the end for the Italian school. 'We aristocrats do not need proofs,' Enriques would say, 'proofs are for you plebeians.'

Zariski was now desperately poor, and only able to continue his studies thanks to the generosity of friendly Italians, high and low. It was during this difficult period that he got to know Yole Cagli, an Italian-Jewish student of literature from Ancona. She gave him lessons in Italian, in return for lessons in Russian. Before long they were engaged and their marriage took place in Kobrin in 1924. The family business had begun to recover, athough later his mother and other members of the family were among the millions who starved to death under the Stalinist oppression.

In Rome the young couple were able to earn something by teaching. Under Enriques' sympathetic guidance Zariski completed his doctorate with a thesis on polynomial equations which can be solved by the use of radicals. 'Zariski, you are with us but not one of us,' Castelnuovo commented, not unkindly, referring to Zariski's insistence on rigour and his feeling that the methods of the Italian school had come to a dead end and were inadequate for further progress in the field of algebraic geometry. Castelnuovo encouraged Zariski to study the innovative work of Lefschetz. Zariski did so with enthusiasm, and under its influence wrote several research papers on combinatorial topology.

Contact between the German and the Italian schools was generally poor at this period. Partly to remedy this, Severi asked Zariski to translate some of Dedekind's works into Italian, while Enriques asked him to write some expository articles on the theory of sets. As Zariski said later, 'It was a pity that my Italian teachers never told me that there was such a tremendous development of the algebra which is connected with algebraic geometry. I only discovered this much later, when I came to the United States.'

Zariski himself was by now fully occupied and his wife Yole was teaching full-time. In 1925 their first child Raphael was born. Already Mussolini's anti-Semitic policies were being put into effect, and Zariski began to doubt whether it would be wise to remain in Italy much longer. Just for one year he was being supported in Rome by a Rockefeller Fellowship, but he needed a regular academic position. He thought about returning to the Soviet Union, but discovered that despite his Marxist background an illegal emigrant like himself would not be welcome.

After trying various other possibilities, Zariski asked Lefschetz if there was anything that might be suitable for him in America. Lefschetz was fifteen years senior to Zariski and already well established in the United States. The best he could do for Zariski was a scholarship at Johns Hopkins University for the year 1927/8. Unfortunately, due to visa problems, Yole and Raphael were unable to accompany him to Baltimore. Zariski found Johns Hopkins 'rather dull'. At the invitation of Lefschetz he gave some lectures at Princeton on his recent research, and wrote back to Yole with some enthusiasm: 'one works very well here—it is a town made for study, totally occupied by university buildings of beautiful architecture. The appearance of the town is attractive; it offers a variety of coloured vistas and finally my eyes find repose, after the annoying monotony of the Baltimore streets. Lefschetz treats me very well, and we have really become friends.' On one occasion when they were discussing the difference between algebra and topology Lefschetz took the view that algebraic geometry was part of topology, and Zariski that it was part of algebra. So Zariski, just to tease Lefschetz a bit, asked, 'How do you draw the line between algebra and topology?' Quick as a flash, Lefschetz came back with, 'Well, if it's just turning the crank, it's algebra, but if it's got an idea, it's topology.'

At the end of his first year at Johns Hopkins Zariski was appointed to the position of associate professor. This strengthened the case for Yole and Raphael to be granted United States visas. Zariski returned to Italy to obtain these and bring his family to Baltimore. In 1932 Yole gave birth to their daughter Vera.

Zariski was attracted by Emmy Noether's modern algebra, not for its own sake but only as the appropriate foundation for algebraic geometry. He was able to deploy both the topological methods developed by Lefschetz and the algebraic methods developed in Göttingen. With the publication of his classic book on algebraic surfaces the importance of Zariski's work became widely recognized. He spent 1934/5 in Princeton as a visitor to the new Institute for Advanced Study, where he was able to get to know Weyl and other German émigrés. In 1936 the Zariskis became American citizens, and he began to play a more prominent role in the American mathematical world—for example he became editor of the *American Journal of Mathematics* and associate editor of the *Annals of Mathematics*. In 1942 he was elected to the United States National Academy of Sciences.

After the Second World War Zariski spent a fruitful year in São Paolo, where André Weil was a colleague. Meanwhile offers were beginning to arrive from other American universities. At first Zariski used these to try to persuade Johns Hopkins to give him a reduced teaching-load so that he could devote more time to research, but without success, and he began to think it was time to move on. In 1947 he accepted an attractive offer from the California Institute of Technology, just before another, more attractive, offer arrived from Harvard. Although much embarrassed by this awkward situation he persuaded the California Institute to release him so that he could take up the Harvard offer, which was for a full professorship. The first Jew to hold tenure in the Harvard mathematics department, he was amazed to discover that his appointment had been strongly supported by the notoriously anti-Semitic Birkhoff.

When she got there Yole was persuaded to give up her work, teaching elementary Italian, and so become like other Harvard wives. In fact the Zariskis rather enjoyed the old-fashioned formal social life for which Harvard was noted. Zariski was a success at Harvard. He was naturally much involved in the 1950 International Congress of Mathematicians held in Cambridge, Massachusetts at which he was interested to see Severi given the cold shoulder as a known fascist sympathizer. One year Zariski gave the Colloquium lectures of the American Mathematical Society at Yale. At Harvard itself he organized what soon became a famous seminar.

In April 1964, when he was sixty-five, Zariski was invited by Harvard to continue in his post for five more years, after the normal retiring age, but was only prepared to do so on a half-time basis. During this period he became president of the American Mathematical Society, at a time when it was becoming somewhat politicized (Zariski thought this undesirable). On the occasion of his seventy-fifth birthday, a bronze portrait bust was placed in the common room of the Harvard mathematics department. Not long afterwards his health began to decline—first he experienced hearing loss and then his mind began to fail. Zariski died at home on 4 July 1986 at the age of eighty-seven.

Critical Genius
Wolfgang Pauli (1900–1958)

Towards the end of his life the physicist Wolfgang Pauli reflected, 'when I was young I believed I was the best formalist of my time. I thought I was a revolutionary. When the big problems would come I would solve them and write about them. The big problems came and passed me by. I was still the classicist and not the revolutionary.' The future Nobel laureate was born in Vienna on 25 April 1900 and given the names Wolfgang Ernst Friederich, his godfather being Ernst Mach, the physicist and philosopher. Pauli's father, also named Wolfgang, came from a respected Sephardic family of Prague named Pascheles, but took the name Pauli after conversion to Catholicism. He had studied medicine at the Charles University of the Bohemian capital, and subsequently had risen to become professor of colloid chemistry at the University of Vienna. Pauli's mother Bertha (née Schutz), the daughter of a well-known Viennese opera singer, wrote for one of the more liberal newspapers.

After she committed suicide in 1927 Wolfgang's father married a young sculptor named Maria Rottler. When he fled to Zurich after Austria was annexed by the Nazis in 1938 she remained in Vienna until the war was over. Highly respected and much honoured he died in 1955.

The boy, his parents' only son, was a prodigy, excelling not only in mathematics and physics but also in philosophy. While still at the gymnasium he began to study the general theory of relativity, which Einstein had just published. It seems likely that in this Pauli was assisted by some of the theoretical physicists at the Institute of Technology. Like his mother, he was strongly against the government which had taken Austria into the war on the German side. He was spared military service because of a weak heart, and so was able to go straight on to university.

Pauli chose to study theoretical physics in Munich under the renowned Sommerfeld, who used to engage his students in the research activity of his institute right from the start. They were introduced to quantum theory and experienced the shock which every physicist felt on encountering the revolutionary theory for the first time. However, the outmoded version which Sommerfeld presented struck Pauli as muddled. His brilliant fellow student Heisenberg, whose bolder departures from the principles of classical physics were soon to be so spectacularly successful, agreed with him. Even so, Pauli, like all of Sommerfield's former students, developed a deep, lifelong respect for his 'highly revered' teacher. Sommerfeld even tolerated Pauli's routine of getting up very late in the morning, teaching in the afternoon, sampling the night-life of Munich in the evening, and returning home late to spend most of the night working.

Klein had commissioned Sommerfeld to write the article on the theory of relativity for his *Encyklopädie der mathematischen Wissenschaften*. Sommerfeld passed on the task to Pauli, still only in his second year of graduate work, because he had already published several excellent papers on the subject. Pauli soon completed a critical monograph of 250 pages which presented the mathematical foundations of the theory as well as its physical significance. He also went into the history of the theory, describing the relevance of the ideas of Poincaré, Lorentz, Hilbert, and Weyl to Einstein's great work. Sommerfeld was elated by his student's performance, in which Pauli demonstrated his mastery of the art of scientific exposition for the first time.

In 1922 Pauli obtained his doctorate and became assistant to Max Born, who had just moved to Göttingen from Berlin. 'Little Pauli', said Born, 'is very stimulating, such a good assistant I will never have again.' In fact Pauli was not exceptionally small although his behaviour was somewhat childlike, and Heisenberg, his successor, was just as intelligent and more disciplined in his behaviour. Anyway, Pauli only stayed in Göttingen one winter before moving to Hamburg. Before leaving, he had met Niels Bohr for the first time; this was to prove a lifelong friendship. Bohr was so impressed by Pauli that he invited him to Copenhagen for the first of many visits. Pauli, with his unsurpassed genius for criticism, became Bohr's favourite partner in debate.

Pauli not only made important contributions of his own but helped to shape the work of others in long, critical discussions. Much of Pauli's effectiveness as a critic was the result of his total disregard for his colleagues' sensitivities. A typical Pauli remark, after reading a paper he did not think much of, was 'it is not even wrong.' Another was 'I do not mind if you think slowly, but I do object when you publish more quickly than you think.' But the best of all may be his intervention after Einstein had made a comment at a colloquium when Pauli remarked to the audience, 'You know, what Mr Einstein has just said is not so stupid.'

Once Pauli had settled down in Hamburg he soon established himself as an influential member of the second generation of quantum physicists. He wrote two important papers with Heisenberg, and although of contrasting personalities and life-styles they remained good friends. In 1924 Pauli habilitated and became *Privatdozent* at Hamburg. Before long he had established the famous exclusion principle, the crowning conclusion to the original quantum theory, soon to be replaced by the proper, mathematically consistent quantum mechanics of Heisenberg, Dirac, Schrödinger, and von Neumann. He also contributed a masterly article on the old quantum theory to the 1926 edition of the *Handbuch der Physic*.

Two years later Hamburg gave him a titular professorship after he refused a call to an *Extra-Ordinarius* post in Leipzig. He looked back on his four years at Hamburg with pleasure, as a beautiful time. In 1928 he moved to Switzerland to become *Ordinarius* at the ETH, after Debye had left Zurich for Leipzig and Schrödinger for Berlin. Thus he found himself the sole lecturer in theoretical physics, although at this time Weyl was also working in the field. Pauli attracted various postdoctoral students, among them the American Oppenheimer, and he had negotiated an assistantship which he used to recruit talented young physicists, some of whom became leaders in the field. One of them was the Viennese physicist Viktor Weisskopf, who was visiting on a Rockefeller Fellowship at the time. When this came to an end he considered joining Kapitza in the Soviet Union but finding the political atmosphere there too repellent he changed his mind and made the rest of his career in the United States. Of the articles Pauli wrote in the next few years the one on wave mechanics which he contributed to the 1933 edition of the *Handbuch der Physic* is outstanding; Oppenheimer used it as the basis for the courses he gave to young American physicists in the following years.

In 1929 Pauli had married the actress Margarete Käthe (Kate) Deppner, from Leipzig, but she soon left him and they were divorced the next year. He began to travel further afield, to Odessa for an international conference, and to lecture at a summer school in America. This was the time of prohibition in the United States, which did not prevent him being occasionally under the influence of alcohol. When Pauli returned to Zurich it was recognized that he was becoming increasingly neurotic. The crisis seems to have been brought on by the suicide of Pauli's mother, two years before, and by his own failed marriage. His father recommended him to consult Carl Jung, who practised in Zurich, and Jung recommended psychoanalysis under a newly qualified analyst, who had just come to work with him. She advised Pauli to make a habit of recording his dreams, which Jung found remarkably interesting.

In April 1934 Pauli, fully recovered from his psychological problems, married Franca Bertram in London, on possibly his first visit to England. She had been the secretary of an important communist politician, perhaps the physicist Friedrich Adler, and held strong opinions, one of which was a dislike of Jung. They had a modest house built at Zollikon, the first municipality adjacent to the city along the lake, where she provided Pauli with a home where he could feel at ease. An eminently practical woman, she looked at the world with realism. This second marriage endured, although there were no children.

Pauli only became aware that he was Jewish quite late, and anti-Semitism did not become a problem for him until the German annexation of Austria in 1938 when Switzerland decreed that visas would be required for holders of Austrian passports. Several physicists, including Pauli, were caught by this. He had already applied to become a Swiss citizen, but without result, and now the matter had become urgent. He wrote to the authorities, 'the intention is to naturalize in Zurich, where I feel at home as I already have for many years.' The reply was that his application could not be considered until he had lived in Switzerland uninterruptedly for twelve years, of which the last six must be in Zurich itself. Also, he must be able to speak in the local dialect. After this rebuff Pauli had to exchange his Austrian passport for a German one, fortunately not marked J for Jew, so that the Paulis were not at risk if they passed through Germany on their travels. At first Pauli did not take the Nazi threat very seriously, although war was now imminent.

Pauli had been offered a visiting professorship at the Princeton Institute for Advanced Study for the winter term 1940/1, but he wanted to get rid of his German nationality before he went. When he asked about his application for Swiss citizenship he was told it was not being considered because one of his colleagues at the ETH did not recommend him, perhaps because he was Jewish. After a trying journey, the Paulis reached New York where von Neumann met them and drove them to Princeton. They found conditions in America relatively normal except that some of the physicists were already engaged on defence work. Pauli began to try to extend his stay for the duration of the war.

The International Education Board had agreed to extend his visiting fellowship for up to four years and the Institute for Advanced Study agreed to supplement this. However the ETH insisted that Pauli should return to Zurich, regardless of the obvious difficulty of crossing the Atlantic in wartime, and would only extend his leave for one year, after which he was liable to dismissal. Pólya was in a similar position. It was argued that the students regarded their absence as somehow immoral. Meanwhile he was enjoying life in Princeton, mainly socializing with émigrés such as the physicist Wigner, the mathematicians Siegel, Weyl, and von Neumann and the art historian Panofsky. The institute offered him permanent membership, after Einstein retired, while Columbia University in New York offered him a full professorship, just after the news of his Nobel Prize was released. The prize was given 'for the discovery of the exclusion principle, also called the Pauli principle', which Pauli had formulated many years before; perhaps the delay could be ascribed to doubts in the physics community as to its validity.

At this point the Paulis returned to Zurich to clear up his position at the ETH and to restart his application for Swiss naturalization. The situation had changed when the news of Pauli's Nobel Prize reached Zurich. Although it was to be three more years before the naturalization process was complete (the key step was to apply in Zollikon rather than Zurich) the problems at the ETH were sorted out and he wrote to decline the offers he had received from America. He became increasingly interested in questions on the borderline between science and philosophy, and collaborated with Jung on a book called *Naturerklärung und psyche* (The interpretation of Nature and the psyche). He was also involved in the planning of the new European research institute of physics, known as CERN and to be located on a site near Geneva. He led an active life, in good health apart from an over-indulgence in alcohol, until he was taken ill while lecturing on 5 December 1958. An operation the following week disclosed a large, inoperable tumour of the pancreas and he died on 15 December at the age of fifty-eight.

Pauli was physically awkward, and this gave rise to the legendary Pauli effect, that something would go wrong as soon as he came into a room. He was a poor experimenter and a bad lecturer. In class he mumbled to himself; his writing on the blackboard was small and disorganized. Although his lectures were not easy to understand his students were fascinated by them. In discussions he was hard to convince, and refused to accept unclear formulations. As Peierls said, 'To discuss some unfinished work or some new and speculative work with Pauli was a great experience because of his understanding and his high intellectual honesty, which would never let a slipshod or artificial argument get by.' Pauli found targets for his caustic wit everywhere. After a long argument with Lev Landau, whose work was as brilliant but not so well expressed as his own, Pauli responded to Landau's protest that not everything he said was nonsense with 'Oh no! Far from it! What you said was so confused that one could not tell whether it was nonsense or not.' The motor clumsiness, the insensitivity to the feelings of others, the mumbling at the blackboard, and other features of his behaviour suggest that like other prodigies Pauli might have suffered from more than a trace of autism.

Although Pauli was only with him in Göttingen briefly he deeply impressed Born, who recalled, 'Ever since the time he had been my assistant in Göttingen I had been aware that he was a genius, comparable with Einstein himself. Indeed from the point of view of pure science he was possibly greater than Einstein. His achievements, the enunciation of the exclusion principle and several major contributions in nuclear physics were certainly of high quality but he was unable to exercise his creative powers with the imagination and intuitive facility possessed by the greatest of his contemporaries.'

Master of Two Cultures
Dennis Gabor (1900–1979)

We now return to Hungary. Dennis Gabor, in Hungarian Gábor Denes, scientist, engineer, inventor, humanist, Nobel laureate, was born in Budapest on 5 June 1900. The eldest in a family of three boys, he was followed by George, who died of pancytopaenia in 1935, and then by André, born in 1903. Dennis knew his paternal grandfather who had been born in 1832 of parents who had settled in Hungary at the end of the eighteenth century, having come from Russia and from Spain.

The family were tall, fair, blue-eyed people, and thought themselves to have been descendants of one of the Russian tribes, the Cerims or Kuzri, who adopted the Jewish faith centuries earlier. The boys' father Bertalan (or Bartholemew) came from the Hungarian town of Eger in 1867. Their mother Adrienne (née Kalman), was an actress who gave up the stage when she married. Her father was a highly skilled watchmaker and the son of an excellent tailor, but Dennis knew very little of his mother's forebears; he thought they were probably Sephardic Jews who settled in Hungary in the eighteenth century. Betalan had been a gifted and ambitious child who hoped to go to university and qualify as an engineer, the profession followed by several other members of the family: unfortunately his father's business failed and as a result he had to leave school early and take a clerical job at the age of seventeen. Nevertheless he worked his way up and succeeded in becoming director of the largest industrial enterprise in Hungary.

The three brothers grew up in a home of culture, where German, as well as Hungarian, was spoken, and the children were provided with French and English governesses in succession so that they became fluent in all four languages. In their early teens the boys had intellectual stimulation not only from an excellent tutor but also from their father's circle of friends, including a doctor and a lawyer who took a special interest in the talented young Gabors. The family took lunch and dinner together and, especially in later years, mealtimes were like the meetings of a discussion group.

Dennis was a voracious reader and was gifted with a prodigious memory. When he was aged about twelve, his father offered him a prize if he could memorize Schiller's long (430-line) epic poem *Das Lied von der Glocke*. Dennis won the prize and could still recite the whole poem in later years. He amused himself translating Hungarian poems into standard German, using the same metre as the original. At home he benefited from a fine collection of histories of the visual arts, including coloured reproductions of famous paintings. He could at once identify the artist of practically any item in a picture gallery. Dennis was also gifted musically and having a marvellous memory and a good voice could sing parts of most operas in their original language.

Family influence was so strong that by comparison his formal education had comparatively little impact on his development. The gymnasium Dennis attended included mathematics and the sciences in its curriculum. After some months the form-master complained that he had a neurotic child on his hands and suggested that Dennis be sent to a special institution catering for unmanageable children. His father realized that the problem was caused by the low standard in the class and persuaded the school to keep him. Dennis gained top marks throughout his school career. He was almost always ahead of the syllabus and did not treat his teachers with due respect.

The physics master was a remarkably conscientious man who constructed teaching aids not provided by the school. Dennis's knowledge of physics even at that early age was superior to that of his teacher due to the fact that Bertalan allowed the boy to buy almost any book he desired, including German textbooks of advanced mathematics and physics. As he claimed, 'Before I went to university I knew all about the mathematics I was to learn there and more electromagnetic theory than I ever learned at the Technical University in Berlin.' Although he never took a degree in mathematics he was a more than competent mathematician, as is obvious from even a casual study of his life's work: all his inventive ideas were based on full mathematical analyses of the relevant details.

Dennis was a somewhat delicate child but at school he developed good physique and athletic ability; later in life he also played a fine game of tennis. He joined the officer training corps and qualified in artillery and horsemanship. In 1917, after passing the *Matura* examination, which qualified him for university entrance, he was called up for military service. This took him to northern Italy, then occupied by the Hungarian forces. Characteristically he took the opportunity to add Italian to his other languages. On demobilization Gabor returned to Budapest.

The collapse of the Austrian monarchy after the war shattered existing economic and social patterns. Moreover, much of the wealth and population of Hungary was transferred to Romania. From being the second capital of the Austrian Empire, Budapest became just the principal town of a small country. In 1919 a communist regime took over, led by Béla Kun. Since a majority of its leaders were Jewish, a wave of anti-Semitism swept the country when the regime fell after four months. Under the fascist regency of Admiral Horthy which followed, Jewish rights were curtailed because Jews were associated with communism. This was racist anti-Semitism, not religious. A *numerus clausus* was imposed, permitting only six Jews in every hundred university students. At the University of Budapest the percentage of Jewish students fell from 34.4 in 1914 to 4.1 in 1939.

At this stage the whole Gabor family adopted the Lutheran faith and Dennis remained in that faith for the rest of his life. In postwar Hungary it was engineering rather than pure science which attracted people of talent and ambition, so that they might be in a better position to earn a living. However, Gabor found that he disagreed so much with the policies of the reactionary government of the time that, in his third year, he decided to leave the country and continue his studies in Berlin. When von Neumann, perhaps the most brilliant star in the constellation of Hungarian scientists who made the same decision, was asked for his opinion as to what contributed to the exodus of so many in the interwar period, he said that it was a coincidence of some cultural factors which he could not make precise: an external pressure on the whole society of that part of central Europe, a subconscious feeling of extreme insecurity in individuals, and the necessity of producing the unusual or facing extinction.

In Berlin Gabor decided to specialize in physics rather than engineering. He had been attending the famous Tuesday physics colloquium at the university, which became the highspot of his week. He was also attending the 'unforgettable' seminar on statistical mechanics conducted by Einstein. This confirmed his resolution to become a physicist, although he preferred to be described as an engineer. After taking a senior research degree in the subject Gabor was recruited by the physics laboratory of the firm of Siemens and Halske but, when Hitler came into power, his contract was not renewed. He returned to Budapest, where he found the political situation had deteriorated further. Several physicists he knew were already thinking of emigrating to England; when he was offered employment by the parent firm of Metropolitan Vickers he did not hesitate. The high-voltage laboratory where he worked was located at Rugby, where he settled down happily, and within two years he had married the daughter of a local railway engineer. He remained there for the next fifteen years but afterwards described it as a sterile period for research, compared with the excitement of Berlin. This was mainly because as an alien he was excluded from the secret research on radar being done at the laboratory, in preparation for the coming war. As we have seen in the profile of Simon, there was a reluctance to entrust secret scientific work to aliens.

In Hungary the first anti-Semitic law on the Nazi model was promulgated in 1939. Quotas were established in the professions and no businesses could be more than partly owned by Jews. Everyone who had acquired Hungarian citizenship since 1914 automatically lost it, even if their ancestors had lived in the country for centuries. In the next ten months, after the Germans occupied Hungary, more than half the Hungarian Jews, including perhaps a third of those living in Budapest, perished as a result. At the end of 1938 Gabor's brother André had come to England on what was meant to be a short visit but Gabor persuaded him to stay and found him work in the ministry of agriculture; later he joined the economics department of the University of Nottingham. Their parents also came to England but returned to Budapest just before Germany's invasion of Poland started the Second World War. Their mother survived the siege of Budapest and shortly after the war came to England, living first with Dennis and later with André.

Meanwhile Gabor was continuing with research and came near to inventing the electron microscope and later the laser. He took out patents on many of his inventions, some of which were commercially valuable. In 1942 he gave a lecture on electron optics in which he anticipated the work on holography which later earned him the Nobel Prize. After twenty years working in industrial laboratories Gabor moved into academia in 1949 when he was appointed reader in electron physics at Imperial College, London. There, during what he later described as some of the happiest years in his scientific career, he led a team of young research students. He was a workaholic but strictly at his own pace, often taking a nap at his desk. He gave special lectures but not regular courses and was spared administrative duties, although he acted as a consultant in industry.

In 1958 Imperial promoted him to a personal chair in applied electron physics. In the first part of his inaugural lecture he focused on scientific questions, including the feasibility of thermonuclear fusion, but in the second part he began to speculate about the future of society. As he explained, 'The future cannot be predicted but futures can be invented. It was man's ability to invent that has made human society what it is. The first step of the inventor is to visualize by an act of imagination a thing or state which does not yet exist and which appears to him as in some way desirable. He can then start rationally arguing backwards and forwards until a way is found from one to the other. For the social inventor the engineering of human consent is the most essential and the most difficult step'. Gabor went on to develop his ideas in what proved to be his most popular book, *Inventing the Future*, which was translated into many languages. In it he expressed critical views about communism, and so he was rather surprised to be elected an honorary member of the Hungarian Academy of Sciences. After Gabor reached retirement age in 1967 Imperial appointed him to a professorial fellowship, which enabled him to retain his old office and the secretarial provision he needed. In February 1969 he made what proved to be his last public appearance when he gave one of the traditional Friday evening discourses at the Royal Institution in London.

In retirement he increasingly devoted his time to writing on social matters. He wrote, 'Now that my future is mostly behind me I am passionately interested in the future which I shall never see, but I hope my writings will contribute to a smooth passage into a very new epoch.' In a series of books and discourses he applied his penetrating intellect to some of the problems of man's survival, problems created by the advance of technology. The Gabors usually spent their summers in Italy, where they had built a villa at Lavinio Lido, a pleasant holiday resort near Anzio, on the Mediterranean coast south of Rome. He was a founder member of the Club of Rome where people of diverse backgrounds met to study problems of natural resources, nutrition, environment, climate, the Third World, income distribution, etc. For some time, Gabor had been considered for a Nobel Prize, and in 1971 he was awarded this in physics for his pioneering work on holography. There followed a cornucopia of honorary degrees and similar marks of distinction. In 1974 he suffered a severe cerebral haemorrhage which left him unable to read or write; later he almost lost the power of speech, although his hearing and intellectual powers were unimpaired. Four years later, after enjoying summer in Italy, he became bed-ridden and died peacefully in a London nursing home on 9 February 1979 at the age of seventy-eight. In his own words, he was one of the lucky physicists who have been able to see one of their ideas grow into a sizeable chapter of physics.

Napoleon of Logic
Alfred Tarski (1901–1983)

When Poland was partitioned between Austria, Germany, and Russia, both Germany and Russia tried to suppress Polish culture; Austria, however, was more liberal. Early in the twentieth century a flourishing school of mathematics developed in Lvov led by Hugo Steinhaus (1887–1972), who studied under Hilbert at Göttingen, and in Warsaw led by Zygmund Janisewski (1888–1920), who studied in Paris. The policy was to concentrate on new fields of research like topology and set theory in which it might be possible to reach international standards more quickly. Although both cities were strongholds of Judaism it was not easy for Jews to obtain regular university posts. The analytic topologist Waclaw Sierpinski (1882–1969), who was a Karaite Jew, succeeded in doing so, but the mathematical logician Alfred Tarski, a converted Jew, encountered great difficulty, as we shall see in this profile. Other famous Polish mathematicians of the younger generation were Stanislaw Ulam (1909–1934) and Samuel Eilenberg (1913–2005) who emigrated to the United States between the wars. Many who stayed in Poland lost their lives in the general slaughter of the Polish intelligentsia by the German invaders.

Born Alfred Teitelbaum in Warsaw on 14 January 1901, Tarski was the elder of two sons born to a successful Jewish businessman of the same name who traded in lumber, and his wife Rosa (née Prussak), the daughter of a textile magnate, who had been a brilliant student in secondary school and was gifted with an exceptional memory. In later years Tarski credited his intellect to his mother but spoke of his father as 'a man of the heart'. He attended a gymnasium for the intellectual elite where his teachers described his ability as extraordinary. Just before Poland regained its independence he enrolled at the University of Warsaw, where lectures were already given in Polish, not Russian; a third of the students were Jewish.

Biology was Tarski's favourite subject at school and he intended to major in this at university. However at the end of the first year he succeeded in solving a challenging problem in set theory posed by the professor of logic which led to his first published paper. At the professor's urging he switched to mathematics and logic, where his breadth of interest and quick mastery of the subject impressed his teachers. At the same time he was working as an instructor at the Warsaw pedagogical institute.

In 1924 Tarski wrote an astonishing paper with the brilliant Polish mathematician Stefan Bamach on the equivalence of geometric figures under finite decomposition. In the same year he met his future wife Maria Witkowska, who had played an active part in Poland's campaign for autonomy. They got married five years later when he was baptized into Catholicism, his wife's religion, and about this time he and his brother changed their name from Teitelbaum to Tarski, because it sounded less Jewish. Their parents, who observed Jewish traditions, disapproved. By this time he had become a *Dozent*, the youngest in the university, and instead of the pedagogical institute taught at the first-class gymnasium where his future wife was also a teacher. The Tarskis had two children: a son Janusz in 1934 and a daughter Krystyna in 1938.

In 1937 Tarski was made adjunct professor—not much better than being *Dozent*—and for the next fifteen years tried to obtain a regular university position. His lack of success has been attributed to the anti-

Semitism which was rife in Poland between the wars (Infeld (1941) has given a vivid picture of what it was like for a Jewish boy to grow up in Cracow at this period). Before the war Polish Jews numbered around 3.5 million, or some 10 per cent of the population. This high density must be part of the explanation for the anti-Semitism which prevailed in Poland; in Italy, for example, the density was much lower and the Jewish minority were more easily absorbed into the general population.

Since it was difficult if not impossible for Polish Jews to rise on the academic ladder in their homeland, Tarski began to consider the possibility of emigrating. Although handicapped by overwork, the research he published even during this period marked him as one of the premier logicians of the century. In 1935 he was awarded a Rockefeller Fellowship to spend nine months in Vienna, where he worked with members of the celebrated Wiener Kreis, including the young Gödel, who was soon to revolutionize mathematical logic. The next year he published a semi-popular text *Introduction to Logic and to the Methodology of the Deductive Sciences*, originally in Polish but later translated into English and many other languages.

In the summer of 1939 Tarski attended a conference at Harvard, intending only to be away for a short time, but while he was in America the Germans invaded Poland and he was stranded in America without money or any means of livelihood. If Tarski had returned to occupied Poland he would probably have perished as did both his parents. He made desperate efforts to rescue his wife and two sons, but despite assistance from the Rockefeller Foundation this proved impossible until the war was over. Meanwhile he was able to obtain a series of temporary positions in the United States, first as a research assistant at Harvard, then as a visiting professor at the City College of New York. A Guggenheim Fellowship enabled him to spend a year with Gödel at the Institute for Advanced Study. Finally, he was recruited by the University of California at Berkeley, where in four years he rose to the rank of full professor.

A charismatic leader and teacher, known for his brilliantly precise yet suspenseful expository style, Tarski's formidably high standards frightened away some of his research students but others survived to become leaders in the field of mathematical logic. Although gregarious and extroverted Tarski had hardly any close friends. He rarely opened up or showed affection. It seemed much easier for him to criticize than to compliment. The very traits that made him an outstanding logician—self-confidence, self-discipline, single-mindedness of purpose, a quick and curious mind, an outgoing personality, and persistence—seemed to pose difficulties in personal relationships, which were not important to him. His working habits were nocturnal, to the despair of his students; he would usually begin work after dinner and continue until dawn the next day. Monday afternoons were devoted to gardening; he was very proud of his garden, which contained some fine specimens. On Sundays the Tarskis would occasionally make excursions into the Californian countryside, usually accompanied by assorted students and colleagues. His intellectual fearlessness was coupled with physical boldness and a total absence of self-doubt.

The family spoke Polish at home, and Tarski's English was fluent and correct but in speech strongly accented. Maria ministered to all his needs and to the upbringing of their children. He had a whole series of affairs, and often made passes at attractive women. At one point Maria left him for several years, after the children were grown up, and came close to seeking a divorce. Tarski was fond of literature, especially poetry. Even in old age he could still recite poems in Polish, German, and Russian. While he was not interested in music he had a taste for the visual arts. He closely followed events in Poland, especially political developments, and although happy enough in America he, like many other European exiles of his generation, retained an affection for the old-world way of life. In 1965 Tarski was elected to the National Academy of Sciences; by then no fewer than seven of the fifty-two mathematical members of the academy were of Polish origin. After he became emeritus in 1968, he was recalled for active duty for another five years. Even after that he still continued to lecture and to supervise graduate students until his death, aged eighty-one, on 27 October 1983 in a Berkeley hospice, from emphysema, a lung condition caused by chain-smoking of cigarettes and cigarillos.

Although Tarski abandoned his Jewish origins, anti-Semitism awakened painful memories of his early years in Warsaw. In 1980 he received a visit from Yuri Ershov, a brilliant young logician from Novosibirsk who was making a lecture tour of the United States. Ershov was involved in the widespread official and semi-official anti-Semitic practices of that time which were peculiar to mathematics. These included the denial of admission of bright young Jewish mathematics students to universities, denial of advancement to graduate study for those who overcame the first hurdle, blocking the publication of Jewish mathematicians' research in leading journals, limitation of invitation to Soviet conferences, refusal of permission to attend international conferences, and rejection of PhD theses. Ershov was a member of the central committee that made the judgements as to the acceptability of the higher DSc theses needed to secure a university chair; those submitted by Jewish mathematicians were rejected almost without exception. Ershov encountered boycotts and other forms of protest wherever he went. Much as Tarski admired Ershov's mathematical work he did not attend the lecture he gave.

Bibliography

Abramowicz, Hirsz (1999). *Profiles of a Lost World: Memoirs of East European Jewish Life before World War II.* Detroit MI: Wayne State University Press.

Ahrens, Wilhelm (1907). *Briefwechsel zwischen CGJ Jacobi und MH Jacobi.* Leipzig: B. G. Teubner.

Alexanderson, G. L. (2000). *The Random Walks of George Pólya.* Washington DC: Mathematical Association of America.

Allibone, T. E. (1980). 'Dennis Gabor', *Biographical Memoirs of Fellows of the Royal Society* 26, 107–48.

Altmann, Simon and Ortiz, Eduardo L. (2005). *Mathematics and Social Utopias in France: Olinde Rodrigues and his Times* (History of Mathematics series vol. 28). Providence RI: American Mathematical Society.

Anchel, R. (1946). *Les Juifs de France.* Paris: J. B. Janin.

Appleyard, Rollo (1930). *Pioneers of Electrical Communication.* London: Macmillan.

Archibald, R. C. (1944). 'Materials concerning James Joseph Sylvester', in *Studies and Essays in the History of Science and Learning offered in Homage to George Sarton on the Occasion of his Sixtieth Birthday.* New York NY: Schuman.

Arms, Nancy (1966). *A Prophet in Two Countries: the life of F. E. Simon.* Oxford: Pergamon Press.

Baird, Davis, Hughes, R. I. G., and Nordman, Alfred (eds) (1998). *Heinrich Hertz.* Dordrecht, Boston, and London: Kluwer Academic Books.

Baron, S. W. (1964). *The Russian Jew under Tsars and Soviets.* New York NY: Macmillan.

Batterson, Steve (2006). *Pursuit of Genius.* Worcester MA: A. K. Peters.

Behnke, Heinrich (1978). *Semesterberichte.* Göttingen: Vandenhoek and Ruprecht.

Bell, E. T. (1937). *Men of Mathematics*. London: Victor Gollancz.

Benbassa, A. (1999). *The Jews of France: A History from Antiquity to the Present* (trans. M. B. DeBevoise). Princeton NJ: Princeton University Press.

Bentwich, Norman (1953). *The Rescue and Achievement of Refugee Scholars: The Story of Displaced Scholars and Scientists 1933–1952*. The Hague: M. Nijhoff.

Beyerchen, A. D. (1977). *Scientists under Hitler: Politics and the Physics Community under the Third Reich*. New Haven CT: Yale University Press.

Birkenhead, Earl of (1961). *The Prof in Two Worlds*. London: Collins.

Blaedel, Niels (1988). *Harmony and Unity: The Life of Niels Bohr* (trans. Geoffrey French). Madison WI: Science Tech. Inc.

Bonne-Tamir, B. and Adam, A. (eds) (1994). *Genetic Diversity among Jews: Disease and Markers at the DNA Level*. Oxford: Oxford University Press.

Born, Max (1978). *My Life: Reflections of a Nobel Laureate*. London: Taylor and Francis.

Botticini, Maristella and Eckstein, Zvi (2005). 'Jewish Occupational Selection: Education, Restriction or Minorities?', *Journal of Economic History* 65, 922–48.

Brewer, James W. and Smith, Martha K. (1981). *Emmy Noether: A Tribute to her Life and Work*. New York NY: Marcel Dekker.

Brian, Denis (1996). *Einstein: A Life*. New York NY: John Wiley and Sons.

Brieskorn, E. (ed.) (1996). *Felix Hausdorff zum Gedächtnis*. Braunschweig and Wiesbaden: Vieweg Verlag.

Bruhns, Karl (ed.) (1873). *Life of Alexander von Humboldt* (compiled by J. Lowenberg, Robert Ave-Lallemant, and Alfred Dove; trans. Jane and Caroline Lassell). London: Longmans Green.

Burkill, J. C. (1971). 'Abraham Samoilovitch Besicovitch', *Biographical Memoirs of Fellows of the Royal Society* 17, 1–16.

Busch, Alexander (1959). *Die Geschichte des Privatdozenten*. Stuttgart: F. Enke.

Charpa, Ulrich and Deichmann, Ute (eds) (2007). *Jews and Science in German Contexts*. Tübingen: Mohr Siebeck.

Cochran, Gregory, Hardy, Jason, and Harpending, Henry (2006). 'Natural History of Ashkenazi Intelligence', *Journal of Biosocial Science* 38, 659–93.

Crilly, Tony (2006). *Arthur Cayley*. Baltimore MD: Johns Hopkins University Press.

Dauben, Joseph Warren (1979). *Georg Cantor: His Mathematics and Philosophy of the Infinite*. Cambridge MA: Harvard University Press.

Dawidowicz, Lucy S. (1975). *The War against the Jews 1933–45*. New York NY: Holt, Rinehart and Winston.

Dent, Bob (1990). *Hungary*. New York NY: W. W. Norton.

Dick, A. (1981). *Emmy Noether 1882–1935*. Basel: Birkhäuser Verlag (originally published in German; trans. Heidi Blocher).

Dieudonné, Jean (1971–80). 'Hermann Minkowski', *Dictionary of Scientific Biography*. New York NY: Scribner.

Dunlop, D. M. (1954). *The History of the Jewish Khazars*. Princeton NJ: Princeton University Press.

Efron, Noah (2006). *Judaism and Science*. Westport CT: Greenwood Press.

Endelman, Todd (2000). *The Jews of Britain 1656 to 2000*. Berkeley CA: University of California Press.

Enz, Charles P. (2002). *No Time to be Brief: A Scientific Biography of Wolfgang Pauli*. Oxford: Oxford University Press.

Evans, Richard J. (2006). *The Third Reich in Power, 1933–1939*. New York NY: Penguin.

Feferman, Anita Boardman and Feferman, Solomon (2004). *Alfred Tarski: Life and Logic*. Cambridge: Cambridge University Press.

Fermi, Laura (1961). *Illustrious Immigrants*. Chicago IL: Chicago University Press.

Feuer, Lewis S. (1984). 'America's first Jewish professor: James Joseph Sylvester at the University of Virginia', *American Jewish Archives* 36 (1984), 151–201.

Fitzpatrick, Sheila (ed.) (1978). *Cultural Revolution in Russia 1928–1931*. Bloomington IN: Indiana University Press.

Fleming, Donald and Bailyn, Bernard (1969). *The Intellectual Migration*. Cambridge MA: Belknap Press of Harvard University Press.

Følsing, Albrecht (1997). *Albert Einstein: A Biography.* New York NY: Viking.

Fort, Adrian (2003). *Prof: the Life of Frederick Lindemann.* London: Jonathan Cape.

Fraenckel, Abraham A. (1930). *Georg Cantor.* Leipzig: B.G. Teubner.

Fraenkel, Abraham A. (1960). 'Jewish Mathematics and Astronomy', *Scripta Mathematica* 25, 33–47.

Frei, Gunther and Stammbach, Urs (1999). 'Heinz Hopf', in I. M. James (ed.), *History of Topology.* Amsterdam: North Holland.

French, A. P. and Kennedy, P. J. (1985). *Niels Bohr: A Centenary Volume.* Cambridge MA: Harvard University Press.

Friedlander, Saul (1997). *Nazi Germany and the Jews: the Years of Persecution, 1933–1939.* New York NY: Harper Collins.

Frisch, O. R. (1970). 'Lise Meitner', *Biographical Memoirs of Fellows of the Royal Society* 16, 405–20.

Gardner, Helen, and Wilson, Robin J. (1993). 'Thomas Archer Hirst— Mathematician Xtravagant', *American Mathematical Monthly* 100, V 827–34, VI 907–14.

Gerber, Jane (1992). *The Jews of Spain: A History of the Sephardic Experience.* New York NY: Free Press.

Gershenfeld, L. (1934). *The Jew in Science.* Philadelphia PA: Jewish Publication Society of America.

Givant, S. R. (1991). 'A Portrait of Alfred Tarski', *Mathematical Intelligencer* 13 (3), 16–33.

Glyn, Lynn B. (2002). 'Israel Lyons: a short but starry career. The life of an eighteenth century Jewish botanist and astronomer', *Notes Rec. Royal Society London* 56 (3), 275–305.

Goldschneider, Calvin and Zuckerman, Alan S. (1984). *The Transformation of the Jews.* Chicago: Chicago University Press.

Goodman, Richard M. (1979). *Genetic Disorders among the Jewish People.* Baltimore MD: Johns Hopkins University Press.

Goodman, R. M. and Motulsky, A. G. (eds) (1979). *Genetic Diseases among Ashkenazi Jews.* New York NY: Raven Press.

Goodstein, Judith R. (1983). 'The Italian Mathematicians of Relativity', *Centaurus* 26, 241–61.

Goodstein, Judith R. (2007). *The Volterra Chronicles: The Life and Times of an Extraordinary Mathematician 1860–1940* (History of Mathematics series vol. 31). Providence RI: American Mathematical Society.

Gordon, Milton (1964). 'Marginality and the Jewish Intellectual', in Peter I. Rose (ed.), *The Ghetto and Beyond*. New York NY: Random House.

Graham, Loren R. (1992). *Science in Russia and the Soviet Union*. Cambridge: Cambridge University Press.

Hardy, G. H. and Heilbronn, H. (1938). 'Edmund Landau', *Journal of the London Mathematical Society* 13, 302–10.

Harrod, Roy (1959). *The Prof: A Personal Memoir of Lord Cherwell*. London: Macmillan.

Heims, Steve J. (1980). *John von Neumann and Norbert Wiener: From Mathematics to the Technologies of Life and Death*. Cambridge MA: MIT Press.

Hertz, Heinrich (1977). *Memoirs, Letters, Diaries*, ed. J. Hertz. San Francisco CA: San Francisco Press.

Highfield, Robert, and Carter, Paul (1993). *The Private Lives of Albert Einstein*. London: Faber & Faber.

Hodge, W. V. D. (1973). 'Solomon Lefschetz', *Biographical Memoirs of Fellows of the Royal Society* 19, 433–54.

Hoffmann, Banesh, with Dukas, Helen (1972). *Albert Einstein: Creator and Rebel*. New York NY: Viking.

Hollinger, David A. (1996) *Science, Jews and Secular Culture: Studies in Mid-Twentieth-Century American Intellectual History*. Princeton NJ: Princeton University Press.

Hollinger, David A. (1998). 'Jewish Identity, Assimilation and Multiculturalism', in Karen S. Mittelman (ed.), *Creating American Jews: Historical Conversations about Identity*. Philadelphia PA: National Museum of American Jewish History in association with Brandeis University Press.

Hollinger, David. A. (2002). 'Why are Jews Pre-eminent in Science and Scholarship? The Veblen Thesis Reconsidered', *Aleph* 2, 145–63.

Hollinger, David A. (2006). *Cosmopolitanism and Solidarity*. Madison WI: University of Wisconsin Press.

Honigmann, Peter (1985). 'Peter Theophil Riess, der erste Jüde in der Preussischen Akademie der Wissenschaften', *Jahrbuch des Institut für Deutsche Geschichte* 14, 181–89.

Honigmann, Peter (1997). 'Alexander von Humboldt und die Jüden', in Chaim Selig Slonimski (ed.), *Zur Freiheit bestimmt: Alexander von Humboldt—eine Hebraische Lebensbeschreibung*, trans. and ed. Kurt-Jürgen Maass. Bonn: Bouvier.

Hooker, P. F. (1965). 'Benjamin Gompertz 1779–1865', *Journal of the Institute of Actuaries* 91, 203–12.

Infeld, Leopold (1941). *Quest: The Evolution of a Scientist.* London: Victor Gollancz.

Isaacson, Walter (2007). *Einstein: His Life and Universe.* London: Simon & Schuster.

Israel, Giorgio (2004). 'Italian Mathematicians, Fascism and Racial Policy', in Michele Emmer (ed.), *Mathematics and Culture.* Berlin-Heidelberg: Springer Verlag.

Jaffe, Bernard (c. 1960). *Michelson and the Speed of Light.* London: Heinemann.

James, I. M. (1997). 'James Joseph Sylvester FRS (1814–1897)', *Notes and Records of the Royal Society of London* 51, 247–61.

James, I. M. (2002). *Remarkable Mathematicians.* Cambridge: Cambridge University Press.

James, I. M. (2003). 'Singular Scientists', *Journal of the Royal Society of Medicine* 96, 36–9.

James, I. M. (2004). *Remarkable Physicists.* Cambridge: Cambridge University Press.

Jones, Steve (1997). *In the Blood.* London: Flamingo.

Karabel, Jerome (2005). *The Chosen: The Hidden History of Admission and Exclusion at Harvard, Yale and Princeton.* Boston MA: Houghton Mifflin.

Kemmer, M. and Schlapp, R. (1971). 'Max Born', *Biographical Memoirs of Fellows of the Royal Society* 17, 17–52.

Kevles, Daniel J. (1976). *The Physicists: The History of a Scientific Community in Modern America.* New York NY: Alfred A. Knopf.

Klein, Martin J. (1970). *Paul Ehrenfest.* Amsterdam: North Holland.

Klier, John D. and Lambrosa, Schlomo (1992). *Pogroms: Anti-Jewish Violence in Modern Russian History*. Cambridge: Cambridge University Press.

Klineberg, Otto (1971). 'Race and Psychology', in *Race and Science* (a Unesco publication). New York NY: Columbia University Press.

Klingenstein, Susanne (1991). *Jews in the American Academy 1900–1940*. New Haven CT: Yale University Press.

Koestler, Arthur (1976). *The Thirteenth Tribe*. London: Hutchinson.

Kojevnikov, Alexei B. (2004). *Stalin's Great Science: The Times and Adventures of Soviet Physicists* (History of Modern Physical Sciences vol. 2). London: Imperial College Press.

Königsberger, Leo (1904). *Carl Gustav Jacob Jacobi*. Leipzig: B. G. Teubner.

Kuhn, H. G. (1965). 'James Franck', *Biographical Memoirs of Fellows of the Royal Society* 11, 53–74.

Küssner, Martha (1982). 'Carl Wolfgang, Benjamin Goldschmidt and Moritz Abraham Stern. Zwei Gaussschuler Jüdischer Herkunft', *Mitteilungen der Gauss-Gesellschaft* 19, 37–62.

Landau, P. E. (2001). 'Olry Terquem (1782–1862): Régénérer les Juifs et transformer le Judaisme', *Revue des études Juives* 160, 169–87.

Langerman, T. Tzvi (ed.) (1999). *The Jews and the Sciences in the Middle Ages*. Aldershot: Ashgate Variorum.

Levinson, Thomas (2003). *Einstein in Berlin*. New York NY: Bantam Press.

Lindemann, Albert S. (1997) *Esau's Tears: Modern Anti-Semitism and the Rise of the Jews*. Cambridge: Cambridge University Press.

Lipman, Vivian D. (1990). *A History of the Jews in Britain since 1858*. Leicester: Leicester University Press.

Lipset, Martin Seymour and Ladd, Everett Carl (1971). 'Jewish Academics in the United States: Their Achievements, Culture, and Politics', *American Jewish Handbook*, 89–128.

Magee, Bryan (1968). *Wagner and Philosophy*. Oxford: Oxford University Press.

Masani, P. R. (1990). *Norbert Wiener 1894–1964*. Basel: Birkhäuser Verlag.

Mason, Joan (1992). 'Hertha Ayrton: A Scientist of Spirit', in Gill Kirkup and Laurie Smith Keller (eds), *Inventing Women: Science, Technology and Gender*. Cambridge: Polity Press and Open University.

Maz'ya, Vladimir and Shaposhnikova, Tatyana (1998). *Jacques Hadamard, a Universal Mathematician* (History of Mathematics series vol. 14). Providence RI: American and London Mathematical Societies.

McCagg, Jr, William O. (1972). *Jewish Nobles and Geniuses in Modern Hungary*. New York NY: Columbia University Press.

McCormmack, Russell (1982). *Night Thoughts of a Classical Physicist*. Cambridge MA: Harvard University Press.

Medawar, Jean and Pyke, David (2000). *Hitler's Gift: Scientists who Fled Nazi Germany*. London: Judy Piatkus.

Mendelsohn, Ezra (1983). *The Jews of East Central Europe between the World Wars*. Bloomington IN: Indiana University Press

Michelson, Dorothy Livingston (1973). *The Master of Light: A Biography of A. A. Michelson*. New York NY: Scribner.

Minkowski, Hermann (1972). *Briefe an David Hilbert*, eds Lily Rudenberg and Hans Zassenhaus. Trier: Spec Paulinus.

Moore, Ruth (1967). *Niels Bohr: The Man and the Scientist*. London: Hodder & Stoughton.

Murray, Charles (2003). *Human Accomplishment*. New York NY: Harper Collins.

Nachmansohn, David (1978). *German–Jewish Pioneers in Science, 1900–1933*. New York NY: Springer Verlag.

Nahon, G. (1989). 'The Sephardim of France', in R. D. Barnett and W. M. Shwab (eds), *The Sephardic Heritage: Essays on the History and Cultural Contribution of the Jews of Spain and Portugal*, vol. 2. Grendon, Northants.: Gibraltar Books.

Nastasi, Pietro and Tazzioli, Rossana (2000). *Per l'archivio della corrispondenza dei matématici italiani: aspetti scientifici e umani nella corrispondenza di Tullio Levi-Civita (1873–1941)*. Palermo.

Neher, André (1986). *Jewish Thought and the Scientific Revolution of the Sixteenth Century* (trans. David Maisel). Oxford: Oxford University Press.

Niewyk, Donald L. (1980). *The Jews in Weimar Germany*. Baton Rouge LA: Louisiana State University Press.

Noether, Max (1898). 'James Joseph Sylvester', *Math. Annalen* 50, 133–56.

Ogilvie, Marilyn Bailey (c. 1987). 'Marital Collaboration', in Privina G. Abir-am and Dorinda Outram (eds), *Women in Science*. New Brunswick NJ: Rutgers University Press.

Pais, Abraham (1982). *'Subtle is the Lord—': The Science and the Life of Albert Einstein*. Oxford: Oxford University Press.

Pais, Abraham (1991). *Niels Bohr's Times: In Physics, Philosophy, and Polity.* Oxford: Oxford University Press.

Pais, Abraham (2000). *The Genius of Science*. Oxford: Oxford University Press.

Parikh, C. (1991). *The Unreal Life of Oscar Zariski*. Boston MA: Academic Press.

Parshall, K. H. (1998). *James Joseph Sylvester: Life and Work in Letters*. Oxford: Oxford University Press.

Parshall, K. H. (2006). *James Joseph Sylvester: Jewish Mathematician in a Victorian World*. Baltimore MD: Johns Hopkins University Press.

Patai, Raphael (1996). *The Jews of Hungary*. Detroit: Wayne State University Press.

Patai, Raphael (1997). *The Jewish Mind*. New York NY: Scribner.

Patai, Raphael and Wing, Jennifer Patai (1989). *The Myth of the Jewish Race* (revised edn). Detroit MI: Wayne State University Press.

Peierls, Rudolf Ernst (1985). *Bird of Passage*. Princeton NJ: Princeton University Press.

Peierls, Rudolf Ernst (2007). *Sir Rudolf Peierls: Selected Private and Scientific Correspondence*, vol. 1, ed. Sabine Lee. London: World Scientific.

Pinkus, Benjamin (1988). *The Jews of the Soviet Union: The History of a National Minority*. Cambridge: Cambridge University Press.

Pinl, Max and Furtmüller, Lux (1973). *Mathematicians under Hitler* (Year Book XVIII of the Leo Baeck Institute). London: Secker & Warburg.

Reid, Constance (1996). *Courant*. Berlin: Springer Verlag (originally published as *Courant in Göttingen and New York* by Springer Verlag, 1976).

Reingold, Nathan (1981). 'Refugee Mathematicians in the United States of America 1933–1941', *Annals of Science* 38, 313–38 (reprinted in Peter

Duren (ed.), *A Century of Mathematics in America*, part I, 175–200. American Mathematical Society 1988).

Richarz, Monika (1974). *Die Eintritt der Jüden in die Akademischen Berufe: Jüdische Studenten und Akademiker in Deutschland*. Tübingen: J. C. B. Mohr (Paul Siebeck).

Richarz, Monika (1976). *Jüdisches Leben in Deutschland*. Stuttgart: Deutsche Verlags-Anstalt.

Richelson, Jeffrey T. (c. 2006). *Spying on the Bomb: American Nuclear Intelligence from Nazi Germany to Iran and North Korea*. New York NY: W. W. Norton.

Rider, Rolin (1984). 'Alarm and Opportunity: Emigration of Mathematicians to Britain and the United States, 1933–1945', *Historical Studies in the Physical Sciences* 15, 107–76.

Rife, Patricia (1992). *Lise Meitner and the Dawn of the Nuclear Age*. Basel: Birkhäuser Verlag.

Ringer, F. (1960). *The Decline of the German Mandarins*. Cambridge MA: Harvard University Press.

Robinson, Ira (1995). 'Hayyim Selig Slonimski and the Diffusion of Science among Russian Jewry in the Nineteenth Century', in Y. M. Rabkin and I. Robinson (eds), *The Interaction of Scientific and Jewish Cultures in Modern Times*. Lewiston NY and Lampeter: Edwin Mellen Press.

Roth, C. (1941). *A History of the Jews in England*. London: Oxford University Press.

Roth, C. (1942). 'The Jews in English Universities', in *Miscellanies of the Jewish Historical Society of England*, part 4.

Roth, C. (1965). *The History of the Jews of Italy*. Philadelphia PA: Jewish Publication Society of America.

Rowe, D. E. (1986). '"Jewish Mathematics" at Göttingen in the era of Felix Klein', *Isis* 77, 422–49.

Rowe, D. E. (2007). 'Felix Klein, Adolf Hurwitz, and the "Jewish Question" in German Academia', *Mathematical Intelligencer* 26/3, 18–30.

Rowe. D. E. and Schulman, Robert (eds) (2007). *Einstein on Politics*. Princeton NJ: Princeton University Press.

Rozental, Stefan (ed.) (1968). *Niels Bohr: His Life and Work as Seen by his Friends and Colleagues*. Amsterdam: North Holland.

Ruderman, David B. (1995). *Jewish Thought and Scientific Discovery in Early Modern Europe*. New Haven CT: Yale University Press.

Rupke, Nicolaas A. (2005). *Alexander von Humboldt: A Metabiography*. Frankfurt-am-Main: Peter Lang.

Ruppin, Arthur (1934). *The Jews in the Modern World*. London: Macmillan.

Sakharov, Andrei (1990). *Memoirs*. New York NY: Alfred A. Knopf.

Salaman, R. N. (1947). 'The Jewish Fellows of the Royal Society', in *Miscellanies of the Jewish Historical Society of England*, part 5.

Schatzky, Jacob (1953). 'Abraham Jacob Stern', in *The Joshua Starr Memorial Volume: Studies in History and Philology*. New York NY: Conference on Jewish Relations, 203–18.

Segal, Sanford (2003). *Mathematicians under the Nazis*. Princeton NJ: Princeton University Press.

Sharp, Evelyn (1926). *Hertha Ayrton 1854–1923*. London: Edward Arnold.

Siegmund-Schultze, R. (1998). *Mathematiker auf der Flucht vor Hitler. Quellen und Studien zur Emigration einer Wissenschaft*. Braunschweig: Vieweg Verlag.

Siegmund-Schultze, R. (2002). *Rockefeller and the Internationalization of Mathematics between the two World Wars*. Basel: Birkhäuser Verlag.

Sime, Ruth Lewin (1996). *Lise Meitner: A Life in Physics*. Berkeley CA: University of California Press.

Singer, Charles (1960). 'Science and Judaism', in Louis Finkelstein (ed.), *The Jews*. New York NY: Harper Brothers.

Slezkine, Yuri (2004). *The Jewish Century*. Princeton NJ: Princeton University Press.

Slonimski, Chaim Selig (1997). *Zur Freiheit bestimmt: Alexander von Humboldt—eine Hebraische Lebensbeschreibung*, trans. and ed. Kurt-Jürgen Maass. Bonn: Bouvier.

Steinberg, Stephen (1974). *The Academic Melting Pot: Catholics and Jews in American Higher Education*. New York NY: McGraw Hill.

Steinschneider, M. (1893–9). *Die Mathematik bei den Jüden*. Bibliotheca Mathematica n.s. vols 7–13.

Stillwell, John (1999). 'Max Dehn', in I. M. James (ed.), *History of Topology*. Amsterdam: North Holland.

Storfer, M. D. (1990). *Intelligence and Giftedness: The Contributions of Heredity and Early Environment*. San Francisco CA: Jossey-Bass.

Stubhaug, Arild (2000). *Niels Henrik Abel and his Times*. Berlin: Springer Verlag.

Süsskind, Charles (1995). *Heinrich Hertz: A Short Life*. San Francisco CA: San Francisco Press.

Veblen, Thorstein (1919). 'The intellectual pre-eminence of Jews in modern Europe', *Political Science Quarterly* 34, 219–31.

Vital, David (1999). *A People Apart: The Jews in Modern Europe 1789–1939*. Oxford: Oxford University Press.

Volkov, Shulamit (2001). 'Jewish Scientists in Imperial Germany', *Aleph* 1, 215–81.

Weber, Robert L. (1980). *Pioneers in Science: Nobel Prize Winners in Physics*, ed. J. M. A. Lenihan. Bristol and London: Institute of Physics.

Weil, A. (1983). *Number Theory: An Approach Through History; From Hammurapi to Legendre*. Boston MA: Birkhäuser.

Weintryb, B. D. (1972). *The Jews of Poland*. Philadelphia PA: Jewish Publication Society of America.

Whitrow, G. J. (ed.) (1957). *Einstein: The Man and his Achievement*. London: British Broadcasting Corporation.

Wiener, Norbert (1953). *Ex-Prodigy—My Childhood and Youth*. New York NY: Simon & Schuster.

Wiener, Norbert (1956). *I am a Mathematician—The Later Life of a Prodigy*. New York NY: Doubleday.

Zbrorowski, Mark and Herzog, Elizabeth (1952). *Life is with the People: The Culture of the Shtetl*. New York NY: Schocken Books.

Zuckerman, Harriet (1977). *Scientific Elite: Nobel Laureates in the United States*. New York NY: Free Press/Macmillan.

Zweig, Stefan (1944). *The World of Yesterday*. London: Cassell.

Credits

INTRODUCTION

Bonne-Tamir and Adam (1994), Botticini and Eckstein (2005), Cochran, Hardy, and Harpending (2006), Goodman (1979), Goodman and Motulsky (1979), Gordon (1964), Hollinger (2002, 2006), Jones (1997), Klineberg (1971), Magee (1968), Murray (2003), Patai (1997), Patai and Wing (1989), Storfer (1990), Veblen (1919).

1 HISTORICAL BACKGROUND

Abramowicz (1999), Anchel (1946), Baron (1964), Benbassa (1999), Dawidowicz (1975), Dent (1990), Dunlop (1954), Endelman (2000), Evans (2006), Fitzpatrick (1978), Gerber (1992), Goldschneider and Zuckerman (1984), Hollinger (1998), Klier and Lambrosa (1992), Koestler (1976), Lindemann (1997), Lipman (1990), Mendelsohn (1983), Nahon (1989), Niewyk (1980), Patai (1996), Pinkus (1988), Roth (1941), Richarz (1976), Ruppin (1934), Vital (1999), Weintryb (1972), Zbrorowski and Herzog (1952), Zweig (1944).

2 JEWS IN ACADEMIA

Behnke (1978), Bentwich (1953), Beyerchen (1977), Busch (1959), Fermi (1961), Fleming and Bailyn (1969), Fort (2003), Graham (1992), Israel (2004), Kevles (1976), Klingenstein (1991), Kojevnikov (2004), McCormmack (1982), Medawar and Pyke (2000), Nachmansohn (1978), Pais (2000), Peierls (1985, 2007), Pinl and Furtmüller (1973), Reingold

(1981), Richarz (1974), Rider (1984), Roth (1942), Rowe (1986), Salaman (1947), Segal (2003), Siegmund-Schultze (1998, 2002), Weber (1980), Zuckerman (1977).

3 SOME FORERUNNERS

Ahrens (1907), Altmann and Ortiz (2005), Efron (2006), Fraenckel (1960), Gerschenfeld (1934), Glyn (2002), Hollinger (1996), Hooker (1965), Karabel (2005), Küssner (1982), Landau (2001), Neher (1986), Ruderman (1995), Singer (1960), Steinschneider (1893–9).

4 YEARS OF OPPORTUNITY

Carl Jacobi Ahrens (1907), James (2002), Königsberger (1904).
J. J. Sylvester James (1997), Parshall (1998, 2006).
Gotthold Eisenstein Weil (1983).
Leopold Kronecker James (2002).
Georg Cantor Dauben (1979), Fraenckel (1930), James (2002).
Albert Michelson Jaffe (1960), Michelson (1973).
Hertha Ayrton Mason (1991), Ogilvie (c. 1987), Sharp (1926).

5 YEARS OF SUCCESS

Heinrich Hertz Appleyard (1930), Baird, Hughes, and Nordman (1998), Hertz (1997), Süsskind (1995).
Vito Volterra Goodstein (2007).
Hermann Minkowski Dieudonné (1971–80).
Jacques Hadamard Maz'ya and Shaposhnikova (1998).
Felix Hausdorff Brieskorn (1996), James (2002).
Tullio Levi-Civita Goodstein (2007), Nastasi and Tazzioli (2000).
Edmund Landau Hardy and Heilbronn (1938).

6 TROUBLED TIMES

Lise Meitner Frisch (1970), James (2004), Rife (1992), Sime (1996).
Max Dehn Stillwell (1999).
Albert Einstein Batterson (2006), Brian (1996), Følsing (1997), Highfield and Carter (1993), Hoffmann (1972), Isaacson (2007), James (2004), Levinson (2003), Pais (1982), Rowe and Schulman (2007), Whitrow (1957).
Paul Ehrenfest James (2004), Klein (1970).
Abram Ioffe Kojevnikov (2004).
Emmy Noether Brewer and Smith (1981), Dick (1968), James (2002).
James Franck Kuhn (1965).

7 EMIGRANTS AND IMMIGRANTS

Max Born Born (1978), Kemmer and Schlapp (1971).
Solomon Lefschetz Hodge (1973), James (2002).
Niels Bohr Blaedel (1988), French and Kennedy (1985), James (2004), Moore (1967), Pais (1991), Rozental (1968).
George Pólya Alexanderson (2000), James (2002).
Richard Courant James (2002), Reid (1996).
Abram Samoiovitch Besicovitch Burkill (1971).
Franz Simon Arms (1966).

8 MODERN TIMES

Heinz Hopf Frei and Stammbach (1999).
Norbert Wiener Hcims (1980), James (2002), Masani (1990), Wiener (1953).
Igor Ivgenievitch Tamm Kojevnikov (2004), Peierls (2007).
Oscar Zariski James (2002), Parikh (1991).
Wolfgang Pauli Enz (2002).
Dennis Gabor Allibone (1980).
Alfred Tarski Feferman and Feferman (2004), Givant (1991).

Image Credits

Jacobi—From Jacobi, Carl (1881). *Gesammelte Werke* (ed. Carl Wilhelm Birchardt). Berlin: George Reinerke.

Sylvester—Private collection of Enthoven family.

Eisenstein—From *Journal für die reine und ungewandte Mathematik*, band 221 (1966).

Kronecker—From Kronecker, Leopold (1895). *Werke* (ed. K. Hensel). Leipzig: Teubner.

Cantor—From Cantor, Georg (1966). *Gesammelte Abhandlungen* (ed. E. Zermelo). Hildesheim: Georg Ohms Verlagsbuchhandlung.

Michelson—From Jaffe, Bernard (c. 1960). *Michelson and the Speed of Light*. London: Heinemann.

Ayrton—Institution of Electrical Engineers, London.

Hertz—From Appleyard, Rollo (1930). *Pioneers of Electrical Communication*. London: Macmillan.

Volterra—From *Lettera matematica pristem* 57–58. Milan: Springer (2006).

Minkowski—From Minkowski, Hermann (1911). *Gesammelte Abhandlungen von Hermann Minkowski* (ed. David Hilbert). Leipzig: Teubner.

Hadamard—Royal Society, London.

Hausdorff—Mathematische Forschungsinstitut, Oberwolfach.

Levi-Civita—From *Lettera matematica pristem* 57–58. Milan: Springer (2006).

Landau—London Mathematical Society.

Meitner—Royal Society, London.

Dehn—Private collection of Frau Elizabeth Reidemeister.

Einstein—Lotte Jacobi Collection, University of New Hampshire.

Ehrenfest—From Klein, Martin J. (1970). *Paul Ehrenfest*. Amsterdam: North Holland.

Ioffe—Soviet Academy of Sciences, Moscow.

Noether—Bryn Mawr College University Library.

Franck—Royal Society, London.

Born—Royal Society, London.

Lefschetz—Royal Society, London.

Bohr—From Bohr, Niels (1981). *Collected Works*. Amsterdam: North Holland.

Polya—Private collection of G. L. Alexanderson.

Courant—Mathematische Forschungsinstitut, Oberwolfach.

Besicovitch—Royal Society, London.

Simon—Royal Society, London.

Hopf—Wissenschaftshistorische Sammlungen der ETH Bibliotek, Zurich.

Wiener—From Wiener, Norbert (1976). *Collected Works with Commentaries* (ed. P. Masani). Cambridge MA: MIT Press.

Tamm—Soviet Academy of Sciences, Moscow.

Zariski—From Zariski, Oscar (1974). *Collected Papers* (ed. H. Hironaka and D. Mumford). Cambridge MA: MIT Press.

Pauli—From Enz, Charles P. (2002). *No Time to be Brief: A Scientific Biography of Wolfgang Pauli*. Oxford: Oxford University Press.

Gabor—Royal Society, London.

Tarski—From *Proceedings of Symposia in Pure Mathematics* vol. 25. Providence RI: American Mathematical Society.

Index